Children exposed to parental substance misuse

Children exposed to parental substance misuse
Implications for family placement

Edited by Rena Phillips

British Association for Adoption & Fostering
(BAAF)
Skyline House
200 Union Street
London SE1 0LX
www.baaf.org.uk

Charity registration 275689

British Library Cataloguing in Publication Data
A catalogue record for this book is available
from the British Library

ISBN 1 903699 27 4

Editorial project management by Shaila Shah
Cover photographs posed by models;
John Birdsall Photography
Designed by Andrew Haig & Associates
Typeset by Avon DataSet, Bidford on Avon
Printed by Creative Print and Design Group

BAAF Adoption & Fostering is the leading
UK-wide membership organisation for all those
concerned with adoption, fostering and child
care issues.

Acknowledgements

One of the best and most challenging aspects of editing this book has been the team effort required. Authors from diverse backgrounds have generously contributed their personal and professional experience, knowledge and expertise. I have been helped and encouraged by Mary Mather and Florence Merredew who acted as consultants to the anthology. We had long and productive teleconferencing sessions and they read and commented on all the various drafts. Interesting conversations with my husband Bill Phillips, one of the contributors, helped to shape my thinking on the important and complex issues the book raises. Phillida Sawbridge made a valuable input to the editorial task. Finally, I am indebted to Shaila Shah for her guidance and support, and to her assistant Jo Francis for her practical help.

Rena Phillips
April 2004

Note about the editor

Rena Phillips is an independent practitioner and researcher. She is currently employed by adoptive families as part-time co-ordinator of a post-adoption support service and is an adoption panel member.

Rena worked in a social work department as an adoption and foster care specialist, and was a teacher and researcher in the Social Work Unit and Social Work Research Centre, Stirling University. Her publications cover adoption, disability, children with complex support needs and social work education. She co-edited *After Adoption: Working with adoptive families* (BAAF, 1996). She was previously chair of BAAF's Research Group Advisory Committee. She is on the peer review panel of the journals *Adoption & Fostering* and *Adoption Quarterly*.

Contents

Foreword

Ten years ago, the problems of children affected by the drug or alcohol misuse of their parents was not a subject of general interest in either health or social care. Today, a Government report estimates that two to three per cent of children under 16 in England and Wales, and four to six per cent of children under 16 in Scotland, have one or both parents affected by serious drug problems, a figure that rises steeply in the looked after children population. Parental drug and alcohol misuse can and does compromise children's health and development at every stage, from conception to adolescence and beyond, and the number of children needing substitute parental care continues to grow. The issue of parental drug and alcohol misuse has moved from being a relatively rare occurrence in social work practice to almost an everyday dilemma.

Professionals can only deal with probabilities. Statistical information is often out of date before it is published. It is still not possible to determine precisely which children will be affected by parental substance misuse and in what way. As the drug testing of pregnant women and the extended follow-up of drug-exposed children becomes widespread, the range of consequences for the affected child has become more apparent. Not all children will have long-term difficulties. Some appear to have no apparent problems at all, while others have very severe problems and there is a spectrum of difficulties between these two extremes. Not all professionals are fully informed of the effects of substance misuse and conflicting advice can add to the dilemmas substitute carers face. The range of opinion from different professionals is academically interesting but of limited help to a parent struggling with a difficult child. This is a field in which there are still more questions than answers.

The challenge for social workers assessing the needs of children exposed to parental substance misuse and making plans for them is complex and immense. How should social workers assess substance-misusing families before taking their children into care? And once in care, how should they assess their needs? And how will foster carers and adopters, once they are found for these vulnerable children, deal with their difficulties? The need for social workers to know more and act sensitively and diligently on this information is undisputed.

When *Bruised before Birth* was published by BAAF ten years ago, it became an immediate bestseller, addressing an identified need, and remaining an invaluable resource for social workers, parents and carers. Ten years on, this anthology builds considerably on what little we knew then. This book is more than a revision of this pioneering work. The contributors are all experts in this challenging area of practice. Medical experts provide up to date information, social workers write of their experiences, including setting up specialist and innovative projects, and those directly affected tellingly describe their experiences. This is a unique collection. No other book exists which can equip social workers in planning and achieving placements for this very vulnerable group of children, some of whom experience drug withdrawal, or present with Foetal Alcohol Spectrum Disorder or learning disabilities that may manifest as they grow up.

Social workers must be equipped with the facts, learn to apply what they know as well as ask pertinent questions about what is still unknown in their practice, and help parents and carers with solutions. This collection will help them to do that. BAAF should be congratulated on this important new publication, which will be backed up with seminars, workshops and training.

Society owes an enormous debt of gratitude to those adults whose generosity and commitment has helped children overcome an uncertain start to life. This book is dedicated to all who seek to give children a second chance.

Dr Mary Mather
Consultant Paediatrician
Chair of the Health Advisory Group, BAAF
April 2004

Introduction

Rena Phillips

Our social worker gave us excerpts of 'Bruised Before Birth', *which was a harrowing read, and we looked on the web for anything else that we could find.* (Adoptive parent)

It is a decade since *Bruised Before Birth – Parenting children exposed to parental substance misuse* was published by BAAF (McNamara, 1994). At that time, relatively little attention was paid to the effects of drugs and alcohol misuse on children's development, and the book filled a gap for adopters and foster carers in their quest for reliable and useful information. The recent rise in concern about parental substance misuse has resulted in other helpful publications (Harbin and Murphy, 2000; Hoggan and Higgins, 2001; Kroll and Taylor, 2003; Tunnard, 2002a, 2002 b). Two major government reports, *Hidden Harm* in England (ACMD, 2003), and *Getting our Priorities Right* in Scotland (Scottish Executive, 2003) have added to our knowledge and understanding in this area. While there remains a great deal to be learned about the consequences for children of parental substance misuse, the emerging picture suggests a very significant and sizeable problem, which is getting bigger, and which has a serious impact on the child protection and looked after children systems.

Against this background of growing attention and concern the time seemed appropriate for BAAF to also turn its attention to this issue and commission an edited collection on parental substance misuse and the implications for family placements. Both topics are, in their own right, demanding and complex and doubly so when considered together. It is interesting to reflect on some similarities between them. They share a long history. Alcohol and other drugs have long been part of life, affecting how people feel, think and act. The basic elements of informal substitute care, as providing family life for children who cannot be cared for by their birth parents, goes back a long time too. Both areas need to be seen in the context of a community perspective involving parents, children, families, friends and neighbourhoods. At the same time, the way people are affected can be very different, as each situation and individual is unique. Both are prone to attract controversy, fuelled by media attention and political pressure, for example, the re-classification of drugs, or the alleged incompetence of local authorities standing as a barrier to an increase in the number of adoptions.

This timely collection is aimed at families and professionals, and we have attempted to make it as "reader friendly" as possible. Inevitably, the subject of substance misuse requires reference to medical and technical terms; this applies particularly in the section on substance misuse in pregnancy. Rather than use a glossary, contributors have provided a brief explanation following their use of such terms. The way terminology is expressed is important in order to avoid language that implies value judgements or negative connotations about substance misuse and parental capacity. The terms "substance misuse" and "problem use" have mainly been used in the book. For a fuller discussion of definitional issues see Chapter 7.

There is a considerable amount of information to absorb in this anthology, but the book is so organised that the reader can dip in and out of chapters. As it is only possible to cover specific areas of the vast literature on substance misuse, websites are given in some chapters which might prove to be of interest and use.

The impact of parental substance misuse on children's development

The substances covered in this book are psychoactive drugs, including alcohol and tobacco. The chapter by Bill Phillips provides a brief introduction to some psychoactive drugs that are commonly misused and difficult to assess. Many of their complex effects on the nervous system are not visible, yet can be very significant.

Pregnancy is a crucial time for a woman misusing drugs. Our guide here is Patricia McElhatton who, through her own research and those of others, reviews the effects of drugs, including tranquillisers and antidepressants, at different stages of development – on the baby in the womb, on the new-born infant and during post-natal development. Withdrawal symptoms, the most commonly reported adverse effect of substance misuse in pregnancy, are outlined. While maternal misuse of drugs potentially affects pregnancy outcomes, this is complicated by some important limitations. There is an association between drug misuse and poverty, physical and psychological health problems, poor ante-natal and post-natal care, inadequate diet and exposure to violence. The use of drugs, or a combination of drugs, may be coupled with alcohol and smoking. Such lifestyle issues make it difficult to establish direct and straightforward cause and effect relationships. There is a lack of good data and evidence on the effects of drug misuse on the foetus and newborn baby and particularly on children's longer-term development. There is more research evidence available on the longer term impact of alcohol misuse on children. Concern about parental drug misuse is relatively recent, and research has concentrated more on pregnancy and the newborn infant rather than on tracking children over time in respect of their psychological development, behaviour and educational progress.

'Why do we talk about illicit drugs first and alcohol second?' – the frustration I heard expressed by a clinical psychologist working in the field of substance misuse was evident. According to Alcohol Concern (the national charity that aims to reduce the level of alcohol misuse) roughly ten times more people die as a result of alcohol misuse than drug misuse. Yet ten times as much money is spent on drug services than on alcohol services (Appleby, 2003). In a recent survey commissioned by the charity across the UK, only seven per cent of men and 22 per cent of women knew what the recommended daily alcohol allowance is. The low level of attention given to alcohol misuse is raised in the chapter by Donald Forrester and Judith Harwin. They conducted the first large-scale national study of social work cases, which showed the high numbers involving parental substance misuse, including alcohol, but also that most social workers have little information and training in this area. A strong message from the research is that social workers under-respond to alcohol misuse as compared with drug misuse. As the authors point out, such findings have clear implications for social work training. They highlight the neglect of substance misuse in the development of policy and guidance in the field of social work and child care. Crucially, the new social work degree courses are required to teach about mental health and disability, but not substance misuse.

In the context of a steady increase in the last two decades in the number of women drinking heavily, and recent evidence that it is increasing faster among younger women than any other group, Moira Plant discusses alcohol consumption in relation to the stage of pregnancy and pattern of drinking. She outlines the condition of Foetal Alcohol Syndrome (FAS), which affects babies born to women who drink heavily in pregnancy, and the attendant physical, cognitive and behavioural problems that can continue into childhood and beyond. A less severe condition known as Foetal Alcohol Effects (FAE) has also been identified to describe more subtle problems. In recent years, the term Foetal Alcohol Spectrum Disorder (FASD) has been used to indicate the wide range of disorders and their severity associated with prenatal alcohol exposure. Throughout the book, contributors make use of the terms FAS, FAE and FASD to describe the effects of alcohol misuse. The subject of drinking in pregnancy has always been highly charged emotionally, including the levels of drinking in relation to possible risks to the unborn child. It is important to be aware that alcohol may affect development at any time during pregnancy and that a safe level of alcohol use in pregnancy has not been established.

As an adoption and foster care practitioner in the late 1970s, I was somewhat surprised to receive a letter from a medical adviser, urging me to think carefully about placing a young child in a smoking household. He was clearly ahead of his time regarding the continuing and increasing debate on the effects of passive smoking. This is an issue now more routinely raised in adoption and fostering panels, especially in relation to younger children and those with conditions such as asthma. The balance that needs to be struck at an individual level, between the health risks to substitute carers who smoke and the benefits of a family placement for a child, are highlighted by Catherine Cosgrove, Catherine Hill and Tagore Charles in their chapter on smoking. As well as looking at the health effects on children living in a smoking environment, they review the significant risks, now well established, associated with maternal use of tobacco in pregnancy. Other important health considerations concern children whose birth parents have high risk factors for blood-borne viruses. BAAF convened a Working Party which produced a Practice Note on hepatitis and HIV in relation to substitute care (BAAF, 1999). Jacqueline Mok, who was a member of this group, brings the topic up to date. She emphasises that despite clinical advances there is still considerable anxiety when these children require family placements. In order for misconceptions or fear not to stand in the way of providing an effective and non-discriminatory service, children, families and professionals need to be well informed as regards the management of blood-borne viruses. Advice on Hepatitis B immunisation can also be found in BAAF's journal, *Adoption & Fostering* (Grant, 2000).

Information and communication

The literature on parental substance misuse contains emotive words such as hidden harm, silence and disclosure, keeping it quiet, concealment and taboo. They convey scenarios of secrecy, stigma and problems of communication.

It is vital to hear directly from children and young people regarding their experiences and feelings of living with parents who misuse substances. Yet services are targeted principally at adults, with children described as 'invisible' (Kroll and Taylor, 2003). Research on this topic is rare. An important exception is a recent study of 36 children and young people which concluded that they are locked into a silence they find difficult to unburden to anyone:

> *The situation that seems to obtain is one where children know that the household revolves around something other than themselves, but that they are not allowed to know what it is and they are not allowed to ask what it is. This persists even once children have worked out that drug dependency is at the heart of their family dynamic.* (Barnard and Barlow, 2003, p 52)

The chapter by Veronica Corbett on the voices of children and young people demonstrates that they know more than their parents think they do, and in turn "keep it quiet" out of a sense of loyalty, embarrassment, fear of being removed from their parents and not wanting to appear different from others. The importance of openness between children and parents on sensitive and problematic subjects echoes the difficult task of adopters talking about adoption to their children.

The Draft Adoption Agencies Regulations, issued for consultation in England in 2003, will require adoption agencies to provide prospective adopters with detailed information on children before they are adopted. This has particular implications for those from a substance misuse background. Family Futures Consortium is a voluntary organisation offering therapeutic support to families who have adopted or are fostering traumatised children. Its work reveals that these families lack information about children's early personal and medical history, that poor or non-existent paediatric assessments leave children with un-diagnosed conditions, and that cognitive testing to ascertain areas of specific learning difficulties is inadequate (Burnell and Vaughan, personal communication). From the contributions to this book by adopters and foster carers, we are left in no doubt that their level of training and information on substance misuse was poor in some instances, reinforcing important questions about social work practice in this area. As Mary Mather in the chapter on working with the medical adviser advocates, to know is to understand. She gives practical and helpful advice on how adopters and foster carers can be empowered to obtain accurate, relevant and up-to-date information.

Children affected by drug and alcohol misuse will have health, social and educational needs that require the co-ordination of different agencies. That substance misuse workers and child care social workers need to talk to each other more is the conclusion to be drawn from Joy Barlow's chapter. Improving collaboration requires that issues be addressed such as joint training, protocols regarding confidentiality and approaches to inter-disciplinary assessments. Family members can be a vital source of information in gauging how substance misuse affects parenting, but assessing risk in the face of denial or minimisation of problems is a complex and challenging task. Donald Forrester alerts us against pro-fessional biases and value-judgements in relation to substance misuse unfairly distorting assessments, and offers guidance on how to engage more productively and sensitively with parents by paying attention to the style and method of interviews.

An important element emphasised in the assessment process is that the question to ask is not the "extent" of the substance misuse by parents, but the "impact" that the misuse has on the child (depending on age and stage of development). The theme of keeping the focus on the child is further elaborated by Di Hart in her contribution on the care planning for children looked after as a result of substance misuse. Very young children may be unable to speak for themselves. The need for early assessment and planning for permanent placements may be compromised by parents who cannot consistently and predictably care for their children, as well as difficulties around rehabilitation attempts. Once children become looked after, they require help in managing conflicting emotions such as relinquishing feelings of responsibility for birth parents and in dealing with the anxiety about their welfare, as well as fears for children that they themselves might misuse substances.

Placement issues

Our knowledge and understanding of the challenges posed by family placements for children with special needs have been steadily growing. What does this book tell us about some of the additional issues they and their new families face in relation to parental substance misuse?

While it has been established that parental substance misuse is associated with an increased risk of children experiencing significant harm, there are many uncertainties and much that we do not yet know. Some children, in addition to the risks they were exposed to during pregnancy, may continue to experience parental abuse and neglect. It does not follow that *all* will have severe problems – who will be affected and how is difficult to determine. Although many children appear normal at birth, they could later be identified with deficits not apparent in their early years. Diagnosis can be difficult as some conditions, for example, Foetal Alcohol Syndrome, may cause similar symptoms to those seen in children with attachment disorders and may occur in addition to such disorders. The inter-relation of problems is commented on by Sara Mayer in the chapter about the needs of black and dual heritage children. An already marginalised group because of parental substance misuse, these children also need to deal with the impact of racism and oppression.

There are trends indicating an increase in the number of babies and infants requiring to be placed for adoption, including those from substance misusing backgrounds. In a position statement by BAAF (2003) on adoption planning for babies, concern is expressed about the substantial delay in achieving placements for them in their new permanent family, including the fact that social workers lack experience in assessing and planning for babies. This can then erroneously be seen as a more straight-forward task and be carried out by workers without the relevant specialist knowledge. This has particular implications for babies who might have suffered undetected neurological damage through parental substance misuse, and whose prospective adopters might likewise be inclined to think that their task is a more straightforward one.

As far as we can tell from the evidence, some genetic influence might contribute to the development of substance misusing behaviour, but environmental factors are considered to have much more influence. Importantly, research is very limited on the substantial number of children affected by parental substance misuse, whose parents can no longer look after them. They are cared for formally or informally by relatives and friends, or are in residential care or have been fostered or adopted. As highlighted previously, longitudinal studies are required, as well as com-parative studies of children in permanent placements and those raised by their birth parents.

When I first met Jennifer Bell and Margaret Simm from the Families for Children Team, Glasgow City Council, they half seriously suggested they title their chapter *Chaos*. This inner city area (with around a quarter of all drug misusers in Scotland) has been described as where 'the drugs time bomb is ticking' and social care services come into contact with second and even third generations of drug misusers (Colvin, 2003). Children placed from such "chaotic" backgrounds have more than the usual number of placement disruptions, even with carers experienced in managing challenging behaviour. A survey undertaken by the team on children from drug-misusing backgrounds revealed more cases involving sexual abuse and a greater number of sibling groups. Both issues have their own attendant set of complex dilemmas. Face-to-face contact with birth parents who misuse substances can lead to adoptees experiencing similar problems themselves. Such potential risk is demonstrated in the chapter by adoptive parents in which, despite difficulties for their family and adopted son in maintaining face-to-face contact in a situation of parental substance misuse, such arrangements were impressively persisted with. The emotional and painful journey described by an adopted young woman, burdened with issues of loss and seeking to work out identity issues, brought her into contact with her birth mother and the world of drugs. She describes her own misuse of drugs and the turmoil this created in her life.

It has been suggested that, if the main attachment of parents is to a substance, this has implications for their capacity to attach to their children (Kroll and Taylor, 2003). Children exposed to parental substance misuse will experience separation and loss in many ways. As mentioned above, a substantial number do not live at home, as parents are in hospital, prison, undergoing treatment for their addiction in residential facilities and, even more dramatically, may have died. The theme of disrupted attachments is pursued by several contributors from different perspectives, thus reinforcing the centrality of this topic in understanding the lives of troubled children. Caroline Archer, taking a neuro-biological approach, charts the difficulties where parents who misuse substances, although physically present, are emotionally unavailable or unpredictable and describes the attachment "disorganisation" that ensues. Alan Burnell and Jay Vaughan put forward their hypothesis that, depending on whether parents misuse mainly drugs or alcohol, different attachment styles ensue and show how this, in turn, affects the remedial parenting and therapeutic packages children require. The emotional and social development of vulnerable children is further explored by Patricia Daley and Sandra Johnson who from their standpoints as educational psychologists explore the role of "inclusive" and "nurturing" schools. Through case examples, they illustrate the range of problems in learning and behaviour that children affected by parental substance misuse can experience in school and they provide guidance as to how the education system can support the needs of children and their carers.

The effects of parental substance misuse can be countered by a variety of protective factors. A very obvious one is the safe, secure and predictable environment of permanent substitute family care. This requires that new families are helped to negotiate a range of adoption support services from social work, health and education services which so far are patchy and under-resourced, particularly when specialist help is required. Caring for the carers is a sentiment often commended, but little acted upon. If we do not look after the carers they cannot look after the children. This is the theme of the chapter by Kate Cairns. Combining the topics of brain development and attachment relationships, she demonstrates that living with children 'who think and feel with a different brain' because of substance misuse harm before birth, can result in secondary trauma for substitute families, impacting on the latter's mental health. Ways are suggested of preventing disorders and treating symptoms. In the context of the imminent changes proposed in the way adoption support is organised and delivered as part of the Adoption and Children Act 2002 (England and Wales), it is important to understand the daily reality that confronts carers. One message is loud and clear: carers are our most skilled and precious resource, yet they are also vulnerable, and their wellbeing must also be protected.

The conclusion of the Advisory Council on the Misuse of Drugs (ACMD, 2003) was that its inquiry into parental drug misuse opened their eyes and minds to a problem most people had been largely unaware of. This anthology has likewise "opened up" many issues. It has attempted to address a wide and complex range of perspectives concerning the needs of children exposed to parental substance misuse, as well as the needs of the adopters and foster carers who support them. Much remains to be learned and understood, with several issues raising particular concern. Social workers need better training in this area of work. More research is required on children's views and experiences of parental substance misuse. Crucially, their long-term progress in family placement in terms of their health, behaviour, education and social and psychological development is as yet largely unknown. Such steps are necessary to make this group of vulnerable children more visible and to respond more effectively to the challenges they, and their adopters and foster carers, face together.

References

Appleby E (2003) 'Policies with bottle', *Community Care*, 23–29 October, pp 42–43

ACMD (2003) *Hidden Harm: Responding to the needs of children of problem drug users*, Report of an Inquiry by the Advisory Council on the Misuse of Drugs, London: Home Office. www.drugs.gov.uk

BAAF (2003) *Adoption Planning for Babies - Position Statement*, London: BAAF

BAAF (1999) *Hepatitis and HIV: Issues related to substitute care, foster care, residential care and adoption*, Practice Note 39, London: BAAF

Barnard M and Barlow J (2003) 'Discovering parental drug dependence: silence and disclosure, *Children & Society*, 17, pp 45–56. www.interscience.wiley

Colvin I (2003) 'The drugs time bomb is ticking', *Community Care*, 10–16 April, p 23

Grant A (2000) 'Looking after carers: argument for the hepatitis B immunisation', *Adoption & Fostering*, 24:4, pp 67–70

Harbin F and Murphy M (2000) *Substance Misuse and Child Care: How to understand, assist and intervene when drugs affect parenting*, Lyme Regis: Russell House Publishing

Hoggan D and Higgins L (2001) *When Parents Use Drugs: Key findings from a study of children in the care of drug-using parents*, Dublin: The Children's Research Centre, Trinity College

Kroll B and Taylor A (2003) *Parental Substance Misuse and Child Welfare*, London: Jessica Kingsley Publishers

McNamara J (1994) *Bruised before Birth: Parenting children exposed to parental substance abuse*, London: BAAF

Scottish Executive (2003) *Getting Our Priorities Right: Good practice guidance for working with children and families affected by substance misuse*, Edinburgh: The Stationery Office. www.scotland.gov.uk

Tunnard J (2002a) *Parental Problem Drinking and its Impact on Children*, Dartington: Research in Practice

Tunnard J (2002b) *Parental Drug Misuse: A review of impact and intervention studies*, Dartington: Research in Practice

SECTION I

Setting the scene

1 Finding out about the past to understand the present
Working with the medical adviser in adoption and foster care

Dr Mary Mather

From healthy babies for the perfect couple . . .

Adoption first became legal in England and Wales in 1926 in response to the orphanages of the First World War and the 1918 influenza epidemic. Adoption, however, only became practical with the development of safe artificial infant feeding, which made it feasible to move newborn babies from their birth mothers to foster mothers.

For the next 50 years, adoption practice was primarily about finding babies for childless couples. The "perfect" adopted baby was newborn, white, healthy and developmentally normal. As the number of prospective adoptive parents was always greater than the number of babies, the former's age, health, material wealth, marital and professional status could be used to restrict the definition of "the perfect adopter". In those early days the medical input to adoption was minimal. Essentially healthy babies were given a brief physical examination to exclude major health problems or congenital malformations. Children unlucky enough to have any medical problems were likely to be labelled as unadoptable. They were placed in local authority nurseries or foster homes and their medical needs were largely forgotten.

Adoption practice focused on three principles: secrecy, anonymity and the sealing of records. Systems were specifically designed to prevent birth and adoptive parents from meeting and sharing information. The medical history of a child's family was often lost as the adopted baby was always given a completely new blank medical record. The emotional needs of adopted children and their families were largely unrecognised. Elements of this early practice remain to this day as each child is still given a new NHS number at the time of legal adoption.

... To finding families for children

By 1970, effective contraception, the legalisation of abortion, increasing acceptance of single parents and improved state welfare benefit led to a dramatic drop in the number of babies needing adoption. Adoption began to be seen as a solution to the care problems of children whose parents were unwilling, unable or judged by the legal system as unfit to care for them. At the beginning of the 21st century, the children for whom adoptive parents are sought are now likely to have complex physical, emotional, developmental and educational needs. Inadequate parenting, abuse and neglect have often been major factors in their early lives. These children are from a variety of ethnic and cultural back-grounds. Many require a placement with their siblings. Many will have had multiple placements in the care system. There is now an acceptance that most children will maintain some form of contact with their birth families and siblings (Mather, 1999). Parents for these damaged children are not easy to find.

Most adopters believe they have little chance of adopting a baby. The statistical evidence, however, is that adoption in the UK is still largely a service for the young child – 3,400 children were placed for adoption in England in the year ending 31 March 2002. Sixty per cent of these children were aged between one and four years of age (Department of Health, 2002). A significant number are the children of drug misusing parents unable to care for them, and who are affected by exposure to drugs before birth. Adopters, foster carers, social workers and paediatricians increasingly have to face the reality of the effect of drugs on children's health and development. What implications do these direct and indirect effects have for children, their families, foster carers and adoptive parents? These questions take on great urgency as the following case scenarios show.

Meet the children

Jon

Jon is a six-month-old baby living with a foster mother. Both his birth parents are drug addicts and after an unsuccessful attempt to rehabilitate him, he will not be returning to their care. His local authority is seeking adoptive parents. His social worker has written:

Jon is a lovely baby with curly brown hair, blue eyes and a cheeky smile. He is meeting all his developmental milestones. His birth parents are white-Scottish and he needs a placement which reflects his ethnic and cultural background.

Adopters are identified very quickly. Over the next few weeks, however, his bewildered adopters, who have fallen in love with his photograph, struggle with an increasingly complex and confusing picture as they discover more background information about their "perfect baby".

Jon was born after a pregnancy with no ante-natal care. For the last six months of pregnancy, his mother lived on the streets neglecting her diet and health. Although principally addicted to methadone, she uses crack cocaine and injects heroin. Both Jon's parents are heavy smokers who abuse alcohol and, occasionally, prescription drugs. Street drugs are expensive and Jon's parents are unemployed. Money to support their drug habit comes from crime and prostitution. Both parents have spent time in prison and domestic violence has featured in their volatile relationship.

Jon's mother arrived at hospital in advanced labour. She was seen, by staff on the labour ward, injecting herself with an unknown drug. Jon was born at an estimated gestation of 36 weeks, about four weeks early. He weighed two kilograms at birth and his urine tested positive for opiates, nicotine and alcohol at delivery. He spent a month on the special care baby unit where he was treated with oral morphine sulphate for prolonged neonatal drug withdrawal. He then spent two months in a residential unit with his parents, while their capacity to care for him was assessed. Following the breakdown of the residential placement Jon now lives with an experienced foster mother.

This story raises a lot of questions, but gives Jon's future adopters little or nothing in the way of hard answers. Will Jon carry a genetic vulnerability to drug and alcohol misuse in later life? In addition to the effects of inter-uterine exposure to drugs, what are the added effects of his mother's lifestyle? How does poor maternal nutrition, sleep deprivation, lack of medical care and domestic violence impact on a developing baby? What are the short and long-term effects of his exposure to nicotine and alcohol?

The British National Formulary (www.bnf.org), the most authoritative source of information on prescription drugs in the UK, lists over 800 prescribable drugs which should 'be avoided or used with caution' in pregnancy. These drugs include alcohol, amphetamines benzodiazepines, nicotine and opiates, all of which are commonly misused by drug users. Trying to assess the effects of drugs on the foetus is difficult, even when the mother is taking a known dose of a prescribed drug and is otherwise healthy and well nourished. It becomes virtually impossible when the mother is using several drugs in varying quantities and her general health and diet are poor.

Jon's adopters are told that, because of his parents' intravenous drug use and his mother's prostitution, he is at increased risk of infection from the blood-borne infections, HIV and hepatitis B and C. This risk of infection is increased by time in prison, where needle sharing is widespread. Jon's mother has returned to her life on the streets. She is no longer in contact with social services and cannot give consent for him to be tested. Can and should Jon be tested and what are the implications of testing?

What are the long-term implications of the prolonged period of neonatal drug withdrawal (neonatal abstinence syndrome)? The symptoms of drug withdrawal vary in severity and can last for days, weeks or even months. The more severe the withdrawal and the longer symptoms last, the greater the impact on bonding between mother and child. The combination of a constantly crying, irritable baby and a stressed, depressed or anxious mother is not the situation in which healthy bonding occurs. Has any potential impairment of Jon's health and development been made worse by failed rehabilitation and placement moves in the early months of life? Will these effects be permanent and what can be done to limit or change them?

For the parents of any newborn child the future holds no certainties. However, these unanswered questions make the decision to care for Jon an anxious, painful and difficult one for his already committed adopters.

Megan, Benjamin and Tyler

Megan six, Benjamin three and Tyler six months are half-siblings. Megan is white and living separately with her birth father under a Residence

Order. Benjamin and Tyler are of mixed heritage. The local authority is seeking adopters for Benjamin and Tyler who are to be placed together and they are consequently advertised in *Be My Parent* as follows:

Benjamin (known as Ben) is an endearing, funny, chatty little boy who thrives on attention. He enjoys riding his bike and going to nursery. He has mild speech delay but has made tremendous progress in his foster home. He will be a challenging but rewarding child to care for. Tyler is a happy settled baby who is waiting to see a cardio-logist about a heart murmur. He is meeting all his developmental milestones. A one or two parent adoptive family who meets the children's cultural, ethnic and religious identity, and who is willing to maintain contact with their sister is needed. A long-term foster family would also be considered.

Any carers for these children will need to cope with additional uncer-tainties. The children's mother was a heavy smoker and an alcoholic whose addiction got progressively worse. While her pregnancy with Megan was relatively uncomplicated, by the time Tyler was born she was drinking large quantities of alcohol on a daily basis. She was frequently incapable of caring for her children. There was mounting professional concern about her children's exposure to domestic violence and the presence of Schedule 1 offenders in the family home.[1] All three children have different fathers. Benjamin's father is a violent man who is currently serving a prison sentence. Tyler's father is unknown.

The children of drug and alcohol users are less likely to be registered with a general practitioner, to be fully immunised or to receive routine developmental checks. Hygiene and diet may suffer. Heavy tobacco smoke in the external environment results in higher rates of sudden infant death and respiratory and ear infections (Advisory Council on the Misuse of Drugs, 2003). Parents preoccupied with addictions have less time to stimulate the child through play and reading and may not give their children the benefits of pre-school education. The child may

---

[1] Offenders who have been convicted of a sexual offence against a child, any offence under the relevant sections of the Children and Young Persons (Scotland) Act 1937 or any assault on a person under 17 years of age leading to that individual's bodily injury.

be left unsupervised or be neglected when the parents are under the influence of drugs or absent from the house obtaining drugs or money to buy them. Children may be exposed to direct physical violence or emotional abuse if the parent or other drug users in the home lose their temper when suffering from withdrawal. Physical, emotional and sexual abuse in these circumstances can never entirely be ruled out.

Julianne

Julianne is 11 and was taken into care when her mother died of a drug overdose. Her maternal grandparents play an important part in her life but are too frail to care for her permanently. Julianne has three younger half-siblings placed with their father and paternal grandparents. Julianne was often the main carer for her siblings and consequently her school attendance was poor. She has a lot of inappropriate knowledge of the drug scene and finds it hard to let go of her adult role and act as a child. She has few friends of her own age. She is very anxiously attached to her present short-term foster carer. Julianne does not want to be adopted because of her loyalty to her birth mother for whom she is still grieving. She is described as follows:

> *Julianne is 11 years old. She has curly red hair and freckles. Her mother died recently and there is no one in her family to care for her. Julianne enjoys swimming and playing on her Play Station. Her schoolwork is making progress in her present foster home. Julianne would like to stay in contact with her grandparents and siblings but she wants a forever family.*

Problem drug use is a chronic relapsing condition, typically marked by dramatic swings between relative stability and chaos. During times of chaos children become vulnerable. Meeting a child's physical, social and emotional needs will frequently conflict with the parent's need for drugs, potentially exposing the child to the effects of neglect, emotional abuse and poverty. When family homes become dysfunctional the children's development and education are neglected.

By the age of 11, affected children are likely to have a variety of behavioural difficulties in response to the circumstances in which they have lived. Children may challenge, withdraw, assume a parental role or deny their feelings. While some, at least on the surface, appear to have adapted and to have survived, others react with demanding behaviour to the emotional and physical chaos of their family life.

Regular school attendance is essential for children; they also need parental support to make progress. A study of 50 primary school age children of problem drug users in Dublin found that their school attendance, their homework and their concentration in class was on average poorer than 50 other children from the same area and socio-economic background (Hogan, 2001). Drug-misusing parents can find it difficult to sustain family routines and be involved with school and schoolwork. Truanting from school may become a problem.

By late childhood, children are likely to have seen their parents using drugs at home and to have seen adults coming to the house to use or deal in drugs. Children may have to assume greater than normal responsibility for their siblings. Parental behaviour involving drug-taking, dishonesty, deceit and criminal behaviour can legitimise and normalise such behaviour in the eyes of the child.

Interviews with children of drug users indicate that the children's understanding of their parents drug problem typically falls into place around the age of 10–12 (Advisory Council on the Misuse of Drugs, 2003). Children can become cautious about exposing family life to outside scrutiny, restricting friendships and thereby incurring social isolation. Teenagers may be left alone to cope with the physical and emotional changes of puberty. Substance misuse by teenagers whose parents have serious drug problems becomes more likely as they get older (Ferguson and Lynskey, 1998). Feelings of isolation and low self-esteem may generate a wish to escape physically through drink or drugs, thus completing the tragic inheritance of wasted potential.

What does this mean for substitute carers?

There are hundreds of studies on the problems of drug users. However, their children have largely escaped the attention of researchers. Data on the drugs taken by pregnant women are not routinely collected in the UK. Problem drug-taking is characterised by the use of multiple drugs, often by injection, and is strongly associated with socio-economic deprivation.

It compromises children's health and development at every stage from conception onward.

The long-term effects of drug use are even more difficult to ascertain. Tobacco was first brought into Britain in the 16th century. It was four hundred years later, in 1957, that the Medical Research Council established the link between smoking and lung cancer. It was another 40 years before the deleterious effects of tobacco smoke on children were recognised.

Parents, doctors and social workers can only deal with probabilities. Statistical information is often out of date before it is even published, and it is still not possible to determine precisely which children will be affected by parental substance misuse and in what way. As the drug testing of pregnant women and the extended follow-up of drug-exposed children has become more widespread, the range of consequences for the affected child has become more apparent. Not all children prenatally exposed to drugs and alcohol will have long-term problems; some appear to have minimal or no apparent problems while others have very severe problems and there is a spectrum of difficulties between these two extremes.

Not all professionals are fully informed of the effects of substance misuse and conflicting advice can add to the dilemmas substitute carers face. The almost unlimited amount of invalidated information available on the Internet, which varies from the excellent to the dangerously misleading, has added to this confusion. The range of opinion from different professionals is academically interesting but of limited help to a parent struggling with a difficult child.

To know is to understand

The information we received at matching was very comprehensive; even though we had our problems we always felt that we understood the reasons why she behaved as she did. (Adopters of a seven-year-old girl)

We all need comprehensive and detailed knowledge about our children in order to parent them sensitively. In addition to the usual roles which all parents undertake, substitute carers have to uncover, discover or simply guess about the past and its continuing influence on the future of their child. Only then can they help their children to repair, rebuild or compensate for what has gone before. No one should ever be asked to parent a child in the absence of *any* of the information that is available to professionals about the child. Foster and adoptive parents need to be archaeologists before they can be the architects of their children's future.

Firstly – making a nuisance of yourself

Comprehensive identification and assessment of problems are likely to facilitate a placement rather than threaten it. Substitute carers require a very honest assessment of the difficulties they are likely to face in meeting a child's needs. Carers must seek every opportunity to obtain as much health information as possible about a prospective child. They need to ask questions, ask them repeatedly and if necessary, make a nuisance of themselves to get the answers.

Carers need to ensure that they see a full record of the child's medical history and the parents' medical history. They should be assertive in their requests to discuss any questions or concerns with the specialists involved with the child. For example, if the child has ever received a psychological or psychiatric assessment, the prospective parents should be given a copy of the report. If the child has been tested for HIV or hepatitis B and C, any prospective carers should make sure that the implications of the test results are explained to them in simple, unambiguous terms.

Health is always more than just physical health. Children are always growing and developing and reports from nursery or classroom teachers give essential information about a child's developmental skills, particularly in the social context. When appropriate, adopters should ask to speak with a health visitor, teacher or other key figure who knows the child in a context outside the social work field. They should request medical and developmental information about siblings, if children are not to be placed together, and the reasons for separation.

Introductions can be a tense and fraught time for all concerned. The potential carers, who have undergone a long assessment process and potentially endured a long wait, may feel their lives have been "on hold" for months. The social worker, who may have been involved in extended legal proceedings, can be equally anxious for a vulnerable child to move into a permanent placement. The process can become rushed and events move at breakneck speed. In addition to the excitement of a long-awaited child, carers are often organising or renovating family homes, tying up loose ends at work in preparation for leave and undertaking tiring journeys to the child's foster family. Medical information, particularly in a superficially healthy child, may not seem a very important issue. In this heady atmosphere many of the questions formulated during the assessment are left unasked, an omission likely to be regretted later.

Secondly – medical assessments must be comprehensive and holistic

The assessment of the child must provide an accurate and realistic picture of physical health and developmental, behavioural and emotional needs. Children affected by drugs or alcohol should not have a pre-placement medical examination done by a doctor who only conducts a physical examination. A comprehensive family medical history and the personal medical history of the child are essential. Health is not just the absence of illness; preventive healthcare is also important. Vision, hearing, dental checks and immunisations matter and, depending on the age of the child, must be done before placement. It is advisable for children with particularly complex or subtle problems to be examined by a community consultant paediatrician or by an experienced agency medical adviser.

Medical advisers are registered medical practitioners, assigned by name to adoption and fostering panels, and increasingly having an additional responsibility for looked after children and fostering services. These doctors are normally paediatricians or general practitioners with a special interest in the work. Whatever their background, the doctors who undertake this role must have an in-depth knowledge of child health and development and understand the long-term consequences of child abuse and neglect. They should have an understanding of the genetic implications of illness in birth parents. An ability to work as part of a multi-disciplinary team is essential, as are good local networks where the skills of obstetricians, psychiatrists, infertility clinics, child protection and special needs services can be shared in the interests of children. Medical advisers should understand the problems that complex children are likely to present to substitute carers and be able to give social workers and carers clear advice.

The medical report produced by a medical adviser, when a child is considered by an adoption or fostering panel, is an important document to which the child will have access in the future. It must therefore be legible and avoid medical jargon and emotive judgements. For many children this information will be the only glimpse of their medical history that they can have access to in the future unless they are still in contact with their birth parents or family to ask for more information. They would not be able to gain access to their parents' health records, GP notes, mental health records and mother's ante-natal records because these records are about another person. They or their adopters could apply for access to the child's record but this would involve knowing which hospital or community service to approach and some knowledge about where the child was living at the time. All this information is very difficult to get hold of, hence the need for comprehensive summaries to be prepared at the time of placement.

Thirdly – the past is important
For a child brought up within his or her birth family, there is little need to depend on accurate medical record-keeping. Most birth parents have an intimate knowledge of their own child's health and development. For children separated from their families the loss or delay in the transfer of medical records, disrupted medical histories and inadequate record keeping is all too common.

A child's medical history starts before conception when the genetic material of both parents is combined to form a new and unique individual. Genetics in substitute care is far from straightforward. Huge information gaps often exist. The family tree may be complicated and tortuous. The mother may be unwilling to divulge the father's identity or may disappear during the legal proceedings.

A child's medical history continues through pregnancy, delivery and the early neonatal period. Pre-birth traumas can include the exposure to violence (including attempted abortion), feelings of ambivalence, rejection or grief in the mother, maternal illness or poor nutrition in addition to the misuse of tobacco, alcohol and drugs.

It is important that adopters have full information about the child's birth. Not only should this include information such as the hospital where the child was born and the child's birthweight, but any possible areas of distress to the infant that could have occurred around the time of delivery. These include instrumental deliveries, caesarean section, prolonged labours, time spent in the special care baby unit and prolonged separation from the mother. Some children may have had repeated or extended early separations from their birth mother. Post-natal depression can make mothers emotionally unavailable to their babies. Many children are subjected to inappropriate attempts at rehabilitation, or may have spent periods of time in a drug withdrawal unit.

A very important and frequently forgotten point is that a child's family history does not stop with his or her permanent placement. It must be kept up to date – family members may die or develop serious illnesses which may be of genetic significance, and siblings can develop a number of health or learning problems. Children and their carers need to know about these issues.

Social workers who are not trained health professionals may be the only people to have contact with birth families. Whereas the social history of the family is often well documented, medical information is frequently sketchy, inaccurately recorded or even worse, omitted on the spurious grounds of confidentiality. All involved in substitute care urgently need updated guidance in the whole area of medical confidentiality to reflect modern adoption and fostering practice.

Intercountry adoption

While information about the past is essential for the future parenting of all children, babies and young children adopted from overseas often present particular problems. These children are adopted from a variety of settings, but are increasingly likely to have been adopted from a background of institutional care. They are also more likely to have been born to parents who have experienced severe poverty and social exclusion and who may have exposed their unborn child to additional risks in pregnancy. Detailed information about the early lives of these children may be impossible to obtain and adopters may forget to ask about exposure to drugs.

Foetal alcohol syndrome (FAS) is an international problem affecting 1.9/1000 live births (Abel and Sokol, 1987). There has been a significant recent increase in alcohol use amongst women in Russia and Eastern Europe with FAS affecting 15/1000 live births. This is likely to be an underestimate as diagnosis of FAS is difficult to detect in newborn children. Heroin and opiate use across Eastern Europe is increasing with Russia having a two per cent prevalence of adult users. Amphetamines account for about 18 per cent of the illegal drug treatment demand in Asia (UN Office on Drugs and Crime, 2003).

Infection with blood-borne viruses is a worldwide and increasing problem. While this increase is not all related to drug misuse, the relative burden of these diseases worldwide at the end of 2002 was: 350 million chronically infected with hepatitis B, 170 million chronically infected with hepatitis C and 42 million chronically infected with HIV. HIV, hepatitis B and hepatitis C prevalence rates are updated annually and posted on the World Health Organisation websites. Further information about the health issues affecting intercountry adopted children can be found in *The Health Screening of Children Adopted from Abroad* (BAAF, 2004).

Fourthly – getting smart about the drug scene
It is only by asking hard and detailed questions that the nature of the potential harm done to a child through drugs can be assessed. Most potential carers initially have little or no knowledge of the drug scene. Despite this they must have a rigorous and systematic approach to obtaining information for the sake of their child. A more comprehensive list of the relevant issues is to be found in the SCODA (The Standing Conference on Drug Abuse) guidelines in Chapter 10. However, the key factors for substitute parents to determine are as follows.

Were the parents able to place the needs of their children before their own need for drugs? Did the child have the protective support of a drug-free partner or supportive relative? Was the drug use by the parent recreational or chaotic and relapsing? Did the parents also misuse alcohol, tobacco and prescription drugs and in what quantities? Was there evidence of co-existing mental health problems? Did drugs cause mental health problems or did poor mental health lead to drug use?

Was the family accommodation adequate for the children and did the parents ensure that rent and bills were paid? Was there adequate food, clothing, warmth and toys? Did the family move frequently? Were the children left with a number of different carers? Were the children left alone while their parents were procuring drugs or were they taken to places where they could be at risk? Did the children attend school regularly and enjoy age-appropriate activities? Were their emotional needs met and were older children taking on a parenting role within the family?

Was there conflict or domestic violence in the children's environment? Were the children living in a drug and alcohol-using community where they witnessed the impact of drugs on other individuals? Was the family home being used to deal drugs? Was injecting equipment kept on the premises and were the children aware of and able to access this? Were the parents sharing intravenous needles and were they aware of the health risks of using drugs and alcohol? Were the children associating with other drug users and experiencing social stigmatisation?

Very few adopters or foster carers ask these questions. However, it is not easy parenting a child without any prior knowledge of what happened during a critical period of their lives. To quote an adoptive mother of a four-year-old who had been found aged 11 months in an underpass with unconscious parents:

We will never know what happened to Chloe during the first 12 months of her life but three years later we are still struggling to cope with her and to understand her behaviour.

Finally . . .

Every child deserves a loving family in which to grow up. When a child has special needs, substitute families are the front line of protection, encouragement and advocacy. Thousands of children have benefited from the generosity and commitment of their substitute parents. Society owes a debt of gratitude to those adults whose devotion and commitment have helped children overcome an uncertain start to life. Second chances are rare but if anyone deserves one it is an innocent, vulnerable child damaged at the very beginning of life.

References

Abel E L and Sokol R J (1987) 'Incidence of Fetal Alcohol Syndrome and economic impact of FAS-related anomalies', *Drug and Alcohol Dependence*, 19, pp 51–70

Advisory Council on the Misuse of Drugs (2003) *Hidden Harm: Responding to the needs of children of problem drug users*, London: Home Office

BAAF (2004) *The Health Screening of Children Adopted from Abroad*, Practice Note 46, London: BAAF

Department of Health (2002) *Children Looked After by Local Authorities Year Ending 31 March 2002 England*, National Statistics, London: Department of Health, www.doh.gov.uk

Ferguson D M and Lynskey M T (1998) 'Conduct problems in childhood and psychosocial outcomes in adolescence: a prospective study', *Journal of Emotional and Behavioural Disorders*, 6, pp 6–12

Hogan D and Higgins L (2001) *When Parents use Drugs: Key findings from a study of children in the care of drug abusing parents*, Dublin: Trinity College

Mather M (1999) 'Adoption: a forgotten paediatric speciality', *Archives of Disease in Childhood*, 81, pp 492–95

Useful resources

The British National Formulary website gives information on prescription drugs in the UK on www.bnf.org

The prevalence of world-wide illegal substance use is updated annually by the UN Office on Drugs and Crime at www.unodc.org/unodc/global_illicit_drug_trends.html

World Health Organisation website gives data on hepatitis at www.who.int/health_topics/hepatitis/en/

World Health Organisation website gives data on HIV/AIDS at www.who.int/health_topics/hiv_infections/en/

2 A brief introduction to the effects of psychoactive drugs

Dr William Phillips

Introduction

This chapter gives a brief introduction to some of the effects of drugs on the brain and mind. These effects are very complex and, though they have been much studied by neurobiologists, psychologists, and pharmacologists, much remains to be discovered. In an attempt to draw some simple but relevant messages from this research, I first explain what psychoactive drugs are and why they are particularly relevant here. Next, I list some of the various ways in which drugs can be classified, which may help clarify differences in the terminology used by different people. I then discuss some of the main drugs within each of four groups, classified by the kind of effect that they have on mental processes. Finally, I will outline some general messages concerning the effects of parental drug use and misuse on child development. Very few technical terms are used; these are printed in bold when they are first discussed, to alert readers to the need to understand how they are being used.

What are psychoactive drugs and why are they important?

Psychoactive drugs are those that affect the mind and brain. They include stimulants, depressants, analgesics and psychedelics. All human cultures use psychoactive drugs and each does so in its own way. Drugs that are strongly prohibited in one culture may be strongly promoted in another. Alcohol provides a well-known example of this cultural relativity, but there are many others. Slowly changing cultures usually have time to avoid the catastrophic effects of drug use, by developing appropriate forms of practice, provision and education concerning the drugs that they use. In rapidly changing global cultures such as ours, however, this is much more difficult. In our society, the availability, distribution and promotion of both long-established and novel psychoactive drugs are running far ahead of all attempts to control them. Parental drug misuse is therefore common, and it creates major and growing problems, both for the individuals concerned and for society as a whole.

Although not all drugs of misuse are psychoactive, most are, and there are good grounds for our focus on them here. Parental use/misuse of psychoactive drugs can affect development of children from conception onwards, and can have long-term consequences for emotional and intellectual life. Post-natal parental drug misuse will have many consequences for the development of the child concerned. Some of these will involve the child's physical development, but most are connected to the child's mental development, and these will be discussed in later chapters. Drug use during pregnancy can cause physical malformations that are easily seen, such as the facial malformations in children with Foetal Alcohol Syndrome. Far more important and far more difficult to assess, however, are the effects on the developing mind and brain. Most of the effects on the brain are not visible and their consequences for behaviour may not become significant for several years, by which time there will be a host of potential causes for any behavioural problems. The difficulty of assessing the effects on the brain and mind must not be seen as implying that such effects are small or unlikely. On the contrary, significant effects are highly probable. It is drugs that have psychological effects that are most commonly misused. These drugs are likely to have even larger effects on embryological brain development, because this is designed to be highly sensitive to the exact conditions in which the development takes place, and because the embryo's mechanisms for limiting the amounts of potentially harmful substances circulating in the blood are not fully established.

Ways of classifying psychoactive drugs

Psychoactive drugs can be classified in several different ways: e.g. by psychological effect, by medicinal use, by neurotransmitter system affected, by chemical structure and by legality. These various ways of classifying drugs leads to differences in terminology. For example, I classify alcohol as a psychoactive drug. When others refer to "drugs and alcohol", the implication is that they are using the word "drugs" as shorthand for "illegal drugs". Legality depends primarily upon historical events and current commercial and political interests. It has little relation to the potential harmfulness or usefulness of the drugs concerned. Drugs are not made harmless by being legal and widely used. Nor are they made harmless by being prescribed for medicinal purposes. Even though such prescribing is usually based, at least in part, upon many decades of research on the drugs concerned, the demands of selecting the appropriate drug and dose and of monitoring its effects are so great that it is not realistic to expect that the advantages will always outweigh the disadvantages. The central point here is that the neurochemical systems being modified by psychoactive drugs are so finely and delicately balanced that using these drugs to advantage is very difficult, even when they are being taken under medical supervision.

Four major classes of psychoactive drugs

Drugs can have many different psychological effects. Here we outline just four major classes: stimulant, depressant, analgesic and psychedelic. There are others, and a single drug can have effects of more than one kind, but in an attempt to make an enormously complex field more comprehensible, only some of the most prominent effects of each drug are mentioned. The best way to understand the psychological effects of any drug is to know what **neurotransmitter systems** it affects and how, and then to relate the effects of the drug to the role of those neurotransmitters in normal psychological function. Taken seriously, this approach would require many years' study of neuropsychopharmacology. A little more will be said about this below, but at this stage it is sufficient to note that **neurotransmitters** are the substances naturally produced by brain cells in order to either increase or decrease the activity of those other brain cells to which they are connected. A neurotransmitter system is therefore the set of connections using that particular neurotransmitter. All mental life depends upon neural activity and thus upon neurotransmitters. Drugs that increase the activity of a neurotransmitter system are called **agonists** of that system and those that decrease it are called **antagonists**. Even within the same class, different drugs can have very different time courses of action, but there is neither space nor necessity to outline these variations here. For more information on the main classes of misused drugs, their prevalence and availability, the many different ways in which they can be taken, their short-term and long-term effects and withdrawal symptoms, see the *Druglink Guide to Drugs* (Drugscope, 2004). This is regularly updated, and further relevant information can be accessed via the website at www.drugscope.org.uk. For an authoritative, in-depth, text on neuropsychopharmacology, I highly recommend Feldman *et al* (1997).

A drug's effects depend not only upon the drug used but also on the "set" and "setting". The "set" involves all the individual's past cultural influences that bear on a person's drug use, together with their relevant prior personal experiences and susceptibilities. The "setting" concerns the immediate circumstances in which the drug is taken, such as whether it is taken in a group situation or not, and, if so, the nature of that social setting. Both set and setting create states of mind that, while not fundamentally changing the kind of effects a drug will have, nevertheless modify or modulate those effects in various ways.

Stimulants

This is a very broad class of drugs with at least four main subtypes: caffeine, nicotine, amphetamine and cocaine. Caffeine acts very specifically as an antagonist of the neurotransmitter adenosine. Adenosine dampens down the general resting level of neuronal excitability when we are awake. In other words, it helps keep us calm. The antagonistic effect of caffeine on adenosine reduces this calming effect and thus increases our resting level of alertness. Substantial amounts of caffeine are found in coffee, tea, Coca-Cola, chocolate and sports drinks. It is widely assumed that caffeine has little or no effect on embryological development, though the effects of large amounts may be significant.

Nicotine is an agonist of the neurotransmitter acetylcholine, whose functions include increasing alertness and focusing attention. Although nicotine is sometimes felt to have a soothing effect, in general it is a stimulant as it increases the activity of an alerting system. Nicotine is one of the most addictive substances known. At least 30 per cent of those who try smoking just once become addicts, and evidence suggests that this is even more than those who try heroin just once. Heroin addicts who also smoke say that it is easier to give up heroin.

Amphetamine and amphetamine-like drugs are synthetic substances that include Dexedrine, "Speed" and Ritalin. They are related to Ecstasy (MDMA) which is mentioned below for its psychedelic effects. Cocaine is a plant-based substance that has been used for many centuries in South America where the coca leaf is widely chewed for its mildly stimulating effect. The dose obtained through this route is many times less than that obtained by users in the West, and particularly by users of crack cocaine, which is a form that has been refined to greatly increase its potency and speed of action. Amphetamines and cocaine are both agonists of the dopamine and serotonin systems. They are both powerful stimulants, and cocaine in particular produces a rush of intensely pleasurable sensations. Effects on the serotonin system are thought to include a strong sense of satisfaction or well-being. They may also be responsible for some of the psychedelic effects that can also be produced by these drugs when taken in large doses or for long periods. Dopamine increases activity by helping to disinhibit actions and, in addition, it produces strong feelings of pleasure by stimulating brain regions specialised to reward appropriate actions. By hijacking neural mechanisms that have evolved to encourage the repetition of actions that contribute to our health and well-being, these substances force repeated taking of the drug, even though that has harmful and sometimes fatal consequences.

Depressants

Depressants are those drugs whose overall effect is to reduce neuronal activity. In large amounts they can therefore lead to stupor, coma or death. In smaller amounts some, such as alcohol, can lead to an increase in behavioural activity. One simple way of thinking of this is that at lower amounts the neuronal activity that is most reduced is that mediating our "inhibitions", e.g. thoughts or tendencies that tell us not to do certain things in the current circumstances. Drugs with depressant effects include tranquillisers, sedatives, such as the barbiturates, and solvents, but by far the most important member of this group in our society is alcohol. At lower doses it can produce a feeling of relaxation and reduce feelings of tension and anxiety, in addition to lessening various inhibitions in relatively harmless ways. But it also reduces inhibitions to aggressive or violent behaviour, and it impairs motor control and intellectual function in many ways. Alcohol is a small and simple molecule that rapidly becomes widely dispersed in the body and affects a whole host of physiological processes. Within the brain it affects many different neurotransmitter systems, but prominent within these is that using the neurotransmitter GABA, which tends to reduce the activity of those brain cells that it affects. Alcohol is an agonist for GABA. It therefore tends to diminish total neuronal activity by increasing the activity of cells with an inhibitory effect.

Psychological dependence on and physiological addiction to alcohol are common. At least 15 per cent of users are described as "dependent". More than 30,000 people die annually in the UK from alcohol-related diseases, and that does not include those due to road crashes or violent outbursts. There is no clear boundary separating those who drink a lot from those who are labelled "alcoholic". Alcohol passes easily through the placenta, and levels circulating in the embryo's bloodstream are higher than in the mother's, because the embryo's mechanisms for breaking down alcohol, such as those in the liver, are not fully functional. Much evidence suggests that the developing brain is very sensitive to the presence of alcohol, and pregnant mothers who drink run the risk of having babies with poorly developed brains and, consequently, with low IQs, hyperactivity, low attention spans and maybe other behavioural problems. At higher amounts, the effects of maternal intake of alcohol become easily visible in what is known as Foetal Alcohol Syndrome (FAS), and more is said about this in a later chapter. FAS includes clear impairments in intellectual functioning, learning ability and behavioural control. The simple point emphasised here is that, though these impairments may be less easily seen with lower amounts of alcohol intake during pregnancy, that in no way implies that they are not there. On the contrary, the available evidence suggests a dose–effect relationship such that even small amounts of alcohol in the foetal bloodstream have some effect, and the greater the amount the greater the effect.

Opiates and other analgesics

The primary effect of analgesics is to moderate or reduce persistent pain, whether of physical or psychological origin. Feelings of warmth and drowsy contentment help cushion the user from the psychological impact of pain, fear and anxiety. They may still be sensed in some way, but they seem to matter less. At higher doses drowsiness and sedation become more prominent. Major members of this class of drug include heroin and the related substances morphine and methadone. Distalgesics and various over-the-counter pain-killers, such as codeine, are also included. Heroin is made from the opium poppy and can be smoked, but to increase the speed with which it reaches the brain, it is more often injected. Initially, heroin rapidly produces sensations of intense pleasure, but it is highly addictive, and with repeated intake, pleasurable sensations decrease, and are replaced by an incessant craving that can only be assuaged by taking the drug again and again. Methadone is a synthetic opiate that is prescribed to help manage heroin addiction. In chemical structure it is closely related to heroin, but it produces milder reactions. It does not produce a rush because generally it is not injected. Its effects are longer lasting than those of heroin and it encourages a more stable lifestyle. Controlled provision by social agencies rather than by illicit traders also makes it easier for addicts to lead worthwhile and enjoyable lives. Methadone is not a cure, however. It, too, is addictive and is often traded on the streets in the same way as heroin. Those who use heroin often combine it with other drugs, such as cocaine or alcohol. The effects of these combinations are highly unpredictable and often lethal.

Drugs such as heroin are agonists for systems that use neurotransmitters called endogenous opiates or endorphins. These are naturally occurring substances that have evolved to dampen down feelings of persistent pain in circumstances where these sensations have no adaptive value, such as during prolonged exercise, e.g. pursuit hunting, or during periods of famine, where prolonged feelings of hunger may have little utility. Both opiate use and withdrawal from opiate use during pregnancy can have serious consequences for foetal development, as discussed in depth in later chapters. The effects of parental opiate use on child care can also be substantial and these are also discussed in later chapters.

Psychedelics

This is a wide and heterogeneous class, in which drugs are loosely grouped together on the grounds that they produce altered states of consciousness or dream-like states, such as heightened awareness of sensory qualities and other perceptual distortions, an altered sense of time and space, hallucinations, delusions and either a sense of detachment or of intense empathy for others. They can also produce paranoia, anxiety, panic and intense agitation. Deaths from overdose are rare, but the delusions can lead to users taking life-threatening actions, such as jumping out of the window in the belief that they can fly. The effects of psychedelics are especially sensitive to the users' beliefs and expectations concerning the drug's effects, and to the social and other circumstances in which the drug is taken. The short-term effects are therefore highly unpredictable, but intellectual functions are generally impaired. The long-term effects can include "flashbacks" of frightening experiences that were had during the "trip", and these may recur for months or years. Acute psychotic episodes may be triggered in those at risk, and long-term psychotic conditions, such as schizophrenia, may be initiated. These drugs are not strongly addictive, but users may become psychologically dependent on them. Drugs in this class are sometimes called "recreational". It includes cannabis (marijuana), Ecstasy (MDMA), LSD, magic mushrooms, mescaline and PCP (Angel Dust). Some of these drugs, such as cannabis and Ecstasy, are in very widespread use.

Cannabis acts as an agonist of a system that uses neurotransmitters with a chemical structure that is very similar to cannabis. The functions of this system include control of the muscles (which may relate to feelings of relaxation) and regulating sensitivity to pain (which may relate to feelings of well-being). In a medical context where the purity of the drug, its manner of delivery and its dose are appropriately controlled, it may have substantial benefits. Unfortunately, as with nicotine, smoking is a highly effective way of getting the drug to the brain, and cannabis smoke has much the same mixture of poisons as do cigarettes. Medicinal use is therefore unlikely to involve smoking.

Ecstasy acts as a strong agonist of the system that uses the neurotransmitter serotonin, as do many other psychedelics. In normal function this neurotransmitter system has many different effects. Several of these relate to the production of a sense of satisfaction. In relation to eating, for example, serotonin is used to signal that enough has been eaten, even if what is being eaten is good and there is more available. Agonists of serotonin are therefore used in medications designed to reduce food intake. Serotonin agonists are also used in the treatment of obsessive compulsive disorders, where someone may keep washing their hands, for example, because they cannot feel satisfied with the washing that they have done. It is therefore not surprising that drugs that strongly stimulate the serotonin system produce strong feelings of satisfaction. Nor is it surprising that heavy use of these drugs can damage this system through overstimulation, leading to the inability to feel satisfaction in anything, and thus to deep and prolonged states of depression. Why increased activity of the serotonin system also produces strong psychedelic effects remains a major scientific mystery.

The consequences of polydrug use

In an attempt to attain some comprehensibility, the above has been written as though people normally use one and only one form of psychoactive drug. This is rarely the case. Considering only legal drugs, the combination of alcohol, nicotine and caffeine is very common. When illegal drugs are added, the number of possible, and frequently used, combinations increases greatly. Alcohol is commonly used in combination with other drugs. When used alone its effects are complex, when used in combination with other psychoactive drugs the consequences become even more so. In assessing the likely outcome of polydrug use, one simple rule-of-thumb is that in most cases two drugs in the same class will combine to produce an effect that is equal to or greater than the sum of their effects when taken separately. For example, two depressants, such as barbiturates and alcohol, can combine to greatly reduce brain activity. Combining drugs from different classes has less predictable consequences. Although there is still much uncertainty concerning the consequences of polydrug use, to me the most remarkable thing is that, despite all of the complexities, much of what has been learned about the effects of each drug when taken separately still has relevance to its effects in the real and complex world of polydrug use.

Summary and conclusions

Psychoactive drugs are most relevant to the concerns of this book because they are by far the most common drugs of misuse, and because both foetal brain development and child-rearing practices will be greatly affected. Even from the brief review given above, it is clear that the use of psychoactive substances is very widespread as they extend far beyond the set of substances sometimes characterised as "hard drugs". Most children will therefore to some extent be affected by pre- and post-natal parental drug use. Much remains to be learned concerning the effects of "normal" or "social" drug use, but the point being emphasised here is that the effects on children born to parents considered to be serious drug abusers may differ in extent rather than in kind from the effects on other children. The long-term or even life-long effects of parental drug misuse may make the child a different person, but that is not necessarily a disabled person.

Neurotransmitters, such as those mentioned above, are central to understanding the psychological effects of drugs. They can be thought of as little keys that fit into locks that open doors to many different kinds of processes within brain cells or neurones. In general, these processes either excite or inhibit the receiving cell in some way. Different neurotransmitters fit into different locks and affect different cells in different ways. Psycho-active drugs can affect these processes by acting as a duplicate key that fits locks designed to receive some naturally produced neurotransmitter. Agonists do so in such a way as to produce the same effects on the receiving cell as would the natural neurotransmitter. Antagonists do so in such a way as to block those processes. There are many different neuro-transmitter systems, and different drugs fit the locks of different systems. Some drugs, and in particular alcohol, act as a kind of skeleton key that fits many different kind of locks and which therefore opens or blocks the doors to numerous different physiological processes. They can therefore have very wide-ranging and complex effects.

Anatomical and physiological studies show that brain function involves the organised activity of vast numbers of molecules in enormous numbers of neurones. Seen from this perspective the neurochemical basis of mental life is hugely complex and highly organised. Furthermore, this organisa-tion is ever changing because the brain is forever reconstructing itself through mechanisms designed to improve its adaptation to the world in which it finds itself. Seen from this neurobiological perspective, the human brain is in no simple sense mechanical or predictable. The level of complexity involved, and its sensitivity to its own particular circumstances, emphasise the essential uniqueness of every human individual.

References

Drugscope (2004) *The Druglink Guide to Drugs*, London: Drugscope Publications

Feldman R S, Meyer J S and Quenzer L F (1997) *Principles of Neuropsychopharmacology*, Massachusetts: Sinauer Associates

The effects of substance misuse in pregnancy

3 The effects of drug misuse in pregnancy

Dr Patricia McElhatton

Introduction

Since the thalidomide tragedy in the 1960s, there has been increased public awareness of the risk that some medicines, when taken during pregnancy, may harm the developing baby (i.e. act as teratogens). However, many women still take medicines during pregnancy (on average three to eight drugs), often before they realise that they are pregnant. In a recent survey in the UK, about 35 per cent of women were found to have taken medicines at least once during pregnancy, and six per cent took medicines during the first three months, excluding iron and vitamins supplements.

An agent is now considered a teratogen if its administration to the pregnant woman causes, directly or indirectly, structural or functional abnormalities in the foetus, or in the child after birth, which may not be apparent until later life (Wilson, 1977; McElhatton, 1999; Schardein, 2000; Peters and Schaefer, 2001). Thus foetal toxicity can occur at any stage of pregnancy, not just in the first trimester (the first three months), although the first trimester is the most vulnerable period for congenital malformations.

A teratogen can induce:
- chromosomal abnormalities;
- impairment of implantation of the fertilised egg in the womb;
- miscarriage (spontaneous abortion/resorption of the early embryo);
- structural malformations, e.g. cleft palate;
- intrauterine growth retardation;
- foetal death – late intrauterine death, stillbirth;
- functional impairment in the neonate (newborn infant), e.g. deafness;
- behavioural abnormalities, e.g. hyperactivity;
- learning difficulties;
- transplacental carcinogen, e.g. cause cancer in childhood or adolescence.

Although the majority of babies are normal at birth, about one in 40 have a birth defect. In about 65 per cent of cases, it is not known why these birth defects occur (Schardein, 2000; Peters and Schaefer, 2001). Therefore, if treatment is required during pregnancy, it is important that doctors are able to give accurate, evidenced-based advice to women about the risks, if any, of medicines prescribed.

At the end of this chapter a brief description is given about the National Teratology Information Service (NTIS). One of its main functions is to provide information and advice, not only about drugs, but also chemical exposures.

Drug misuse in pregnancy

This is one of the most difficult and emotive of all drug safety issues that raises concerns regarding both maternal and foetal toxicity. It often presents parents and clinicians with ethical, medico-legal and emotional dilemmas as to whether the pregnancy should continue.

Drug misuse causes serious health problems (Department of Health, 1995; Nutt, 1996; Gilstrap and Little, 1998; Briggs *et al*, 1998; Schardein, 2000; McElhatton, 2000). It has been estimated that 22 per cent of all misusers are females of childbearing age (15–39 years). Overall, 91 per cent misuse heroin, methadone or other opiates; 35 per cent misuse stimulants and other substances such as cannabis (25%), benzodiazepines (22%) and hallucinogens (7%). At least 25 per cent use more than one drug and 38 per cent inject their main drug. There is an increase in the number of young people misusing and becoming addicted to taking drugs and a corresponding increase in the number of women who misuse drugs during pregnancy. Evidence concerning foetotoxicity from paternal exposure is lacking.

The results of a study of anonymous urine testing, in 1,000 pregnant women attending an inner city maternity hospital, showed that 11 per cent had evidence of substance misuse, with the most common drug being cannabis (8.5%). Other substances were also found: opiates (1.4%), cocaine (1.1%), cyclizine (0.4%), methadone (0.3%) and dextropropoxyphene (0.3%) (Farkas *et al*, 1995). These results were very different from those found in a survey of all maternity units in the UK asking about pregnant drug misusers, performed about the same time (Morrison and Siney, 1995). A mean rate of 0.8 per cent was reported with wide regional variation of 0.1–5 per cent.

One of the difficulties in assessing the effects of a particular drug of misuse on the developing foetus is that the pregnant woman is often taking several drugs at the same time. In order to determine the effects of any single factor, it is desirable to compare a group of similar individuals experiencing this factor or with another "control" group which is similar, except for such a factor. However, in substance-misusing pregnant women, there are a variety of complicating factors which makes it difficult to study the effects of a given drug on pregnancy. The majority of studies have raised more questions than answers. The following potential confounding factors must be addressed, but are difficult to control (McElhatton, 2000):

- difficulty of selecting suitable control groups (drug users *vs*. non-drug users);
- the dose and purity of the substance;
- other drug use, including alcohol, smoking, caffeine;
- women enrol in the study but fail to keep follow up appointments, i.e. they "drop out" of the study;
- infections (sexually transmitted diseases, HIV);
- ill-defined nutritional status;
- obstetric and neonatal risk factors such as the drug-related adverse effects on maternal and foetal health, particularly infections, breathing difficulties, prematurity.

Maternal exposure to drugs of misuse has been associated with foetal and neo-natal toxicity. In most cases it is not clear whether this is a direct drug effect or due to deficits in socio-economic lifestyle. Particularly in the case of "hard drugs" (heroin and cocaine), the effects on the health of the unborn baby are frequently enhanced as a result of polytoxins, including alcohol and nicotine. In socially deprived environments, malnutrition, infections and traumatisation can also have an additional teratogenic effect. Thus in the case of drug-dependent pregnant women, miscarriages, premature births, intrauterine growth retardation and foetal death cannot necessarily be attributed to a single substance. In newborns, the presence of drugs can be established not only in the urine, but just as reliably in the meconium (faeces of newborn) using radioimmunological procedures (Dahlem, 1992).

Recreational drugs can be classified into several groups according to their pharmacological effects:

- *opiates* such as heroin, opium, morphine and codeine;
- *stimulants* such as cocaine and amphetamines; and
- *psychedelics* such as cannabis or marijuana, LSD, phencyclidine, mescaline and psilocybin.

In this chapter the main classes of recreational drugs such as opiates, cocaine and amphetamines will be reviewed, as well as other drugs often taken at the same time such as benzodiazepines (tranquillisers) and anti-depressants, that also have the potential to cause significant dependence.

Opiates

Opiate abuse (heroin, morphine) has been associated with a number of pregnancy complications such as miscarriage and placental abruption (a third trimester complication that results from the haemorrhage and accumulation of blood between the placenta and the wall of the uterus). The latter inevitably interferes with foetal oxygenation and often necessitates the need for emergency caesarean section delivery. Other complications are breech presentation, premature delivery, multiple pregnancy and previous caesarean section (Finnegan, 1979; Ostrea and Chavez 1979).

Heroin (diacetylmorphine)

What is it?

Heroin is a semi-synthetic morphine derivative that acts like morphine. Although its medical use is prohibited in most countries, it has become one of the major substances of misuse, mostly used by injection into a vein or by inhalation through the nose.

What effects does it have on the developing baby (foetus) in the womb?

Congenital malformations: There are several extensive reviews of studies and case reports of children with birth defects born to heroin-using women (Schardein, 2000; Briggs *et al*, 1998; Gilstrap and Little, 1998). Although a number of anecdotal reports of children born with congenital anomalies have been published, the data are difficult to interpret. Heroin-using women often have lifestyles that may influence pregnancy outcome. They often misuse other drugs, alcohol and cigarettes and have poor nutritional and health status (HIV, hepatitis B and C). Moreover, the dose of heroin used, and the period of pregnancy during which it was used, are usually unknown.

No consistent pattern of malformations has been observed, and there is no clear evidence that heroin caused these malformations (Boer *et al*, 1994; Day *et al*, 1994a and b; Glantz *et al*, 1993; Ostrea and Chavez, 1979). The data are insufficient to state that there is no risk, because the number of mother–child pairs studied is small. The overall conclusion is that the diverse nature of the congenital anomalies makes definition of a single heroin syndrome difficult.

Effects on growth and survival in the womb: The most consistent findings are: poor growth (intrauterine growth retardation – IUGR), small head size (decreased head circumference), and increased deaths around the time of delivery (perinatal deaths). Sudden withdrawal of opiates during pregnancy can cause foetal death, and in the last three months of pregnancy cause premature labour contractions.

What effects does it have on the newborn infant (neonate)?

Neonatal survival: There is underweight in about 41–45 per cent of newborns, together with premature delivery and premature rupture of the membranes. The depression of breathing, characteristic of opiates, can be responsible for an increase in infant deaths. It is not clear whether the retardation in post-natal development is directly related to drug exposure in the womb, or to deficiencies in the care after birth.

Neonatal withdrawal syndrome: It is estimated that 40–80 per cent of babies born to heroin-addicted women develop a withdrawal syndrome lasting from several days to several months. It is characterised by exaggerated, jerky movements (hyperactivity), breathing difficulties (respiratory distress), abnormal sleep patterns, fits (convulsions/seizures), fever and diarrhoea (Franck and Vilardi, 1995; Kaltenbach *et al*, 1998). These serious withdrawal symptoms usually begin within 24 to 72 hours after birth. In ten per cent of babies, brain seizures and other symptoms are delayed for ten to 36 days after the birth. The risk of life-threatening withdrawal symptoms is especially high when the mother's dependency is unknown. Careful monitoring of the baby and timely preventive treatment (prophylaxis) with phenobarbitone are needed.

Sudden Infant Death Syndrome (SIDS): Abnormal breathing patterns during sleep may persist for a prolonged period, but usually less than three weeks. This has been suggested as a factor in the increased incidence of SIDS. However, there may be other social and health problems in the families concerned that make interpretation of such reports very difficult. Recently there has been an important extensive review of risk factors associated with SIDS (Sullivan and Barlow, 2001).

Longer-term development: Subsequent growth of these children appears to be normal in most cases although head circumference may continue to be somewhat smaller than expected (Coles, 1993; Ornoy *et al*, 1998). There is no clear evidence of abnormal brain development in most of the children studied.

Heroin substitutes

Methadone

Methadone can be substituted for heroin to reduce pregnancy risks and to prevent the onset of withdrawal symptoms, but is itself addictive. The goal of methadone treatment is a reduction of the dose received to 40 mg a day.

Neonatal breathing difficulties and withdrawal symptoms may also occur with methadone (Koren, 1994). The withdrawal symptoms are often more severe and persistent than with heroin, and there may be a higher risk of SIDS (Bunikowski *et al*, 1998). Overall, methadone may be more beneficial for the mother, but more toxic for the newborn.

Buprenorphine

Some addiction treatment centres are now using sublingual (under the tongue) buprenorphine, an opiate analgesic similar to morphine, instead of methadone (Ling *et al*, 1998). However, buprenorphine itself is addictive and can cause dependence. The effects on the developing baby and newborn have been inadequately studied. In all cases of heroin abuse or opiate substitution, neonates should be observed for many days or weeks, so that any serious delayed withdrawal symptoms can be picked up quickly and be treated (Schaefer and Peters, 2001).

Stimulants

Cocaine, crack cocaine (coke, snow)

What is it?

Cocaine is a local anaesthetic that has a potent, short-acting stimulant effect on the central nervous system. Recreational cocaine use is by nasal inhalation of powder (snorting) or intravenous injection. Intranasally, absorption into the blood stream takes about 20 minutes, but there may be a delay because of blood vessel constriction (vasoconstriction). Intravenous injection is less popular than smoking or insufflation (inhalation/snorting). Taken by mouth (orally) cocaine is absorbed slowly due to its vasoconstrictor effect in the stomach, and the effects come on more slowly and are less intense. Therefore it is a less common method of taking cocaine.

Crack is the free base of cocaine which can be smoked and is often mixed with tobacco or cannabis, and can also be inhaled. Intravenous use, or smoking crack, brings about an effect within a few minutes. To maintain the psychoactive effects and euphoria, the process must be repeated frequently, often termed "a run" or "a binge".

What effects does it have on the developing baby (foetus) in the womb?

Until the beginning of the 1980s, cocaine was considered to be a non-toxic drug prenatally. During the last 20 years, an extensive medical literature on the effects of maternal cocaine use in pregnancy has developed that must be interpreted with great caution (Eriksson and

Zetterstrom, 1994; Day *et al*, 1994a; Gilstrap and Little, 1998; Briggs *et al*, 1998; Richardson and Day, 1999; Schardein, 2000). A great number of confounding factors are present in human studies that often make it difficult to attribute any adverse effects to the taking of cocaine.

Congenital malformations: There is considerable disagreement among experts as to whether or not cocaine and crack themselves actually cause congenital malformations or whether the adverse effects are due either to reporting bias (a need to blame something for causing the malformation observed) or other confounding factors such as multiple drug use (drug interactions) and lifestyle (poor nutrition, ill health). The malformation may not have been caused by cocaine.

A meta-analysis of data (a quantitative method of combining the results of independent studies and synthesising summaries and conclusions, which may be used to evaluate therapeutic effectiveness taking into account different limitations of each of the studies) in 45 papers on cocaine-associated developmental toxicity indicated that adverse outcomes were found only when non-drug using women were used as controls (Lutiger *et al*, 1991). However, foetal toxicity did not appear to be associated with cocaine when compared with a control group of multiple, non-cocaine drug users. Similarly, no evidence of cocaine induced vascular disruption effects (interrupting the normal functions of the blood vessels and circulation) was found in a survey of the Atlanta Congenital Defects Program between 1968 and 1989 (Martin *et al*, 1992). According to current experience, sporadic use in early pregnancy when the mother's liver function is intact, and when there are no additional damaging factors such as alcohol, malnutrition, other drugs, infections, and trauma, does not appear to significantly increase the risk of birth defects.

However, numerous developmental disturbances have been attributed to repeated use of cocaine or crack during pregnancy – microcephaly (abnormally small head), heart defects, effects on the skeletal system (abnormal bone development), blockage of the intestines (intestinal atresia) and genitourinary problems (abnormalities of the genitals and urinary bladder/kidney tract). Many of these abnormalities are thought to be associated with the effects of cocaine on the foetal circulation, such as bleeding and blood clots (infarcts) in these organs and in the placenta. As a result, this can cause focal disturbances in differentiation (the ways cells develop into different types in order to perform different functions) and growth throughout the pregnancy (Delaney-Black *et al*, 1994; Hume *et al*, 1994; Martinez *et al*, 1994).

A distinctive pattern of anomalies, a "Fetal Cocaine Syndrome" has been proposed by some clinicians (Robin and Zackai, 1994; Fries *et al*, 1993) but not by others (Little *et al*, 1996). The features include low birth weight, microcephaly, large fontanelles, prominent glabella (smooth elevation of the frontal bone just above the bridge of the nose), marked periorbital and eyelid oedema (abnormal collection of fluid resulting in swelling around the eye socket), low nasal bridge, short nose and small toenails.

Effects on growth and survival in the womb: Exposure to cocaine and its derivatives has been associated with an increased incidence of placental abruption, bleeding, miscarriage, intrauterine growth delays and prematurity. These effects are often linked to foetal deaths and stillbirths.

What effects does it have on the newborn infant (neonate)?

Neonatal survival: The functional symptoms observed in newborns are less noticeable than in the case of heroin use, and are more apt to be of a toxic nature than connected to withdrawal.

Maternal and neonatal brain haemorrhage, and brain infarcts (blood clots) have been reported (Schaefer and Spielman, 1990; Behnke *et al*, 1998; Frank *et al*, 1998; Little *et al*, 1999; Bellini *et al*, 2000). These neonatal haemorrhages together with high blood pressure in the arteries (neonatal arterial hypertension), IUGR (intrauterine growth retardation) and premature delivery may result in an increased risk of perinatal deaths.

Neonatal withdrawal syndrome: Features include sleep disturbances, tremors, weak suck, increased muscle tone (hypertonus), increased startle response, vomiting, shrill crying, sneezing, tachypnoea (abnormally fast rate of breathing), soft stools, fever and necrotising enterocolitis (inflammation and death of tissues in the intestines as a result of bacterial toxins). In addition, behavioural disturbances, EEG changes and SIDS have been reported (LaGasse *et al*, 1999). However, the existence of a syndrome attributable to withdrawal remains speculative.

Sudden Infant Death Syndrome (SIDS): In a meta-analysis of ten published studies, that included a total of 12,163 infants whose mothers had misused cocaine during pregnancy, the frequency of SIDS was significantly greater than expected (Fares *et al*, 1997). The incidence of SIDS in cocaine exposed babies appears to be 5–8 times higher than in the general population (Bauchner and Zuckerman, 1990). There has also been a case report of one pregnant bodypacker (a person who hides drugs in her body) who had swallowed cocaine contained in pellets wrapped in latex and plastic wrap (Greenberg and Shrethra, 2000). The concern here is whether or not all of the pellets could be removed from the mother's body without damaging the pellets and thus causing leakage of high concentrations into the mother and foetus/neonate. High levels can persist in the neonate and cause toxicity and morbidity.

Longer-term development: There are concerns that *in utero* exposure to cocaine, may cause adverse behavioural changes in children post-natally (Chasnoff *et al*, 1985; Scanlon, 1991). There are many limitations on how such data can be interpreted (Nulman *et al*, 1994; Zuckerman and Frank, 1994; Frank *et al*, 1998, 2001). Some neurobehavioral abnormalities, that have been noted in neonates born to cocaine-using women, have also been seen on ultrasound scans of the foetuses during late pregnancy (Hume *et al*, 1989).

Studies of the cognitive and behavioural effects of prenatal cocaine exposure report learning disorders and attention deficit at three years of age (Griffith *et al*, 1994; Richardson and Day, 1999). However, longer-term follow-up of these children is required to determine the clinical significance of such effects.

Amphetamines

What are they?
Amphetamines (methamphetamine, speed, Ecstasy), which have remained popular drugs of abuse since the 1960s, are central nervous system stimulants that have vasoconstrictor effects (similar to cocaine). Amphetamines are known to cause maternal anorexia (possibly leading to malnutrition), hypertension and reduced blood flow to the placenta. This may result in reduced oxygen and nutrients to the foetus at the sites of newly developing organs.

What effects do they have on the developing baby (foetus) in the womb?

Congenital malformations: There are conflicting data as to whether amphetamines and related compounds have been associated with an increased risk of congenital malformations in human pregnancy.

A number of case reports associate amphetamine exposures during pregnancy with various malformations such as congenital heart disease, anencephaly/exencephaly (the top of the skull fails to form which leaves the often underdeveloped brain exposed), limb reduction defects and biliary atresia (bile ducts between the liver and intestines are absent) (Briggs *et al*, 1998; Little *et al*, 1998; McElhatton *et al*, 2000; Schardein, 2000). However, no clear causal relationship could be established. There has been no indication, as yet, that occasional use of amphetamines in women with intact liver function leads to an increase in congenital anomalies. The summation of data from several studies, of about 3,000 women taking amphetamines during pregnancy, has produced no conclusive evidence of an overall increase in the malformation rate or an increase of any specific type of malformation.

Growth and survival in the womb: Chronic use of amphetamines has been associated with an increased risk of placental abruption, miscarriage, intrauterine growth retardation and premature delivery. Severe maternal toxicity, often resulting in the death of the mother, has also been associated with toxic effects on the foetus, especially the foetal heart, e.g. cardiac arrest. These can seriously compromise foetal and neonatal survival.

What effects do they have on the newborn infant (neonate)?

Neonatal survival: Preterm delivery and a reduction in birth weight have been reported in some newborns exposed to amphetamines, but in most instances the mother took other drugs of abuse.

Neonatal withdrawal syndrome: Withdrawal symptoms such as jitteriness, drowsiness and respiratory distress may develop, suggesting an amphetamine syndrome (Heinonen *et al*, 1977; McElhatton, 2000; McElhatton *et al*, 2000; Schardein, 2000; Peters and Schaefer, 2001).

A recent study of 228 pregnant users indicated an increased risk of minor anomalies and neurological disturbances in exposed pregnant women compared with unexposed controls (Felix *et al*, 2000). However, in this study as in others, respondents were using other drugs including tobacco and alcohol.

Sudden Infant Death Syndrome (SIDS): An increased risk of perinatal mortality has been reported. There is very little information specifically related to amphetamine abuse and SIDS, although the effects are thought to be very similar to cocaine.

Longer-term development: There are few studies on long-term development, and they have produced conflicting results. Among 65 children studied to age 14, a significant increase in learning difficulties in school was found. However, the majority of the mothers had used not only amphetamines but also opiates and alcohol during pregnancy, smoked more than ten cigarettes a day and were in a problematic psycho-social situation. By age 14, only ten per cent of the children had lived with their biological mothers for the whole period since birth (Cernerud *et al*, 1996). Overall, there is no clear evidence to indicate whether or not prenatal amphetamine exposure causes long-term effects on growth and development.

Amphetamines derivatives and designer drugs

There is an ever-changing number of designer drugs available on the market very similar in structure and activity to amphetamine, e.g. methylamphetamine and Ecstasy (MDMA-methylenedioxymethamphetamine). However, the information about their effects in pregnancy is scarce.

Methylamphetamine (speed, ice, crank and crystal meth)

Methylamphetamine is the preferred amphetamine of abuse, possibly because of its greater stimulant effects on the central nervous system and the heart. This drug allegedly has been associated with congenital malformations of the head such as exencephaly, of the eyes, and with cleft palate, as well as behavioural abnormalities. Several reports have attempted to address the behavioural problems but the findings are extremely variable, and no causal relationship has been established.

Ecstasy

Ecstasy (MDMA) and related substances, MDA – methylenedioxyamphetamine (methcathinone, "cat", "Eve") and MDEA –

methylenedioxyethamphetamine, have very powerful effects on the release and actions of serotonin, the nerve transmitter substance. It has been suggested that serotonin can act as a teratogen (cause congenital malformations or other developmental defects).

It is important to realise that tablets often described as Ecstasy can contain anything from relatively "pure" MDMA, amphetamine sulphate, to LSD. Other substances that have also been sold as Ecstasy include ketamine (which can be addictive) and dried hallucinogenic mushrooms. Ecstasy tablets have also been frequently contaminated with substances such as warfarin (an anti-coagulant) used therapeutically to help prevent blood clotting, and also commercially in very large doses as a rat poison, and strychnine (a potent nerve poison). Therefore, in the event of adverse pregnancy outcome, it is extremely difficult to establish whether or not it was caused by "Ecstasy" or other drugs and contaminants.

There have been two small prospective case series published from the Teratology Information Services in the Netherlands and in the UK describing the effects of Ecstasy use in human pregnancy (McElhatton et al, 1999; Rost van Tonningen-van Driel et al, 1999).

The Netherlands data reported on 43 pregnancies (45 outcomes – one set of triplets) in which exposure to Ecstasy occurred. Forty-one were exposed in the first three months, the most vulnerable period for congenital malformations. Only 21 were exposed to Ecstasy alone, while 22 took other drugs of abuse (cocaine, cannabis and alcohol). There were: 39 live-born normal babies, one infant with neonatal withdrawal symptoms, one live-born infant with a congenital heart defect (exposed to Ecstasy alone at six weeks of gestation), two miscarriages and three elective terminations of pregnancy (ETOP). One elective termination occurred following prenatal diagnosis of omphalocoele (the abdominal wall had not closed).

In the UK study there were 136 pregnancies; 74 used only Ecstasy and 62 took a variety of other drugs as well as alcohol. There were 78 live-born infants, 66 were normal, but 12 had congenital anomalies (15.4%), which is significantly higher than the expected incidence of 2–3 per cent. The incidence of miscarriage was within the expected range, but ETOPs were higher than expected. There was no evidence to indicate that the

ETOPs were due to prenatal diagnosis of congenital malformations. Only one severely malformed foetus was electively terminated at 22 weeks.

The 12 malformations (six on only Ecstasy) included two infants with congenital heart defects (CHD) and six with musculoskeletal anomalies. As this study had only a small number of subjects, it did not have sufficient statistical power to prove or disprove that exposure to Ecstasy caused the congenital malformations reported. Overall, there is insufficient information to establish whether or not a single exposure to Ecstasy alone, with no maternal toxicity, is associated with an increased risk of foetal malformations. Nevertheless, 12 malformations, among 78 live-born infants, and one severely malformed foetus electively terminated at 22 weeks raises concerns. Further studies are needed to determine the clinical significance of these data.

One other recent study has looked at the characteristics of pregnant women who took Ecstasy during pregnancy (Ho *et al*, 2001). They found that 132 women who used MDMA were significantly younger, single and had more unplanned pregnancies. They were also more likely to have smoked cigarettes, drunk alcohol and taken other illicit drugs. However, the outcome of these pregnancies was not reported.

Overall, the effects of Ecstasy on the developing baby are poorly understood. No information was found on the long-term effects on development and behaviour. Further studies are needed to address these issues.

Psychedelics

Cannabis (marijuana, Indian hemp, hashish)

What is it?
Along with alcohol, nicotine and Ecstasy, cannabis (tetrahydrocannabinol is the active component) is one of the most commonly used drugs in women of child-bearing age and in pregnant women. In the UK, the recent relaxation of the law governing the possession of cannabis is likely to exacerbate this problem. Relatively little is known about its effects during pregnancy. Compared with nicotine there is thought to be a five-fold increase in the concentration of carbon monoxide, and a three-fold increase in the tar content in the blood. Chronic use of cannabis may

result in accumulation of tetrahydrocannabinol in fatty tissues. There is limited information on the use of cannabis to reduce nausea and vomiting and for pain relief, and further studies are needed to determine the clinical significance of these reported effects.

What effects does it have on the developing baby (foetus) in the womb?

Congenital malformations: Cannabis crosses the placenta and can lead to a decrease in foetal heart rate. There are conflicting data as to whether cannabis and related compounds are associated with an increased risk of congenital malformations in human pregnancy. Although there are a few case reports of congenital malformations after maternal use, no pattern of malformations was seen (Briggs *et al*, 1998; Gilstrap *et al*, 1998; Schardein, 2000). The overall rate of birth defects after use of cannabis during pregnancy is not increased.

Growth and survival in the womb: There is no clear evidence to suggest that cannabis causes intrauterine growth retardation, miscarriage or premature delivery when factors such as the number of previous live-born babies, alcohol and tobacco use are taken into consideration.

What effects does it have on the newborn infant (neonate)?

Neonatal survival: A meta-analysis of moderate or occasional use of cannabis did not provide conclusive evidence that it had any significant effects on birth weight (English *et al*, 1997). There are anecdotal reports that prolonged perinatal exposure to cannabis is associated with an increased incidence of perinatal mortality, but clear evidence to substantiate this is lacking.

Neonatal withdrawal syndrome: There are anecdotal reports that prolonged perinatal exposure to cannabis is associated with withdrawal symptoms such as tremor, increased startle response and abnormal visual responses, but clear evidence to substantiate these effects is lacking.

Sudden Infant Death Syndrome (SIDS): No evidence has been found associating prenatal cannabis exposure with SIDS.

Longer-term development: One long-term study found that speech and memory performance among four-year-olds whose mothers had consumed cannabis regularly (several times a week or daily) during pregnancy was significantly affected (Fried and Watkinson, 1990). The same study also found a significantly decreased head circumference (smaller heads) in the older children, that had not been noticeable at birth (Fried *et al*, 1999). The clinical significance of this has yet to be determined. Other reports indicate that there are no significant adverse effects on visual responses, mental, motor or language development. There is, as yet, no indication that the anecdotal reports of chromosome breaks (spontaneous disruption along the length of the chromosome) attributed to cannabis have any clinical relevance.

There are a number of other illicit drugs that are less frequently used on their own but are often used in combination with other drugs, e.g. "sniffing drugs" as well as some of the psychedelic drugs described below including phencyclidine, mescaline, psilocybin and LSD. There is very little reliable information on the effects of these drugs when used in pregnancy.

Phencyclidine (PCP, Angel Dust)

This substance is an arylcyclohexylamine which has hallucinogenic properties. It is easily manufactured and is a cheap way of stretching out other drugs (LSD, mescaline, cocaine). It is taken by mouth or smoked mixed with marijuana, tobacco and oregano. It alters the way in which neurotransmitters work in the brain and central nervous system. Depending on the dose and site of action, phencyclidine can have either a stimulating or a depressant action. In cases of severe intoxication, depression of the central nervous system is evident. It has been suggested that phencyclidine abuse is associated with microcephaly as well as facial asymmetry, but a causal relationship has not yet been proven (Briggs *et al*, 1998; Schardein, 2000). However, intrauterine growth retardation and post-natal interactional deficits, as well as other neurological deficits and typical symptoms of opiate withdrawal, have been observed. It is difficult to know if these findings are due to an effect of the phencyclidine, or to other socio-economic or biological factors.

LSD (Lysergic Acid Diethylamide)

LSD is a hallucinogenic drug but there is no epidemiological evidence to suggest that there is a causal relationship between LSD use and congenital malformations. In older work, the suspicion was raised that LSD could cause chromosome breaks and malformations of the eyes, skeletal and central nervous systems. There are two small prospective studies that have reported the birth of normal infants following first trimester exposure to LSD (Briggs *et al*, 1998; Schardein, 2000). A possible increase in spontaneous abortions has also been suggested, but not proven.

Sniffing drugs

"Sniffing drugs" i.e. solvent misuse is common in some areas, particularly by adolescents. The toxic effect of high doses of organic solvents such as toluene, benzene, chlorinated hydrocarbons, "nitro thinner" and butane lighter fluid on the maternal and foetal central nervous system and kidneys is unknown. A succession of case descriptions gives the impression that damage similar to that in Foetal Alcohol Syndrome may occur following toluene sniffing during pregnancy.

Other drugs

Benzodiazepines (tranquillisers)

What are they?

Benzodiazepines (e.g. clobazam, diazepam, lorazepam, medazepam, midazolam, nitrazepam, oxazepam, temazepam and triazolam) have anxiolytic (explanation), anti-convulsant, hypnotic-sedating and muscle relaxing properties. Temazepam is a drug which is commonly available on the street. The amount of time that benzodiazepines remain in the body is very variable. Benzodiazepines with a very short action of less than six hours are used in anaesthesia and in the treatment of insomnia, e.g. midazolam and triazolam. Others which act for up to 24 hours, e.g. lorazepam, oxazepam and temazepam are used as sedatives and hypnotics. The longer acting ones (up to several days) are mainly used as sedatives and anxiolytics, e.g. clobazam, diazepam, medazepam and nitrazepam. In therapeutic doses for short periods of time they can be very beneficial. Prolonged use and misuse can cause adverse physical and psychological effects.

What effects do they have on the developing baby (foetus) in the womb?

Congenital malformations: Benzodiazepines cross the placenta. There is controversy about the risk of malformations after exposure to benzodiazepines in the first trimester. In some studies prenatal exposure to benzodiazepines has been associated with cardiac malformations, facial clefts and multiple malformations (Rodriguez-Pinilla, 1999), but other studies do not confirm this association (McElhatton, 1994; Patuszak *et al*, 1996; Dolovich *et al*, 1998; Ornoy *et al*, 1998).

Growth and survival in the womb: There is no clear evidence to indicate that occasional therapeutic doses of benzodiazepines are associated with adverse effects on growth or miscarriage.

What effects do they have on the newborn infant (neonate)?

Neonatal survival: The rate of metabolism (the speed at which chemicals in the body act on the drug) in the neonate is very low. Where adverse effects on foetal survival have been reported, they tend to be related to both the dose and the length of time for which it was taken by the mother, often in combination with other drugs. However, benzodizepines may accumulate in the foetus in a greater concentration than in the mother. After birth the drug may remain in the baby for a long time (due to the immaturity of the liver), resulting in sedation.

Neonatal withdrawal syndrome: The regular use of benzodiazepines in the last three months of pregnancy prior to delivery may cause the "floppy infant syndrome" (lethargy, poor muscle tone, sucking problems, apnoea (temporary inability to breathe)), cyanosis (bluish discoloration of the skin) and hypothermia and neonatal withdrawal symptoms (e.g. increased muscle tone and reflexes, and tremors).

Sudden Infant Death Syndrome (SIDS): Benzodiazepines as such are not normally associated with an increased risk of SIDS.

Longer-term development: Data on long-term effects are scarce.

Antidepressants

What are they?

Antidepressants cause increased concentrations of the nerve transmitter substances such as noradrenaline, serotonin and dopamine, but the mode of action differs for each antidepressant or group of antidepressants. Depression and the wish to self harm are often reported to occur among drug misusers, for which they may be prescribed antidepressant drugs. Antidepressant drugs may interact with drugs of abuse, often enhancing their effects and producing toxicity. Many people, who may not be drug misusers in the true sense of the term, often become addicted to antidepressants and suffer serious withdrawal symptoms.

The main groups of antidepressants are:

a) tricyclic antidepressants (TCAs) – many of which have been on the market for a long time (e.g. amitriptyline, imipramine, clomipramine, dothiepin, lofepramine). The TCAs taken in overdose are associated with severe toxicity such as abnormal heart rhythms (cardiac arrhythmias) and fits. In pregnant women this can have serious adverse effects in both the mother and the developing baby (Garbis and McElhatton, 2001).

b) Serotonin reuptake inhibitors (SSRIs) e.g. citalopram, fluoxetine fluvoxamine, paroxetine and sertraline, which are equally effective but better tolerated than TCAs. Less is known about the newer related drugs that prevent reuptake of serotonoin and noradrenaline (SNRIs) such as venlafaxine. The SSRIs are also safer than other antidepressants for the mother and fetus, in women with suicidal ideation, as they are associated with less severe toxicity.

c) Monoaminoxidase inhibiters (MAOIs) inhibit the enzyme monoaminoxidase, which is responsible for the breakdown of nerve transmitters. The inhibition is either reversible (newer MAOIs, e.g. moclobemide, phenelzine and tranylcypromine) or irreversible (older MAOIs, e.g. isocarboxazid, phenelzine and tranylcypromine). MAOIs have been associated with a high incidence of toxicity. There is a possible interaction between tyramine, which is present in high protein content food and drinks, and MAOIs, that may manifest itself as an acute hypertensive crisis (sudden severe increase in blood pressure).

Hypericin Hypericum (St. John's Wort, SJW) is a herbal medicine which is used as an antidepressant. As SJW interacts with a number of drugs including antidepressants, and data on its use during pregnancy are not yet available, it is best avoided

What effects do they have on the developing baby (foetus) in the womb?

Congenital malformations: There is no clear evidence to indicate that TCAs are associated with an increased risk of congenital malformations (Patuszak *et al*, 1993; Brunel *et al*, 1994; McElhatton *et al*, 1996; Ericson *et al*, 1999).

Among the SSRIs and SNRIs, most data are available on fluoxetine and venlafaxine, but these groups as a whole have not been associated with an overall increase in the malformation rate (Patuszak *et al*, 1993; Brunel *et al*, 1994; Chambers *et al*, 1996; McElhatton *et al*, 1996; Goldstein *et al*, 1997; McConnell *et al*, 1998). In six prospectively assessed studies and surveys, no increased incidence of major malformations was seen in over 1,200 newborns (Gold, 1999). Despite the fact that the MAOIs have been on the market for a number of years, there are few data available on their effects in pregnancy (Heinonen *et al*, 1977).

Growth and survival in the womb: Goldstein (1995) studied the effects of third trimester fluoxetine exposure on the newborn, and states that it is unlikely that such exposure results in significant post-natal complications. Pregnancy induced hypertension is a common complication of pregnancy and is often sudden and unexpected in onset. MAOIs can make this condition worse and may lead to alterations in placental blood flow, particularly placental hypoperfusion – variations in blood pressure and blood flow may alter the amounts of oxygen and nutrients supplied to the foetus from the mother via the placenta. This may have serious consequences for foetal growth and development (Mortola, 1989; Miller *et al*, 1990).

What effects do they have on the newborn infant (neonate)?

Neonatal survival: Antidepressants when used chronically, or particularly near delivery, have the potential to cause neonatal withdrawal symptoms. Short-term withdrawal symptoms such as jitteriness, irritability and convulsions have been reported (Schimmell *et al*, 1991; Bromiker and Kaplan 1994; Dahl *et al*, 1997; Kent and Laidlaw 1995). Neonatal withdrawal symptoms after maternal fluoxetine use near term have been reported by Spencer (1993), Chambers *et al* (1996) and Mhanna *et al* (1997). To date, the most severe symptoms seem to be associated with prolonged use of paroxetine or venlafaxine. The last authors mention that paediatricians should be aware that some babies are more likely to bleed for no apparent reason if exposed to fluoxetine.

Sudden Infant Death Syndrome (SIDS): No evidence has been found to indicate that exposure to antidepressants only was associated with SIDS.

Longer-term development: Nulman *et al* (1997) found that *in utero* exposure to TCAs did not affect the neurodevelopment (global IQ, language and behavioural development) in 80 pre-school children. Similar findings were reported after *in utero* exposure to fluoxetine in 55 preschool children. Overall, the long-term effects of antidepressants belonging to any group are not known.

Conclusions

Maternal exposure to drugs of abuse has been associated with foetal and neonatal toxicity. Intrauterine growth retardation, reduced birth weight and head circumference, meconium stained fluids, prematurity, and an increased incidence of neonatal death are common in infants born to drug misusers. In most cases it is not clear whether this is solely a direct drug effect or due to deficits in socio-economic lifestyle and post-natal care or a combination of the two.

Neonatal withdrawal symptoms, which may last up to several weeks, occur in a high proportion of babies. The features are variable and include tremor, hypertonicity, irritability, diarrhoea, vomiting, abnormal sleep patterns and altered visual response patterns to light stimulus.

Evidence concerning foetotoxicity from paternal exposure is lacking. There are limited and inconsistent data on the possible adverse effects of drugs of abuse on postnatal development.

Drug-dependent mothers and their babies may represent a unique group, and if variables are to be identified which may affect pregnancy outcome, perhaps intra-group as well as inter-group comparison should be made. Comparison of infants of drug-dependent mothers with a good outcome with those of a poor outcome might be an effective approach.

* * *

The National Teratology Information Service (NTIS)

The service provided by NTIS

NTIS is based in the Newcastle Centre of the National Poisons Information Service (NPIS) in the Regional Drug and Therapeutics Centre. It is funded by the Department of Health to provide a national, 24-hour service on all aspects of toxicity of drugs and chemicals (e.g. pesticides, carbon monoxide) in pregnancy throughout the UK. All enquiries are confidential.

Most enquiries are from health professionals, the majority of which are answered by phone on the same day. Urgent enquiries that arise outside office hours are dealt with via the Newcastle Centre of the NPIS. In the year 2002, NTIS answered 5,715 enquiries about drug and chemical exposures in pregnancy. There were an additional 17,496 "hits" by registered healthcare professionals on the pregnancy summaries hosted by the Toxbase website.

The UK National Teratology Information Service is a founder member of the European Network of Teratology Information Services (ENTIS) established in 1990 and it is one of the largest of the 24 centres in Europe. The main task of ENTIS is for members to collaborate and share data, with the objective of preventing birth defects.

NTIS works closely with the Health and Safety Executive (HSE) to monitor the potential teratological hazards associated with chemical exposures in the environment, at work and in the home.

Main functions of NTIS

- Provision of an individual risk assessment for a pregnant woman exposed to drugs or chemicals.

- Pre-conception advice for men and women concerning drug and chemical exposures.
- Provision and interpretation of background risks as well as specific information on drugs and chemicals for healthcare personnel.
- Proactive monitoring of specific hazards and risk assessment.
- Prospective follow-up of selected cases to expand data for use in future enquiries.
- Support for the National Poisons Information Service within the UK.

Prospective follow-up procedures

Selected enquiries are followed up to obtain information on the outcome of pregnancy. Follow-up is attempted for all cases of poisoning and all occupational and environmental exposures during pregnancy. In addition, enquiries involving drugs on a priority list are also followed up, e.g. drugs under intensive surveillance by the Committee on Safety of Medicines, known or suspected human teratogens and drugs for which there are few safety data.

Outcome data

The confidential outcome information provides valuable prospective data for inclusion in FETIS, a database initially developed by the ENTIS, and will expand the grounds on which to base advice in subsequent enquiries. This follow-up data can also be used to generate hypotheses that can be tested in epidemiological studies.

Data have been obtained on approximately 5,000 pregnancies, e.g. the effects of Ecstasy in pregnancy; the safety of new antidepressants; the safety of the use of antidotes in pregnant women who take iron or paracetamol overdoses during pregnancy; the potential reproductive hazards associated with exposure to carbon monoxide or dry-cleaning fluids.

NTIS can be contacted in the following ways – all enquiries are confidential: Monday – Friday, 8.30 am–5 pm

Telephone: (0191) 232 1525
Fax: (0191) 260 6192

Out of office hours
Telephone: (0191) 232 1307 (*urgent* enquiries only)
Fax: (0191) 223 1308

National Teratology Information Service (NTIS)
Regional Drug and Therapeutics Centre
Claremont Place
Newcastle upon Tyne NE2 4HH
www.ncl.ac.uk/pharmsc/entis.htm

References

Bauchner H and Zuckerman B (1990) 'Cocaine, sudden infant death syndrome, and home monitoring', *J Pediatr*, 117:6, pp 904–06

Behnke M, Eyler FD, Conlon M *et al* (1998) 'Incidence and description of structural brain abnormalities in newborns exposed to cocaine', *J Pediatr*, 132, pp 291–94

Bellini C, Massocco D and Serra G (2000) 'Prenatal cocaine exposure and the expanding spectrum of brain malformations', *Arch Intern Med*, 160, p 2393

Boer K, Smit B J, van Huis A M and Hogerzeil H V (1994) 'Substance use in pregnancy: Do we care?', *Acta Paediatr (supplement)*, 404, pp 65–71

Briggs G G, Freeman R K and Yaffe S J (1998) *Drugs in Pregnancy and Lactation*, Baltimore: Williams and Wilkins

Bromiker R and Kaplan M (1994) 'Apparent intrauterine fetal withdrawal from clomipramine hydrochloride', *JAMA*, 272, pp 1722–23

Brunel P, Vial T and Roche I *et al* (1994) 'Suivi de 151 grossesses exposées à un traitement antidépresseur (IMAO exclus) au cours de l' organogenèse', *Therapie*, 49, pp 117–22

Bunikowski R, Grimmer I and Heiser A *et al* (1998) 'Neurodevelopmental outcome after prenatal exposure to opiates', *Eur J Pediatr*, 157, pp 724–30

Cernerud L, Eriksson M, Jonsson B, Steneroth G and Zetterström R (1996) 'Amphetamine addiction during pregnancy: 14-year follow-up of growth and school performance', *Acta Paediatr*, 85, pp 204–08

Chambers C D, Johnson K A and Dick L M *et al* (1996) 'Birth outcomes in pregnant women taking fluoxetine', *N Engl J Med*, 335, pp 1010–15

Chasnoff I J, Burns W J, Schnoll S H and Burns K A (1985) 'Cocaine use in pregnancy', *N Engl J Med*, 313, pp 666–69

Coles C D (1993) 'Saying "goodbye" to the "crack baby" ', *Neurotoxicol Teratol*, 15, pp 290–92

Dahl M L, Olhager E and Ahlner J (1997) 'Paroxetine withdrawal syndrome in a neonate', *Brit J Psychiatry*, 171, pp 391–92

Dahlem P, Bucher H U, Ursprung Th, Mieth D and Gautschi K (1992) 'Nachweis von Drogen im Mekonium', *Monatsschr Kinderheilkd*, 140, pp 354–56

Day N L, Richardson G A and McGuahey P J (1994a) *Prenatal Exposure to Toxicants: Developmental consequences*, Baltimore: The Johns Hopkins University Press

Day N L, Richardson G A, Geva D and Robles N (1994b) 'Alcohol, marijuana, and tobacco: effects of prenatal exposure on offspring growth and morphology at age six', *Alcohol Clin Exp Res*, 18:4, pp 786–94

Department of Health (December 1995) *Sensible Drinking*, London: HMSO

Delaney-Black V, Covington C and Sokol R J (1994) 'Maternal cocaine consumption: birth outcome and child development', *Fetal Matern Med Rev*, 6, pp 119–34

Dolovich L R, Addis A, Regis Vaillancourt *et al* (1998) 'Benzodiazepine use in pregnancy and major malformations or oral cleft: meta-analysis of cohort and case-control studies', *Br Med J*, 317, pp 839–43

English D R, Hulse G K, Milne E, Holman C D J and Bower C I (1997) 'Maternal cannabis use and birth weight: a meta-analysis', *Addiction*, 92, pp 1553–60

Ericson A, Källén B and Wiholm B E (1999) 'Delivery outcome after the use of antidepressants in early pregnancy', *Eur J Clin Pharmacol*, 55, pp 503–08

Eriksson M and Zetterstrom R (1994) 'Amphetamine addiction during pregnancy: 10-year follow-up', *Acta Paediatr (supplement)*, 404, pp 27–31

Fares I, McCulloch K M and Raju T N K (1997) 'Intrauterine cocaine exposure and the risk for sudden infant death syndrome: a meta-analysis', *J Perinatol*, 17, pp 179–82

Farkas A G, Colbert D L and Erskine K J (1995) 'Anonymous testing for drug abuse in an antenatal population', *Br J Obstet Gynaecol*, 102, pp 563–65

Felix R J, Chambers C D, Dick L M, Johnson K A and Jones K L (2000) 'Prospective pregnancy outcome in women exposed to amphetamines', *Teratology*, 61, p 441

Finnegan L P (1979) 'Pathophysiological and behavioural effects of the trans-placental transfer of narcotic drugs to the fetuses and neonates of narcotic-dependent mothers', *Bull Narcotics*, 31, pp 1–59

Franck L and Vilardi J (1995) 'Assessment and management of opioid withdrawal in ill neonates', *Neonatal Netw*, 14:4, p 83

Frank D A, Augustyn M and Zuckerman B S (1998) 'Neonatal neurobehavioral and neuroanatomic correlates of prenatal cocaine exposure: problems of dose and confounding', *Ann N Y Acad Sci*, 846, pp 40–50

Frank D A, Augustyn M and Knight W G (2001) 'Growth, development, and behavior in early childhood following prenatal cocaine exposure: a systematic review', *JAMA*, 285:12, pp 1613–25

Fried P A and Watkinson B (1990) '36- and 48-month neurobehavioral follow-up of children prenatally exposed to marijuana, cigarettes and alcohol', *Develop Behavioral Pediatrics*, 11, pp 49–58

Fried P A, Watkinson B and Gray R (1999) 'Growth from birth to early adolescence in offspring prenatally exposed to cigarettes and marijuana', *Neurotox Teratol*, 21, pp 513–25

Fries M H, Kuller J A and Norton M E *et al* (1993) 'Facial features of infants exposed prenatally to cocaine', *Teratology*, 48, pp 413–20

Garbis H and McElhatton P R (2001) In Schaefer C (ed), *Drugs During Pregnancy and Lactation*, London: Elsevier

Gilstrap L C and Little B B (1998) *Drugs and Pregnancy*, Chapman & Hall

Glantz J C and Woods J R Jr (1993) 'Cocaine, heroin, and phencyclidine: Obstetric perspectives', *Clin Obstet Gynceol*, 36:2, pp 279–301

Gold L H (1999) 'Treatment of depression during pregnancy', *J Women's Health and Gender-Base Medicine*, 8, pp 601–07

Goldstein D J (1995) 'Effects of third trimester fluoxetine exposure on the newborn', *J Clin Psychopharmacol*, 15, pp 417–20

Goldstein D J, Corbin L A and Sundell K L (1997) 'Effects of first-trimester fluoxetine exposure on the newborn', *Obstet Gynecol*, 89, pp 713–18

Greenberg M I and Shrethra M (2000) 'Management of the pregnant bodypacker', *J Toxicol-Clinical Toxicol*, 38, pp 176–77

Griffith D R, Azuma S D and Chasnoff I J (1994) 'Three-year outcome of children exposed prenatally to drugs' *J Am Acad Child Adolesc Psychiatry*, 33:1, pp 20–27

Heinonen O P, Slone D and Shapiro S (1977) *Birth Defects and Drugs in Pregnancy*, Littleton, MA: Publishing Sciences Group Inc

Ho E, Karimi-Tabesh L and Koren G (2001) 'Characteristics of pregnant women who use Ecstasy (3,4-methylenedioxymethamphetamine)', *Neurotoxicology &Teratology*, 23, pp 561–67

Hume R F Jr *et al* (1989) 'In utero cocaine exposure: observations of fetal behavioral state may predict neonatal outcome', *Am J Obstet Gynecol*, 161, pp 685–90

Hume R F Jr, Gingras J L, Martin L S *et al* (1994) 'Ultrasound diagnosis of fetal anomalies associated with in utero cocaine exposure: further support for cocaine-induced vascular disruption teratogenesis', *Fetal Diagn Ther*, 9, pp 239–45

Kaltenbach K, Berghella V and Finnegan L (1998) 'Opioid dependence during pregnancy: effects and management', *Obstet Gynecol Clin North Am*, 25:1, pp 139–151

Kent L S W and Laidlaw J D D (1995) 'Suspected congenital sertraline dependence', *Br J Psychiatry*, 167, p 412

Koren G (1994) *Maternal-Fetal Toxicology: A clinician's guide*, Marcel Dekker

LaGasse L L, Seifer R and Lester B M (1999) 'Interpreting research on prenatal substance exposure in the context of multiple confounding factors', *Clin Perinatol*, 26:1, pp 39–54

Ling W, Charuvastra C and Collins J F *et al* (1998) 'Buprenorphine maintenance treatment of opioid dependence: a multicenter, randomized clinical trial', *Addiction*, 93, pp 475–86

Little B B, Wilson G N and Jackson G (1996) 'Is there a cocaine syndrome? Dysmorphic and anthropometric assessment of infants exposed to cocaine', *Teratology*, 54, pp 45–149

Little B et al (1998) Drugs and Pregnancy, London: Chapman and Hall

Little B B, Snell L M and Trimmer K J et al (1999) 'Peripartum cocaine use and adverse pregnancy outcome', Am J Hum Biol, 11, pp 598–602

Lutiger B, Graham K, Einarson T R and Koren G (1991) 'Relationship between gestational cocaine use and pregnancy outcome: a meta- analysis', Teratology, 44, pp 405–14

Martin M L, Khoury M J, Cordero J F and Waters G D (1992) 'Trends in rates of multiple vascular disruption defects, Atlanta, 1968–1989: Is there evidence of a cocaine teratogenic epidemic?', Teratology, 45, pp 647–53

Martinez J M, Fortuny A and Comas C et al (1994) 'Body stalk anomaly associated with maternal cocaine abuse', Prenat Diagn, 14:8, pp 669–72

McConnell P J, Linn K and Filkins K (1998) 'Depression and pregnancy: use of selective serotonin reuptake inhibitors in pregnancy', Prim Care Update Ob/ Gyns, 5, pp 11–15

McElhatton P R (1994) 'A review of the effects of benzodiazepine use during pregnancy and lactation', Reproductive Toxicology, 8, pp 461–75

McElhatton P R, Garbis H M, Elefant E, Vial T, Bellemin B, Mastroiacovo P, Arnon J, Rodriguez-Pinilla E, Schaefer C, Pexieder T, Merlob P and dal Verme S (1996) 'The outcome of pregnancy in 689 women exposed to therapeutic doses of antidepressants. A collaborative study of the European Network of Teratology Information Services (ENTIS)', Reproductive Toxicology, 10:4, pp 285–94

McElhatton P R (1999) 'The principles of teratogenicity', Current Obstetrics & Gynaecology, 9:3, pp 163–69

McElhatton P R Bateman D N, Evans C, Pughe K R and Thomas S H L (1999) 'Congenital anomalies after pre-natal ecstasy exposure', Lancet, 354, pp 1441–42

McElhatton P R (2000) 'Fetal Effects of Substance Abuse', J Toxicol-Clinical Toxicol, 38, pp 194–95

McElhatton P R, Pughe K R, Evans C, Porter K, Bateman D N and Thomas S H L (2000) 'Is exposure to amphetamine-like drugs in pregnancy associated with malformations?', J Toxicol-Clinical Toxicol, 38, pp 195–96

Mhanna M J, Bennett J B and Izatt S D (1997) 'Potential fluoxetine chloride (Prozac) toxicity in a newborn', *Pediatrics*, 100, pp 158–59

Miller B M, Rosario P G, Prakash K *et al* (1990) 'Neonatal intestinal perforation: the "crack" connection', *Am J Gastroenterol*, 857, pp 67–9

Morrison C and Siney C (1995) 'Maternity services for drug misusers in England and Wales: a national survey', *Health Trends*, 27, pp 15–7

Mortola J F (1989) 'The use of psychotropic agents in pregnancy and lactation', *Psychiatric Clinics of North America*, 12, pp 69–87

Nulman I, Rovet J and Altmann D *et al* (1994) 'Neurodevelopment of adopted children exposed in utero to cocaine', *Can Med Assoc J*, 151, pp 1591–97

Nulman I, Rovet J and Stewart D E *et al* (1997) 'Neurodevelopment of children exposed in utero to antidepressant drugs', *N Engl J Med*, 336, pp 258–62

Nutt D J (1996) 'Addiction: brain mechanism and their treatment implications', *Lancet*, 347, pp 31–6

Ornoy A, Arnon J and Shechtman S *et al* (1998) 'Is benzodiazepine use during pregnancy really teratogenic?', *Reprod Toxicol*, 12, pp 511–15

Ornoy A (2001) 'The role of environment in the neurodevelopmental modulation in children exposed in utero to illicit drugs or maternal diseases', *Reprod Toxicol (abstract)*, 15, p 449

Ostrea E M Jr and Chavez C J (1979) 'Perinatal problems (excluding neonatal withdrawal) in maternal drug addiction: a study of 830 cases', *J Pediatr*, 94, pp 292–95

Patuszak A, Schick-Boschetto B and Zuber C *et al* (1993) 'Pregnancy outcome following first- trimester exposure to fluoxetine (Prozac)', *JAMA*, 269, pp 2246–48

Patuszak A, Milich V and Chan S *et al* (1996) 'Prospective assessment of pregnancy outcome following first trimester exposure to benzodiazepines', *Can J Clin Pharmacol*, 3, pp 167–71

Peters P and Schaefer C (2001) 'General commentary to drug therapy and drug risks in pregnancy', in Schaefer C (ed) *Drugs During Pregnancy and Lactation*, London: Elsevier

Richardson G A and Day N L (1999) 'Studies of prenatal cocaine exposure: assessing the influence of extraneous variables', *J Drug Issues*, 29:2, pp 225–36

Robin N H and Zackai E H (1994) 'Unusual craniofacial dysmorphia due to prenatal alcohol and cocaine exposure', *Teratology*, 50:2, pp 160–64

Rodriguez-Pinilla (1999) 'Prenatal exposure to benzodiazepines: a case-control study', Presentation on the 10th Annual Conference of the European Network of Teratology Information Services

Rost van Tonningen-van Driel M M, Garbis Berkvens J M and Reuvers Lodewijks W B (1999) 'Zwangerschapsuitkomst na ecstacygebruik; 43 gevallen gevolgd door de Teratologie Informatie Service van het RIVM', *Ned Tijdschr Geneeskd*, 143:1, pp 27–31

Scanlon J W (1991) 'The neuroteratology of cocaine: background, theory, and clinical implications', *Reprod Toxicol*, 5, pp 89–98

Schaefer C and Spielman, H (1990) 'Cocaine and pregnancy – shades of the thalidomide tragedy', *Gerburtschilfel Fravenheilkd*, 50, pp 899–900

Schaefer C (2001) 'Recreational drugs', in Schaefer C (ed), *Drugs During Pregnancy and Lactation*, London: Elsevier

Schardein J L (2000) *Chemically Induced Birth Defects*, New York: Marcel Dekker

Schimmell M S, Katz E Z and Shaag Y *et al* (1991) 'Toxic neonatal effects following clomipramine therapy', *J Toxicol Clin Toxicol*, 29, pp 479–84

Spencer M J (1993) 'Fluoxetine hydrochloride (Prozac) toxicity in a neonate', *Pediatrics*, 92, pp 721–22

Sullivan F M and Barlow S M (2001) 'Review of risk factors for Sudden Infant Death Syndrome', *Paediatric and Perinatal Epidemiology*, 15, pp 144–200

Wilson J G (1997) *Current Status of Teratology*, New York: Plenum Press

Zuckerman B and Frank D A (1994) 'Prenatal cocaine exposure: nine years later', *J Pediatr [editorial]*, 124, pp 731–33

4 Parental alcohol misuse
Implications for child placements

Professor Moira Plant

Introduction

The problems associated with heavy drinking in pregnancy have been known for many years. However, the difficulties and joys of raising children with alcohol-related birth damage are complex. The most important point is that with the right conditions these children can be helped to reach their full potential. The severity of the damage mainly depends on the frequency of high dose drinking during pregnancy and it is necessary to accept that they can have life-long problems. Children do not "grow out" of alcohol-related birth damage but with support and help they can live fulfilling lives. It is also important that, for the sake of both the children and the substitute parents who are thinking of caring for them, there is a clear understanding of the commitment involved.

Drinking and alcohol-related problems in the UK

Over the past two decades there has been a steady increase in the number of British women drinking heavily. A recent survey of 2,000 adults found that the highest proportion of women drinking at a level classified as "at risk" were aged 18 to 24 years (Plant *et al*, 2002). This measure of "high risk" means drinking above 35 "units" per week (Royal College of Psychiatrists, 1986). A UK "unit" of alcohol is equivalent to one small glass of wine, one pub measure of spirits, or half a pint of normal strength beer, lager or cider. Extra strength beers and lagers may contain up to five units in a pint. Home measures of wine and spirits may be two to three times larger than pub measures.

Surveys carried out in the UK and many other countries have invariably shown that men are heavier drinkers than women and men also report having more alcohol-related problems than women. In relation to drinking in pregnancy it is obviously the woman's drinking which is of more importance. However, there is evidence that heavy drinking by the father is related to heart anomalies in the baby (Abel, 1998). Given that many heavy drinking women have partners who also drink substantial quantities, this can lead to even more problems for their offspring.

Another factor that can affect the health of the baby is the pattern of drinking. In the UK it is commonplace for people to drink heavily during one or two sessions at the weekend and little during the week. Although this pattern is beginning to change with more people drinking wine with meals during the week, high dose weekend drinking (sometimes referred to as binge drinking) remains a distinctive feature in the UK and in other countries in North-West Europe. As noted below, this is relevant to the patterns of adverse effects on the foetus.

Effects of heavy drinking in pregnancy

The subject of drinking in pregnancy has always been a highly charged emotional topic. The long running debate about the possible risks to the unborn child of heavy drinking in pregnancy is ongoing (Plant, 1997; 2000). More recently, the debate expanded to include the question of whether lower levels of alcohol consumption, those that would be described as "moderate" or "social" drinking, can harm the foetus. This is still open for discussion, with disagreement between the Royal Colleges in the UK. For example, the Royal College of Obstetricians and Gynaeco-logists (1999) suggests 'limit to no more than one standard drink a day'. Most of the other Royal Colleges suggest one or two units once or twice a week. This latter advice is reiterated by the UK Midwives Information and Resource Service (MIDIRS, 2003).

As noted earlier the pattern of drinking is important. Evidence at this point suggests that the severity of alcohol-related damage to the baby is linked to the frequency of high dose drinking. The other factor, which needs to be highlighted, is the stage of pregnancy when the high dose drinking occurs. In relation to maternal ingestion of alcohol or other drugs, the most vulnerable time for organ development in the foetus occurs during the first 12 weeks (Abel, 1998). This is certainly not to suggest that it is safe to drink heavily at any time in the pregnancy – it most certainly is not. Later in the pregnancy, during the second and third trimester, the foetus is growing rapidly. This includes brain growth, so heavy drinking at this time will mean that the child is born smaller and not so well developed. This can lead to problems in early childhood such as difficulties with sleeping, feeding, reduced co-ordination and poor concentration.

The effects of heavy drinking in pregnancy were first described in 1973 by three American paediatricians, Ulleland, Smith and Jones (Jones and Smith, 1973). They coined the term "Foetal Alcohol Syndrome" (FAS). The syndrome included four categories. These were:

- *Pre- and post-natal growth deficiency* The babies were short in length, light in weight, with a smaller than normal head circumference and they did not "catch up" with healthy children as they grew older. Such children are often identified at failure to thrive clinics.
- *Physical anomalies* The best known of these traits is the particular cluster of facial features common to these children. These include short upturned nose, receding forehead and chin, asymmetrical ears and short palpebral fissures (the measurement between the inner corner of the eye and the outer corner of the eye). Other anomalies include heart and kidney problems.
- *Central nervous system dysfunction* This is the most severe problem for the child and parent or other care provider. It includes severe learning difficulties, which as parents with these children report also means severe living difficulties.
- A fourth and final category included the key requirement that the birth mother had to have an 'an identifiable drinking problem'.

This latter category is of interest. The original articles published by this group included the term 'chronic alcoholic mothers'. However, this acknowledgement of the severity of maternal drinking was gradually minimised with the passage of time. This redefinition has led to much of the confusion that now exists in the field.

Working on the premise that if drinking a lot of alcohol when pregnant damages the child severely, then drinking a little alcohol will still damage the child albeit to a lesser extent, a further diagnosis was identified at this time. This was termed "Foetal Alcohol Effects" (FAE). Recently the two people who were at the forefront of raising awareness of alcohol-related harm, Lemoine in France and Jones in the USA, have recommended that use of this term be discontinued. Their view is that the term has been 'used as a dustbin' for any unexplained anomalies, thus exaggerating the likely extent of alcohol-related anomalies, and distorting attempts to monitor their true incidence (Kaskutas, 1995).

In 1996 the Institute of Medicine in the USA defined a new diagnostic paradigm. The major difference in this was the inclusion of a much more prominent criterion of maternal alcohol exposure as part of the diagnosis. FAS was divided into three categories:

- FAS with confirmed maternal alcohol exposure;
- FAS without confirmed maternal alcohol exposure;
- Partial FAS with confirmed FAS maternal alcohol exposure.

The second category, FAS without confirmed maternal alcohol exposure, was added because the reality is that a high proportion of these children are fostered or adopted and it is only when they are in these more stable environments that problems are identified and referrals for assessment are made. It is also the case that in some countries, evidence of the maternal drinking history is not always available at the time of adoption. The third category of partial FAS relates to the fact that some children have a few of the features of FAS, but not enough to qualify for a diagnosis of the full syndrome.

A fourth category included alcohol-related birth defects, while a fifth and final category described "neurological hard and soft signs" which included behavioural problems (Plant et al, 1999).

More recently the term "Foetal Alcohol Spectrum Disorder" (FASD) has been introduced to facilitate a more accurate view of this wide range of disorders, starting with minor individual anomalies and up to the clear diagnostic categories noted above as FAS. The strength of this term is that it gives the clear message that there is a range of severity, rather than an "all or nothing" dichotomy. Studies show that even in severe cases of FAS/FASD, the features are not always consistent (Abel, 1998). Indeed not all children with FAS have severe learning difficulties (Streissguth et al, 1991). However, some degree of damage is usually present. The most common factors, present in all children, are disordered thinking, learning and memory impairment, and crucially an inability to understand the consequences of their actions.

The extent of FAS/FASD

The prevalence of FAS/FASD is not known in most populations. There is no routine monitoring of this condition in most countries, including the UK. It has been suggested that FAS/FASD births may typically occur in one to two per 1,000 live births (Abel, 1998). In some populations, such as indigenous/First Nation (Indian) people in Canada and the USA, FAS/FASD appears to be far more prevalent (Plant *et al*, 1999). This may be a combination of many factors including poverty, poor nutritional status and binge drinking patterns which lead to high blood alcohol levels. Even so, the possibility that any woman who is alcohol dependent or who has "alcohol problems" may give birth to a baby who has been damaged by maternal heavy drinking should be taken seriously. Such babies have special needs.

Heavy paternal drinking

There is evidence to suggest that cardiac problems such as ventricular-septal defect (hole in the heart) are found more commonly in children born to alcohol dependent fathers (Bielawski and Abel, 1997; Abel, 1998).

Problems after birth

Key factors at this age include remaining light in weight and short in length for age, difficulties with feeding and sleeping, irritability and increased risk of infections due to depressed immune function. A particularly difficult aspect for parents to accept is that children with FAS/FASD have problems forming attachments with their primary carers. Difficulties in socio-emotional development are common and appear to continue into adulthood (Jacobson and Jacobson, 2003). These problems have been found in the children regardless of how supportive the home life has been. Recently this difficulty with forming attachments has meant that some children with FASD have been diagnosed as having attachment disorders.

As noted above, children with full-blown FAS/FASD do not catch up as other small-for-dates babies do. This often means frequent feeds. Add to this the problems noted above and the picture of a very demanding and exhausting baby becomes clear. Depressed immune function is often associated with FAS and the high rate of chest and ear infections can necessitate a lot of care early in the child's life (Abel, 1998). As well, the low muscle tone often found in these children affects their strength, endurance and general mobility.

Unfortunately a classic aspect of FAS/FASD is that the child becomes very distressed if held or cuddled. In fact the very behaviour which a parent would normally use to calm or comfort a distressed baby may, in this case, lead to further distress (Hinde, 1993). This heightened sensitivity to touch can lead to problems of discomfort with clothes. Some parents find that even the tiny seams inside socks are uncomfortable to the child, and they need to turn the socks inside out.

In babies and younger children it is important to be aware of how easily they will feel overwhelmed in situations where there is a lot of noise and movement. The short attention span, which is so much a part of the syndrome, means that as children begin to take an interest in toys the adult should only give one toy at a time, then put it away and bring out something else. Presenting more than one toy at a time leads to confusion, which increases anxiety.

Young children

Key problems for young children (toddlers) include continuing lack of concentration and impulsivity. As they reach the age for nursery school, it may be possible for children with FASD to attend a regular nursery. However, this is only possible if staffing allows for working in smaller groups. The children should not be expected to sit as long as other children – their short attention span does not allow them to do this. They will need constant monitoring as their ability to relate to children of their own age may be limited (Jacobson and Jacobson, 2003).

Primary school age

Key factors at this stage include short attention span, inability to learn from past mistakes, difficulty in adapting to new experiences and, frustratingly for child, parent and teacher, the inability to transfer what has been learned from one situation to another.

For children with less severe alcohol-related harm, learning difficulties and problems in handling social interactions may not become apparent until they start school. It may then become clear that they are not able to function in a group of children of their own age. Individual alcohol-related defects might mean that there are few intellectual deficits but a number of behavioural problems. These children can be very demanding and highly distractible. They have poor impulse control and do not understand "social rules". Children with FAS/FASD cannot be selectively attentive, so if there is a lot of noise or distraction, they cannot stay focused. They usually do well with one-to-one attention, but as soon as there are more than three or four children in the group, they cannot concentrate. Sadly this can be misinterpreted as the child being lazy, easily distracted or not caring (see section on adopters and foster carers).

It is important to be aware that these problems are not under the child's control. He or she is not wilfully difficult or disruptive, and does not understand why things are going wrong. For these reasons frequent breaks are recommended. They can be easily overwhelmed in large busy spaces and will not be able to concentrate. Any instructions have to be given in small simple steps, making sure they understand one step before moving on to another. They need everything repeated again and again no matter how many times they have performed it before. Consistency and structure are key.

If the adults become frustrated, imagine how much more difficult it is for the children, whose frustration often leads to acting out or becoming withdrawn. Added to this, difficulties with impulse control may mean that they can cause a great deal of disruption in the classroom.

A further major problem in living with children with FAS/FASD is the difficulty they have in understanding the link between cause and effect. This often means that they do not understand that if they do something wrong then they will be punished. It is not that they are "trying to get away with" behaving badly, but rather that they genuinely do not see the connection and so will often end up feeling very badly treated and even more isolated.

Sometimes teachers prefer to assess a child themselves, rather than look through a child's notes before they meet. If the child has been labelled with some behavioural disorder, the teacher may wish to provide a "fresh start". In many cases this is a very positive opportunity. However, in relation to children with FASD, it may give rise to expectations that are too high for them to meet. Teachers need to know what to expect of these children, and to understand that most of the problems are medical, and not disciplinary in nature.

Secondary school age

As children with FAS/FASD grow, it can be very difficult for them to see their peers passing them in terms of developmental milestones and moving up to other classes, when they themselves remain behind. Even so, being in a class with younger children can be more realistic and appropriate, and not so stressful. Furthermore, due to their growth deficiency they will not "stand out" as older.

As the children get older, any classroom activities have to be tailored to them individually. What they need are adaptive skills such as decision-making, health and personal care and, very importantly, self-esteem and awareness of safety issues. As one young adult told me, 'I do not need to know Shakespeare but I do need to know how to get from home to school and back and how to know if I am getting the right change when I go shopping'. A constant worry for parents is that these children are highly vulnerable and have no sense of risk or danger. A statement such as 'Don't go with strangers' will be met with 'What's a stranger?'

Children with FAS/FASD are also at risk, wanting friends so desperately, or believing anything they are told that they can be easily manipulated. They are the ones always left holding the incriminating object, when everyone else has run away. Young adults are still beset with problems of low self-esteem, which will continue to affect them academically. More seriously for some, persisting problems such as not fitting in at school may lead to truancy and delinquency.

Adolescent to adult

This time in life can be amongst the most frightening both for the young person and parents. A wish for independence has to be balanced against a realistic assessment of skills. Difficulty with understanding and working out the value of money can lead to problems when shopping. Problems with grasping the concept of time will make it hard to keep appointments, even important ones such as job interviews (Morse and Weiner, 1996).

Adolescence can bring increased risk of mood and anxiety disorders. Depression is common at this time and concerns and worries about everything can freeze or panic the young person if he or she does not know what to do. Sadly there is also an increased risk of involvement with the law. As has been seen earlier in life, there is little point in punishing children with FAS/FASD, if they do not understand what they are getting punished for. Accordingly, the ideal is to put structures or boundaries in place so that they will be less likely to get into trouble in the first place. This means close supervision and the development of awareness by the carer of the types of situations which are particularly risky. This is necessary in order to work out ways of avoiding such dangers. The young person with FAS/FASD generally does not do "bad" things on purpose.

Challenges for adopters and foster carers

As noted above, the majority of children with FAS/FASD are fostered or adopted because continued heavy and harmful maternal drinking means that most of their birth mothers are unable to care for them. Caring for a child with FAS/FASD is very demanding. People who are going to foster or adopt a child with these difficulties must be informed of what this will mean. FAS/FASD does not go away or get better. Most children with FAS/FASD will need some form of sheltered environment for the rest of their lives and few will be able to live alone without help and support (Morse and Weiner, 1996; Abel, 1998).

Families thinking of fostering or adopting a child with FAS/FASD will need patience, resourcefulness and the energy to constantly repeat even the most obvious things. There may be many times when adoptive parents become angry and frustrated with the child and with professionals who do not appear to be helping. For some, a clear-cut diagnosis brings mixed feelings. There is relief at understanding that many of the behaviours the child shows are not due to poor parenting or the child acting out for the sake of it, but there is also the shattering of dreams and hopes for the child's future. There are concerns as to the care of the child as parents get older and not so fit to look after an adult constantly needing care. The question 'What will happen to her/him after I am gone?' gets asked more frequently.

The vulnerability of these children is a constant worry to parents. Long after other children have learned about not going with strangers children with FAS still will not understand the risks. As they get older this problem will cause increased disquiet to parents. Many report feeling burnt out and tired. It is of real importance that parents of children with FAS/FASD find ways of getting support and help, enabling them to have a break. To make this possible, the babysitters or other carers must have knowledge of FAS/FASD and it is important that parents feel they have the right to be clear about what works with their child and what does not. It cannot be stressed enough that *parents have the right to have input into their child's care*. This becomes even more important in relation to school and teachers. Parents and teachers must work together for these children. Teachers need to accept that parents, who live with the child all the time, have a very good idea of what works and what does not work. Parents need to feel confident they have the right to say that one thing will work and another will not. Teachers need to be prepared to listen.

It is also necessary for children to know what it is that causes them so many problems. Understanding that something is wrong with them, something that happened before they were born, can help them come to terms with their problems. It is not necessary or appropriate to blame the birth mother. For them to be able to tell people: 'I'm not lazy. I don't forget things on purpose. It is because I have FAS/FASD,' can be empowering and take some of the pressure away. A young adult said, when he found out why he was having all these problems: 'To know it wasn't just me, there was something wrong with me, really helped me and now the light shines right on me. Like I just grew.'

Diagnosis or labelling

There have been many debates over whether providing a diagnosis of FAS/FASD is appropriate or indeed necessary. Originally the view was that nothing could be done to improve the life and functioning of children with this diagnosis. Therefore the "label" would simply mean that they would be left without any stimulation or help to develop to the best of their capabilities. It is now quite clear that there are many aspects of this syndrome that can be helped with the right care and attention. For this reason scientists and clinicians with a special interest in FAS/FASD now agree that early assessment is important to allow for early identification. Continuing regular assessment is also needed to ensure special needs are met and development is encouraged appropriately. The child needs to be supported and encouraged frequently as low self-esteem is an ongoing problem, which affects the child's willingness and ability to try new things. For helpful and more practical information readers are advised to look at books such as *Fantastic Antone Succeeds* (Kleinfeld and Westcott, 1993) and *Fantastic Antone Grows Up* (Kleinfeld *et al*, 2000), both available from www.amazon.co.uk.

As noted earlier, an important point to remember is that with the right conditions children with these problems can be helped to reach their full potential. These factors include a diagnosis before the age of six years to enable appropriate support and a stable, nurturing home for at least 70 per cent of their lives. Not all mothers with drinking problems need to have their children taken into care. However, if the mother continues to drink in a problematic way, it is unlikely that children with FAS/FASD will have the sense of stability, consistency and nurturing which is so important for them. This sense of a contained, secure, safe environment appears to be particularly important between the ages of eight and 12 (Streissguth and Kanter, 1997).

Genetics . . . or will my child develop a drinking problem?

Much time and a great deal of money have been spent looking for the "alcoholic gene". Alcohol problems constitute complex disorders and although certain genes may be involved in the expression of specific aspects, at this point no single gene has been identified (Couzigou *et al*, 1999). In fact the great majority of people who drink heavily enough will eventually experience some form of adverse effects. However, it is clear that the environment in which the child is raised, particularly in the early years, is a powerful determinant (Streissguth and Kanter, 1997). Growing up in an environment where there is stability rather than chaos, social drinking rather than problem drinking and nurturing rather than abuse and neglect, will have a positive effect on how nearly children with FAS/ FASD can reach their full potential.

Sources of information

For accurate up-to-date information on the web: www.fas-info.uwe.ac.uk (UK based); www.ccsa.ca/fas (Canadian based)

Acknowledgements

The Alcohol & Health Research Trust (A&HRT) is an independent charity. The work of the Trust and its team has been supported by charities, research councils, the beverage alcohol industry, government departments, healthcare trusts, the police, universities, the European Union and the World Health Organisation. Particular thanks are due to the University of the West of England, Bristol.

References

Abel E L (1998) *Fetal Alcohol Abuse Syndrome*, New York: Plenum Press

Bielawski D M and Abel E L (1997) 'Acute treatment of paternal alcohol exposure produces malformations in offspring', *Alcohol*, 14, pp 397–401

Couzigou P, Begleiter H and Kiianmaa K (1999) 'Alcohol and Genetics', in Macdonald I (ed) *Health Issues Related to Alcohol Consumption*, Oxford: Blackwell Science

Hinde J (1993) 'Early intervention for alcohol-affected children', in Kleinfeld J and Wescott S (eds) *Fantastic Antone Succeeds!: Experiences in Educating Children with Fetal Alcohol Syndrome*, Fairbanks, Alaska: University of Alaska Press

Jacobson J L and Jacobson S W (2003) 'Effects of prenatal alcohol exposure on child development', National Institute on Alcohol Abuse and Alcoholism Publications, Maryland, USA and on www.niaga.nih.gov/publications

Jones K L and Smith D W (1973) 'Recognition of the fetal alcohol syndrome in early infancy', *The Lancet*, 2, pp 999–1001

Kaskutas L A (1995) 'Interpretation of risk: The use of scientific information in the development of the alcohol warning label policy', *International Journal of the Addictions*, 30, pp 1519–48

Kleinfeld J and Wescott S (1993) *Fantastic Antone Succeeds!: Experiences in educating children with fetal alcohol syndrome*, Alaska: University of Alaska Press

Kleinfeld J, Morse B and Wescott S (2000) *Fantastic Antone Grows Up: Adolescents and adults with fetal alcohol syndrome*, Alaska: University of Alaska Press

MIDIRS (2003) 'Alcohol in pregnancy', Informed Choice leaflet, Bristol UK Midwives Information and Resource Service – www.midirs.org

Morse B A and Weiner L (1996) 'Rehabilitation approaches for fetal alcohol syndrome', in Spohr H L and Steinhausen H C (eds) *Alcohol, Pregnancy and the Developing Child*, Cambridge: Cambridge University Press

Plant M L (1997) *Women and Alcohol: Contemporary and historical perspectives*, London/New York: Free Association Press

Plant M L (2000) 'Drinking during pregnancy', in Plant M A and Cameron D (eds) *The Alcohol Report*, London: Free Association Books, pp 34–38

Plant M L, Abel E L and Guerri C (1999) 'Alcohol in pregnancy', in Macdonald I (ed) *Health Issues Related to Alcohol Consumption*, Oxford: Blackwell Science

Plant M L, Plant M A and Mason W (2002) 'Drinking, smoking and illicit drug use among British adults: gender differences explored', *Journal of Substance Use*, 7, pp 24–33

Royal College of Obstetricians and Gynaecologists (1999) *Alcohol Consumption in Pregnancy*, London: Royal College of Obstetricians and Gynaecologists

Royal College of Psychiatrists (1986) *Alcohol: Our favourite drug*, London: Tavistock Publications

Streissguth A P, Aase J M, Clarren S K, Randels S P, LaDue R A and Smith D F (1991) 'Fetal alcohol syndrome in adolescents and adults', *Journal of the American Medical Association*, 265, pp 1961–67

Streissguth A P and Kanter J (1997) *The Challenge of Fetal Alcohol Syndrome: Overcoming secondary disabilities*, Seattle: University of Washington Press

Thomas S E, Kelly S J, Mattson S N and Riley E P (1998) 'Comparison of social abilities of children with fetal alcohol syndrome to those of children with similiar IQ scores and normal controls', *Alcoholism: Clinical and Experimental Research*, 22:2, pp 528–33

5   The effects of smoking tobacco

Dr Catherine Cosgrove, Dr Catherine Hill and Dr Tagore Charles

Introduction

The detrimental effects of smoking on the health of an individual have been known for centuries. However, a proven association between smoking and lung cancer was not demonstrated until 1950 (Doll and Bradford Hill, 1950). The impact of smoking on children is more complex, as one has to consider the effects of having biological parents who have smoked, the effects on the child of living in a smoking environment, and the effects on the health of the child's carer. Some parents may smoke before, during and after pregnancy, others may stop or start at any of these time points. Some children may be removed from a non-smoking environment into an environment of smoking or vice versa. In deciding what is best for a particular child a decision must be made which takes into account their psychological, social and physical health needs. This chapter focuses on the impact of smoking on the child, while recognising the difficulty of teasing out confounding factors.

Historical perspective

Tobacco is a native plant of the American continent and was brought to England in 1565. Initially it was a drug of the rich, but it later spread to all sections of society. As early as the 1600s, the supposed health benefits of tobacco were being questioned and King James I produced a proclamation in which he said that smoking is a 'custome loathsome to the eye, hateful to the nose, harmful to the brain, dangerous to the lungs'. The initial heavy import duty he levied was later lowered, as the reduction in smoking substantially reduced the revenue from the tobacco trade. It was also early in the 1600s that the addictive nature of tobacco was remarked upon, and in the 1700s that cancers began to be attributable to it. In the 20th century, with the advent of cigarette-making machines and with the distribution of cigarettes to soldiers in their ration boxes, there was a great increase in tobacco consumption, to a peak of 8.8 g per adult per day. The suffragette movement made it more socially acceptable for women to smoke, and tobacco companies branded cigarettes for women, using imagery of power and liberation (Royal College of Physicians Tobacco Advisory Group, 2000). Over the later part of the last century there has been a growing movement to restrict the consumption of tobacco, which has been relentlessly resisted by the tobacco companies. In the 21st century efforts are escalating to try to protect the public against the effects of passive smoking (Donaldson, 2003). In February 2002 the World Health Organisation (WHO) declared that the tobacco epidemic is one of the greatest public health challenges facing the European Region (Warsaw Declaration for a Tobacco-free Europe, 2002).

Epidemiology of smoking

Despite the well-known detrimental health consequences of smoking, nationally 27 per cent of people over 16 years of age smoke (Census Data, 2001), while worldwide prevalence rates of 47 per cent of men and 12 per cent of women are recorded (WHO, 1997). In the UK the prevalence of smoking from 1992 to 1997 remained unchanged, with a slight rise up to 2001, when 32 per cent of males and 26 per cent of females were smoking. Significantly half of all children worldwide are exposed to tobacco smoke at home.

Worldwide male smoking rates are in slow decline, but tobacco use amongst women has increased and is expected to rise to 20 per cent by 2025. This may reflect tobacco marketing specifically targeting women (Richmond, 2003). Smoking is more common in younger women: 42 per cent of 15–24 year olds, compared with 21 per cent in those aged 35 and over. Risk factors for smoking have been identified in women who are unskilled manual employees, and those who are unemployed are nearly six times more likely to smoke than women in professional and non-manual groups. Women who leave education early, and who are not married, are also more likely to smoke when compared with women as a whole (Royal College of Physicians Tobacco Advisory Group, 2000).

Of particular concern to the future health of children is the prevalence rate of smoking amongst pregnant women. In 1999, 30 per cent of all pregnant women in the UK were recorded as smoking (Owen and Penn, 1999; Royal College of Physicians Tobacco Advisory Group, 2000), compared to 13 per cent in the US (Pickett *et al*, 2003). Pregnant women with larger families and those in rented accommodation are more likely to smoke. Many women make substantial efforts in pregnancy to quit smoking, but even with the most effective "best practice" interventions, the reduction in maternal smoking is only 20 per cent (Pickett *et al*, 2003).

Pharmacology

There are approximately 4,000 substances in cigarette smoke, many of which have been shown to be deleterious to health. The major toxic constituents that have been extensively studied are nicotine and carbon monoxide. Nicotine acts directly on the nervous system via nicotinic receptors, producing central nervous system effects of pleasure and increased vigilance, and peripheral effects of increased catecholamine (stress hormones) production. This produces a rapid pulse rate, a rise in blood pressure, and a rise in glucose, cortisol and free fatty acids. Carbon monoxide interferes with the transport of oxygen in the blood, producing an increase in the red blood cell content in the blood, and may produce subtle impairment of central nervous function. Many of the other thousands of substances found in cigarette smoke have been shown to be carcinogens and irritants.

The health effects of smoking during pregnancy on the developing foetus and newborn baby

The impact of maternal smoking on the foetus can include miscarriage and stillbirth, preterm birth, birth defects and intrauterine growth retardation.

Miscarriage and stillbirth

The risk of miscarriage is increased by a quarter and the risk of stillbirth is increased by a third in women who smoke (Royal College of Physicians, 1992). The effects of toxic components in the tobacco smoke on both the placenta and foetus cause the increased risk. A major contributing factor is the reduction in blood flow to the placenta caused by nicotine tightening blood vessels (Ness *et al*, 1999).

Preterm birth

Premature babies are twice as common in women who smoke when compared to those who do not smoke (Royal College of Physicians, 1992). Some reasons for this appear to be problems with the placenta. Many studies have shown an increased risk of placental abruption (placenta separating from the wall of the womb), placental praevia (low lying placenta) and pre-eclampsia (high blood pressure and reduced flow of blood in the placenta) in women who smoke (Higgins, 2002). There are substantial risks to a baby who is born prematurely, and these risks increase the earlier in gestation the baby is delivered. Prematurity increases neonatal mortality and morbidity (disease), increasing the risk of respiratory, cardiovascular, neurological and gastrointestinal disease as well as long-term disability.

Birth defects

Population studies have suggested that cigarette smoking while pregnant also increases the risk of having a child with cleft lip, cleft palate and cardiovascular abnormalities. The risk of cleft lip/palate has been shown to be 1.3 times more likely if the mother smokes, with this risk increasing to 1.8 for the category of mothers with the highest daily number of cigarettes smoked (Chung *et al*, 2000).

Intrauterine growth retardation

Babies born to mothers who smoke are on average 200 g lighter – interestingly if the father smokes they are also lighter, but to a less marked extent. Some of this growth reduction can be improved if the mother stops smoking by 32 weeks gestation (Higgins, 2002). The WHO defines a full-term newborn child weighing less than 2,500 g (5 lbs 8ozs) as 'low birth weight', which increases the risk to the health of the infant, and furthermore recognises maternal cigarette smoking as the principal cause of underweight babies. There is a growing body of evidence to suggest a link between low birth weight and adult diseases such as hypertension, stroke, obesity and myocardial infarction (Barker, 2001). Smoking is one of the few risk factors for low birth weight where an intervention, such as smoking cessation programmes, can improve outcome.

The health effects on the child and adult whose mother smoked during pregnancy

A WHO report summarises the data pertaining to the effect that prenatal smoking has on foetal respiratory and cardiovascular development. It states that infants born to mothers who smoke have lower lung volumes, lower lung compliance and lower expiratory airflow velocities (Cook and Strachan, 1999). It is suggested that this is due to alterations in lung collagen and elastin content. The changes in lung volume and function in babies born to mothers who have smoked during pregnancy can be detected in premature babies, suggesting that many of the deleterious effects occur early in pregnancy (Le Souef, 2000). Airway sensitivity, which is associated with wheeze, is also increased in these babies. In older children, current environmental exposure may be to blame for the reduction in lung function shown in children born to parents who smoke. However, there is growing concern that damage to the airways of foetuses and infants leads to poor lung function in later life (Stocks and Dezateux, 2003). Systolic blood pressure is higher amongst children born to mothers who smoke, but it is not known if this continues into later life, with all the attendant mortality and morbidity (Higgins, 2002).

The health effects on the child of living in a smoking environment

Concerns about the health effects of breathing other people's tobacco smoke have recently come to the forefront of political debate, with the Chief Medical Officer in Britain challenging the government to introduce a total ban on smoking in public to protect individuals and vulnerable children from the toxic effects of passive smoking.

Sudden Infant Death Syndrome (SIDS)

Sudden Infant Death Syndrome or cot death is defined as the sudden death of an infant that remains unexplained by clinical or post-mortem examination. It is the most common cause of death between one to 12 months of life (Anderson, 1997; Stocks and Dezateux, 2003); in Britain the incidence is 0.53 per thousand live births. Almost 50 studies have examined the relationship of smoking and SIDS, and all have indicated an increased risk (Mitchell *et al*, 1997). These studies have shown that the risk of SIDS is increased five times by maternal smoking, or double if all possible confounding factors are accounted for. This risk also increases if only the father smokes (Mitchell *et al*, 1997; Brooke *et al*, 1997), making it likely that it is the environmental smoke that accounts for much of these data. There are some research papers, however, that hypothesise that *in utero* exposure to tobacco smoke may also play some role, through an abnormality of lung development (Anderson and Cook, 1997), or a central nervous system abnormality leading to sleep apnoea (where children stop breathing briefly when asleep). The recent "Back to Sleep" campaign appears to have produced a substantial reduction in the number of cot deaths in the UK; this has been achieved by encouraging the appropriate positioning of the child in their cot (on their back), avoiding overheating, together with a smoke-free environment (Dwyer and Ponsonby, 1996).

Respiratory disease

There is convincing evidence from a large body of research that parental smoking is associated with an increased prevalence of asthma and respiratory symptoms in children. Risks of asthma and respiratory symptoms depend on the age of the child and number of parents smoking (Cook and Strachan, 1997). For younger children the risk increases by 1.6 times if either parent smokes, rising to 1.7 if the mother smokes. For older children the risk increases by 1.2 to 1.3 if either parent smokes, and 1.3 to 1.4 if the mother smokes. In children with established asthma, parental smoking is associated with more severe disease. Pneumonia is 1.6 times more likely in children exposed to environmental tobacco smoke than in those who are not (Cook and Strachan, 1997). After general anaesthesia, environmental tobacco smoke exposure has been associated with an increased frequency of respiratory symptoms in the post-operative period (Drongowski *et al*, 2003). It has been estimated that, in the USA, between 136 and 212 children under five years of age die each year from lower respiratory tract infections attributable to smoking (DiFranza and Lew, 1996).

Dental caries
Recent work suggests that not only current smoking in adults, but also passive smoking by children contributes to the burden of dental caries (Aligne *et al*, 2003). There are many possible confounding factors for this observation and more work is needed to prove a truly causative effect.

Otitis media
A recent meta analysis suggests that children who are exposed to environmental tobacco smoke are 1.6 times more likely to suffer otitis media (middle ear infection) (DiFranza and Lew, 1996). In the USA it has been estimated that between 354,000 and 2.2 million episodes of middle ear infection are attributable to environmental tobacco smoke, with the associated morbidity of hearing loss, surgery, speech delay, schooling difficulties and social isolation.

Behaviour and academic achievement
Research has highlighted the effect of nicotine on the developing brain. An aetiological link has been suggested between foetal exposure to nicotine, and difficulties with maths and language and behavioural problems (Higgins, 2002; Richmond, 2003). Carbon monoxide in maternal cigarette smoke binds more strongly to foetal haemoglobin than adult haemoglobin, therefore reducing oxygen to the foetus, which may lead to neurological and developmental abnormalities (Stocks and Dezateux, 2003). There have been a number of studies on *in utero* smoke exposure and anti-social behaviour in children and young adults – these show a strong association but further studies are needed to prove causation (Brook *et al*, 2000; Wakschlag and Pickett, 2002).

Children more likely to smoke themselves
Addiction to tobacco most frequently starts during the teenage years. Indeed 89 per cent of adults who smoke began before 18 years of age, and parental attitudes and smoking habits have been shown to affect this greatly. One-quarter of children aged 15 years smoke (Royal College of

Physicians Tobacco Advisory Group, 2000), and this rate is increasing in many countries (Bricker *et al*, 2003). People who start smoking younger than 16 years of age are more likely to be current smokers at age 35 years, when compared with those who begin smoking at an older age (Le Souef, 2000).

There are thought to be three important etiological factors in the onset of smoking in childhood: exposure to social and environmental models of smoking, personality traits and family genetics.

Girls appear particularly at risk of smoking if a parent smokes, with more than 20 per cent smoking if their mother smokes, as opposed to seven per cent if neither parent smokes (Royal College of Physicians, 2000). Taken as a whole, children living with parents who smoke are nearly three times more likely to be smokers than those whose parents do not smoke. Conversely, children are seven times less likely to smoke if they perceive a strong disapproval from their parents. If both parents quit smoking, the children's chances of smoking are reduced by 39 per cent, and if one parent stops smoking the children's chances of smoking are reduced by 25 per cent. However, in one study the risk of a child smoking, if living with ex-smokers, was still shown to be elevated when compared with children living with non-smoking parents (Bricker, 2003). This was true even if the parents had stopped smoking before the birth of the child, making the authors hypothesise about inherited addictive factors.

It has been difficult to tease out all the confounding variables related to addiction to tobacco. Environmental factors, family and peer pressures, advertising and cost are all very strongly related to smoking initiation and continuation. Studies of twins have suggested a genetic link in that concordance was higher for smoking in genetically identical twins than in non-identical twins (Carmelli *et al*, 1992). The heritability estimates for smoking in twin studies have ranged from 46 to 84 per cent, and suggested genes involved include differences in the specific receptors for nicotine, and those involved in the way nicotine is removed from the body (Batra *et al*, 2003). This is a complicated issue and further research is ongoing to try to improve knowledge in this area.

Morbidity and mortality from fires started by cigarettes

Fire and burns are the leading cause of death in the home for children. One study has shown that 29 per cent of fatal fires were caused by cigarettes (Shai and Lupinacci, 2003). In the USA there are over 300 fire-related injuries to children per year initiated by smoking materials (DiFranza and Lew, 1996). In the UK, 10 per cent of fires ignite with smoking related material, leading to between 130 and 180 deaths per year, or one in three of all deaths from fires (Census Data, 1998 and 1999).

The effects of smoking on the caregiver's health

When considering all issues concerning the well-being of a child, the health and well-being of the carer also need to be considered, and smoking is a significant risk factor for early death and disability. In 1997, cigarette smoking accounted for an estimated one in five of all adult deaths, or for the loss of 205,000 years of life under age 65. Life tables can be used to predict the impact of smoking on an individual's life expectancy: more than one in four men aged 35 who continue to smoke can expect to die before age 65, compared with one in nine non-smokers. For women the figures are one in seven and one in 12 respectively (Royal College of Physicians Tobacco Advisory Group, 2000). These figures can be made more precise by considering other risk factors, such as diabetes, high cholesterol, etc. and may relate to a substantial reduction in the life expectancy of the carer. In this way, the benefits to the child of a certain home environment can be reviewed in the light of the risk of that placement failing due to the poor health of the carer.

Smoking cessation

The above discussion demonstrates that there are many reasons why promoting smoking cessation is important in consideration of a child's welfare. Nicotine is highly addictive and is thought to be the major factor inhibiting smokers from stopping (Royal College of Physicians, 1992). Of those smokers who attempt to stop smoking, over 90 per cent will remain as smokers 12 months later (Le Souef, 2000). In a meta-analysis on the Cochrane database of 18 studies, using both intervention and control groups only four achieved a reduction in children's environmental tobacco smoke exposure (Roseby *et al*, 2003). Of these four studies, one conducted in China was school based, and involved letters written by the children asking their father to stop. Two studies employed a three-month counselling intervention, and one used a half-hour motivational interview. Experiments performed on women during pregnancy to try to encourage smoking cessation have had very mixed results. Some studies suggested that targeting women immediately after birth might prevent a relapse to smoking. Partner support and attitude are thought to be extremely important. There have been improved results with nicotine replacement therapy and bupropion (an agent used to reduce craving in nicotine withdrawal) in promoting smoking cessation in the general population (up to a doubling of successful cessation). People have therefore wondered about these products for pregnant women, but there are concerns at present over safety implications.

Conclusion

On 21 May 2003, the WHO's 192 member states unanimously adopted the world's first public health treaty, the WHO Framework Convention on Tobacco Control. In this Treaty they state that second-hand smoke is a real and significant threat to public health and that children are at particular risk. The Treaty obliges Party States to adopt, implement and promote measures to protect from exposure to tobacco smoke (World Health Organisation, International Treaty for Tobacco Control, 2003).

While the negative health implications of tobacco on the child before and after birth are now well known, the methods of reducing the child's exposure are less clear. Tobacco is such a highly addictive substance that most smoking cessation programmes have had poor results. Preventing the onset of smoking should be the priority, but the huge influence of the tobacco companies, particularly in the developing world, has hampered these strategies. While governments need to curb the influence of the tobacco companies, implement smoke-free environments and encourage public health measures for smoking cessation, professional bodies always need to encourage what is in the best interests of the child. This should include an assessment of the impact of smoking on a child placed in substitute care.

References

Aligne C A, Moss M E, Auinger P and Weitzman M (2003) 'Association of paediatric dental caries with passive smoking', *Journal of the American Medical Association*, 289:10, pp 1258–64

Anderson H R and Cook D G (1997) 'Passive smoking and Sudden Infant Death Syndrome: review of the epidemiological evidence', *Thorax*, 52:11, pp 1003–9

Barker D (2001) *Fetal Origins of Cardiovascular and Lung Disease*, New York: Marcel Dekker

Batra V, Patkar A A, Berrettini W H, Weinstein S P and Leone F T (2003)'The genetic determinents of smoking', *Chest*, 123:5, pp 1338–40

Bricker J B, Leroux B G, Peterson A V, Kealey K A, Sarason I G, Anderson M R and Marek P M (2003) 'Nine-year prospective relationship between parental smoking cessation and children's daily smoking', *Addiction*, 98:5, pp 585–93

Brook J S, Brook D W and Whiteman M (2000) 'The influence of maternal smoking during pregnancy on the toddler's negativity', *Archive of Pediatric Adolescent Medicine*, 154, pp 381–385

Brooke H, Gibson A, Tappin D and Brown H (1997) 'Case-control study of Sudden Infant Death Syndrome in Scotland, 1992–5', *British Medical Journal*, 314:7093, pp 1516–20

Carmelli D, Swan G E, Robinette D and Fabsitz R (1992) 'Genetic influence on smoking: a study of male twins', *The New England Journal of Medicine*, 327, pp 829–833

Census Data, United Kingdom www.statistics.gov.uk/CCI/SearchRes.asp? term=smoking+prevalence/ Website accessed 27/09/2003

Chung K C, Kowalski C P, Kim H M and Buchman S R (2000) 'Maternal cigarette smoking during pregnancy and the risk of having a child with cleft lip/palate', *Plastic and Reconstructive Surgery*, 105:2, pp 485–91

Cook D G and Strachan D P (1997) 'Health effects of passive smoking, 3, Parental smoking and prevalence of respiratory symptoms and asthma in school age children', *Thorax*, 52:12, pp 1081–94

Cook D G and Strachan D P (1999) 'Health effects of passive smoking, 10, Summary of effects of parental smoking on the respiratory health of children and implications for research', *Thorax*, 54, pp 357–366

DiFranza J R and Lew R A (1996) 'Morbidity and mortality in children associated with the use of tobacco products by other people', *Paediatrics*, 97:4, pp 560–8

Doll R and Bradford Hill A (1950) 'Smoking and carcinoma of the lung: preliminary report', *British Medical Journal*, 2, pp 739–748

Donaldson L (2003) *Annual Report of the Chief Medical Officer*, London: Department of Health, Update 36

Drongowski R A, Lee D, Reynolds P I, Malviya S, Harmon C M, Geiger J, Lelli J L, and Coran A G (2003) 'Increased respiratory symptoms following surgery in children exposed to environmental tobacco smoke', *Paediatric Anaesthesia*, 13:4, pp 304–10

Dwyer T and Ponsonby A L (1996) 'Sudden Infant Death Syndrome: after the "back to sleep" campaign', *British Medical Journal*, 313:7051, pp 180–181

Higgins S (2002) 'Smoking in pregnancy', Current Opinion in *Obstetrics and Gynaecology*, 14:2, pp 145–51

Le Souef P N (2000) 'Pediatric origins of adult lung diseases, 4, Tobacco related lung diseases begin in childhood', *Thorax*, 55:12, pp 1063–7

Mitchell E A, Tuohy P G, Brunt J M, Thompson J M D, Clements M S, Stewart A W, Ford R P K and Taylor B J (1997) 'Risk factors for Sudden Infant Death Syndrome following the prevention campaign in New Zealand: a prospective study', *Paediatrics*, 100:5, pp 835–40

Ness R B, Grisso J A, Hirschinger N, Markovic N, Shaw L M, Day N L and Kline J (1999) 'Cocaine and tobacco use and the risk of spontaneous abortion', *The New England Journal of Medicine*, 340:5, pp 333–339

Owen L A and Penn G L (1999) '*Smoking and Pregnancy: A survey of knowledge, attitudes and behaviour 1992–1999*', London: Health Education Authority

Pickett K E, Wakschlag L S, Dai L and Leventhal (2003) 'Fluctuations of maternal smoking during pregnancy', *Obstetrics & Gynecology*, 101:1, pp 140–7

Richmond R (2003) 'You've come a long way baby: Women and the tobacco epidemic', *Addiction*, 98:5, pp 553–7

Roseby R, Waters E, Polnay A, Campbell R, Webster P and Spencer N (2003) 'Family and carer smoking control programmes for reducing children's exposure to environmental tobacco smoke', *Cochrane Database Systematic Reviews* (3): CD001746

Royal College of Physicians Tobacco Advisory Group (2000) *Nicotene Addiction in Britain*, www.rcplondon.ac.uk/pubs/books/nicotene/

Royal College of Physicians Working Party (1992) 'Smoking and the young', *Journal of the Royal College of Physicians of London*, 26:4, pp 352–356

Shai D and Lupinacci P (2003) 'Fire fatalities among children: an analysis across Philadelphia's census tracts', *Public Health Reports*, 118:2 pp 115–26

Stocks J and Dezateux C (2003) 'The effect of parental smoking on lung function and development during infancy', *Respirology*, 8, pp 266–285

Wakschlag L S and Pickett K E (2002) 'Maternal smoking during pregnancy and severe antisocial behavior in offspring: A review', *American Journal of Public Health*, 92:6, pp 966–974

Warsaw Declaration for a Tobacco-free Europe www.euro.who.int/eprise/main/ WHO/Progs/TOBCONF/ConfDocs/ (accessed 11/03)

World Health Organisation (1997) *The Smoking Epidemic: A fire in the global village*, Press release WHO/61 www.who.int/archives/inf-pr-1997/en/pr97-61.html

World Health Organisation (2003) *An International Treaty for Tobacco Control*, www.who.int/features/2003/08/en/

6 Placement of children born to women with blood-borne viruses

Dr Jacqueline Mok

Introduction

In this chapter, "blood-borne viruses" (BBVs) is used as a generic term to cover Human Immunodeficiency Virus (HIV), Hepatitis B virus (HBV) and Hepatitis C virus (HCV). They are so called because they are carried in the blood stream, and can be spread by activities which involve coming into contact with blood. Children whose birth parents are at a high risk of acquiring blood-borne viral infections tend to be over-represented in those who require substitute care. Considerable anxiety still exists when dealing with these children, despite advances made in the management of HIV and the hepatitis viruses. Such concern can distract from the needs of the child and cloud thinking about the placement. It is therefore important that those providing services for looked after and accommodated children are well versed in the topic of blood-borne viruses.

Factors which put the child or birth parents at risk of contracting a blood-borne virus infection include:

* having lived in an area of high prevalence of blood-borne viruses;
* needle-sharing injecting drug use;
* a history of multiple sexual partners (heterosexual, homosexual or bisexual);
* unprotected sexual activity from a "high risk" partner (consenting or abusive);
* injections from non-sterile needles, including accidental or inflicted needle stick injuries;
* recipient of blood transfusions, haemodialysis and organ/tissue donation prior to routine screening for blood-borne viruses;
* extensive or prolonged contact with blood or body fluids on broken skin or mucous membranes (eyes, mouth or genital tract).

Mother to child transmission

Where the birth mother is found to have a blood-borne virus infection, the child is at risk of acquiring the infection through vertical (mother–child or perinatal) transmission. Perinatal transmission can occur during pregnancy (intrauterine), during labour and delivery (intrapartum), or after delivery through breastfeeding (postpartum). Most of the information on modes of transmission has come from research into HIV, summarised by Bulterys and Lepage (1998) and Fowler *et al* (2000). In the absence of breastfeeding, intrauterine transmission accounts for 25–40 per cent of infection, and 60–75 per cent of transmission occurs during labour and delivery. Among women who breastfeed, approximately 20–25 per cent of vertical infections are believed to be associated with intrauterine transmission, 60–70 per cent with intrapartum transmission or very early breastfeeding; and 10–15 per cent with later postpartum transmission through breastfeeding. Intrapartum transmission can occur during labour through maternal–foetal exchange of blood or during delivery by contact of the infant's skin or mucous membranes with infected blood or other maternal secretions. Most infections transmitted through breastfeeding probably occur during the first few weeks to months of life.

In many parts of the world, pregnant women are screened for HBV, and when an infectious carrier (HB surface or e antigen positive) is identified, the newborn is given immediate protection with Hepatitis B immunoglobulin followed by an accelerated course of Hepatitis B vaccination, with a booster injection at one year. Under these circumstances, the majority of babies are protected against HBV infection and can breastfeed. It is vital that the full course of vaccinations is completed, and this is especially difficult to implement if the baby is moved from one placement to another.

In the USA and many parts of the UK, HIV testing has been added to antenatal screening in high-prevalence areas (Centers for Disease Control and Prevention, 2001a; Department of Health, 2002). Because of recent advances in both anti-retroviral and obstetric interventions, pregnant women infected with HIV who are identified in the antenatal period can reduce the risk of transmitting HIV to their infants to approximately two per cent. The pregnant woman is offered counselling which involves interventions to decrease mother–child transmission. These include assessing her own health and the effects of HIV on her immune system; anti-retroviral treatment for herself and the newborn; and a planned caesarean section and advice against breastfeeding (Leroy *et al*, 1998; International Perinatal HIV-1 Group, 1999; The European Mode of Delivery Collaboration, 1999; Public Health Service task Force, 2003).

Where a child is thought to be at risk of a blood-borne virus infection because the mother has been diagnosed with an infection, it may be possible to assess the degree of risk with some certainty, if there is access to stored samples from the mother. Some virus laboratories store frozen samples of serum and, with the mother's consent, these can be tested for HIV, HBV or HCV. For example, if stored samples during the pregnancy and after the child's date of birth test negative, the risk of the child being infected by vertical transmission are nil, and placement plans can proceed normally.

Clinical features of blood-borne virus infection

An adult or child infected with HIV, HBV or HCV can remain in good health, with no signs or symptoms of illness. Only the appropriate blood test can establish if the person is infected with a blood-borne virus. The following medical terms are used to describe children born to women with a blood-borne virus infection:

- *Indeterminate infection status* (for HIV and HCV infection) – this describes the child who has not been tested; or the infant under 18 months in whom no definitive tests have been performed, and a positive antibody test could reflect passively-acquired maternal antibodies. If indicated, it may be useful to request more sensitive tests (PCR (polymerase chain reaction)), with consent from the mother.
- *Uninfected* – the child born to a mother with a blood-borne virus infection is uninfected if an appropriate test has been negative. No further testing is required, and no special arrangements are necessary for substitute care.
- *Infected* – a laboratory diagnosis of infection requires evidence of the virus (genetic amplification by PCR testing, positive virus antigen or culture, or positive antibody test in the older child). Many infected

children show no clinical evidence of ill health, and the only way to diagnose infection is with the appropriate blood test.

Hepatitis B virus infection

HBV infection is a major global public health problem which has not received as much attention as HIV because there is a safe and effective vaccine, and infected people are largely asymptomatic. However, HBV can affect the liver and cause an acute and serious illness with jaundice, vomiting, anorexia and abdominal pain leading to liver failure. With supportive treatment, 90 per cent of adults make a full recovery and have no further problems. The virus remains in about ten per cent of infected people, and the person is described as an infectious carrier. About a quarter of carriers will develop chronic hepatitis, cirrhosis and primary liver cell carcinoma. When infected by vertical transmission, the majority of children will remain carriers (Dupuy et al, 1978) and pose a risk to others in the community. This is obviously a situation where antenatal screening and immunisation can play an important role in preventing vertical transmission from mother to child.

Hepatitis C virus infection

The virus responsible for this infection was identified in 1989, although the disease, previously described as non-A, non-B hepatitis, was recognised earlier. HCV has become the most significant cause of chronic liver disease in the developed world. Areas of high prevalence include the USA, Southern Europe, Egypt and Japan. In the UK, studies have shown that the frequency of HCV infection amongst injecting drug users vary from 60 to 80 per cent, the prevalence being higher in people who have been in prison (Department of Health, 2001). Transmission from mother to child is low (about five per cent), although this risk is greater if the mother is co-infected with HIV. Unless there is co-infection with HIV, no special precautions are required for the care of a pregnant woman with HCV – normal delivery is advised and breastfeeding does not appear to alter the risk of infection (European Paediatric Hepatitis C Network, 2001).

The illness may present with jaundice in 25 per cent of patients, but non-specific symptoms (flu-like illness, lethargy and headache) are more common. The longer-term outlook is not yet known, but infected people have a higher risk of chronic hepatitis, cirrhosis and liver cancer. The majority of children who have HCV infection will be indistinguishable from other children, and will remain undiagnosed unless there is a high index of suspicion regarding their own, or the mother's, risk activities. Under these circumstances, advice should be sought from a paediatrician who is knowledgeable about mother–child transmission of HCV, and the appropriate tests requested. If found to be infected with HCV, the child will require regular monitoring of health, growth and blood tests. The blood tests look for the degree of liver involvement (liver function tests), levels of HCV in the blood (viral load) and the sub-type of HCV responsible for the infection. Response to treatment depends on the sub-type. A liver biopsy may be necessary, if contemplating treatment. There are currently trials examining various treatment options, mainly in adults.

Human Immuno-deficiency Virus (HIV) infection

Since the first descriptions of the Acquired Immune Deficiency Syndrome (AIDS) in the late 1970s, much has been learnt about its causation, modes of transmission, clinical spectrum, natural history and treatment options. There has also been an improved understanding of the emotional, social and economic consequences of the diagnosis. Nonetheless, there is still a stigma attached to a diagnosis of HIV/AIDS, and decisions can be influenced by fear, ignorance and prejudice. Workers who are know-ledgeable will be better able to deal confidently with issues arising from the need for placement of children infected with, or affected by, HIV and AIDS.

HIV-infected women (or their children's carers) should be informed of the importance of follow-up for their children. Any child whose HIV infection status is unknown should be offered early diagnostic testing so that treatment can be given to prevent *Pneumocystis Carinii* Pneumonia (PCP). Uninfected children who are exposed to anti-retroviral therapy should be assessed for potential short- and long-term side effects. Identi-fication of an HIV-infected mother indicates that her family needs or will need medical and social services as her disease progresses. Therefore, health and social care workers should ensure that referrals to services address the needs of the entire family.

Children, like adults, can be infected with HIV and appear perfectly healthy as well as grow normally. Like HBV and HCV infection, the only way to diagnose infection is through a high index of suspicion and appropriate blood tests. Infected children should be followed up to determine the need for prophylactic therapy and anti-retroviral treatment, and to monitor disorders in growth and development that often occur in infancy. The most commonly performed laboratory tests are a full blood count, immune function tests (CD4 and CD8 counts) and the amount of HIV in the blood (viral load). Where indicated, other blood tests or X-rays will be requested by the paediatrician. Some children infected with HIV will have mild non-specific signs (such as thrush, enlarged lymph nodes, liver or spleen) or present with moderate non-specific illnesses (such as pneumonia, meningitis or gastro-enteritis). At the other extreme, they can present acutely ill, at any age, with AIDS-defining illnesses like PCP, Burkitt's lymphoma and disseminated chicken pox or tuberculosis (Centers for Disease Control and Prevention, 1994).

Several prospective studies (Grubman *et al*, 1995; The European Collaborative Study, 2001; Thorne *et al*, 2002) have highlighted the good outlook for children with HIV, even before the use of highly active anti-retroviral treatment (HAART). With the advent of HAART, children infected by vertical transmission are now leading normal lives. Many therapeutic trials are now in place, to assess the best combinations of drugs and the optimum duration of treatment for children (AIDS Treatment Information Service website).

Long-term survival

With or without therapeutic interventions, children who have been infected in infancy will reach adolescence and adulthood. The blood-borne virus infections, including HIV, are recognised as chronic childhood diseases. Children infected vertically who have survived their first ten years are mainly free of serious symptoms. As they enter adolescence, additional services are needed (Thorne *et al*, 1999). Any adolescent with a long-term illness is likely to feel different from his or her peers, and may rebel against all advice, including those regarding medical treatments. All blood-borne viruses (especially HBV and HCV) affect the liver, and infected individuals need to be judicious in the use of alcohol and drugs which also affect the liver. Girls need to know how to dispose of blood-stained sanitary towels safely, to avoid horizontal spread of the viruses. Young people will need support to make decisions about disclosure of their diagnosis, medical care, sexual health, emotional needs, lifestyle choices and future plans. As they become sexually active, they will become a potential source of transmission to their sexual partners and babies.

Confidentiality and the public right to know – who needs to know?

Children and families with blood-borne virus infections are entitled to the same degree of privacy and confidentiality as all other families. Even if not infected by the virus, the child will have experienced multiple episodes of ill health, hospitalisation and perhaps bereavement because of infected family members. Some children will have acted as carers for ill family members, or assumed the care of younger siblings when the parents are not able to. Young carers may miss school and lose out on normal childhood experiences, but are afraid to divulge family secrets for fear of being removed from home. Children and young people infected with, or affected by, blood-borne viruses tend to come from families where there are already many existing uncertainties and problems – homeless-ness, unemployment, domestic abuse, drug misuse, imprisonment as well as worries about parental physical and mental health. They therefore require sensitive and expert support and counselling (Thorne *et al*, 1999).

The concept of privacy in Article 16 of the Convention on the Rights of the Child (General Assembly of the United Nations, 1989) recognises the child's right to retain maximum control of all aspects of his or her life. Information about any medical diagnosis should only be divulged to others on a need-to-know basis, when it is in the best interests of the child and with consent of the parents and child (if appropriate). When dealing with blood-borne virus infections, there may be a balancing act between the rights of the child and the interests of the wider public. Children and young people infected by any blood-borne virus have a right to attend school with no special arrangements unless they require a modified curriculum on health grounds. These cases are best dealt with in a multi-agency forum, attended by the parents and child if appropriate. With consent from the parent and child, professionals closely involved with the child and family should share relevant information and reach a plan to address the child's needs. Where a child is looked after by the local authority, whether in day care, foster care or residential care, the carers need full information about the child's health in order to fulfil their responsibilities towards the child (Department of Health, 1992; The Scottish Office, 1992). The interests of other children using the service will also need to be considered. Training issues which arise for all carers are:

- awareness of the UN Convention on the Rights of the Child;
- information about consent and confidentiality;
- health needs of the infected child, together with implications of regular visits to hospital, blood tests and medications;
- implications of possible deteriorating health, developmental regression and end of life care;
- possible reactions from family members, friends, schools and the community;
- health and safety practices – enforcement of universal good hygiene practices and infection control policies;
- first aid procedures which include the action required in the event of injuries to children (bites, cuts, nose bleeds);
- reporting structure when such incidents occur, including access to medical advice;
- what and how to communicate, in the case of such incidents, to parents of other children using the facility.

Compared to HIV and HCV, HBV is highly infectious as the virus is present in large quantities in blood and body fluids. The risk of transmission posed by an accidental injury depends on factors such as whether the skin is broken, the depth of puncture wound and if blood is present on the device (Table 1).

Table 1
Transmission risks for blood-borne infections, following needle stick injuries

Virus	Transmission risk	Post-exposure treatment
HBV	1 in 3, especially if e antigen positive	Immunoglobulin and vaccine
HCV	1 in 30	None
HIV	1 in 300	HAART, if considered high risk

Children's rights to know versus parents' rights to confidentiality – what to tell?

When the child is infected

As with all medical diagnoses, the decision about what the child needs to know usually lies with the parents, working closely with the paediatrician. However, a diagnosis of an infection with a blood-borne virus, especially HIV, carries a stigma associated with parental lifestyle and risk activities. For these reasons, many parents object to the child receiving any information about his or her diagnosis. Parents also fear that children may be indiscriminate in who they tell. The child may need to know for purposes of giving consent to investigations or treatment. It is extremely difficult to prescribe multiple treatments and achieve compliance with medications if the child does not understand the nature of his or her illness and the purpose of treatment. Depending on the maturity of the child, there may be circumstances in which the child has both a need and a right to know which will over-ride the wishes of the parent (The Children Act, 1989; The Children (Scotland) Act, 1995). The paediatrician should work with the parents, acknowledging their responsibilities and rights as parents, but always subject to the over-riding consideration of the best interests of the child. Often, explanations to the child can involve phrases like 'a virus in the bloodstream', or 'something wrong with the immune system', without usage of terms like AIDS or HIV. The parents should always be informed that, if the child asks a direct question about his or her illness (e.g. Have I got HIV?), a truthful answer will be given. That would also provide an opportunity to explore other questions and fears in the child's mind.

When the parent is infected

The wider family or local authority may wish to make plans for children of infected parents, because of deteriorating mental or physical health of the parent. In the past, there has been an exaggerated concern about confidentiality regarding the parent's diagnosis. Children do not have a right to know their parent's medical diagnosis, but Articles 12 and 13 in the UN Convention on the Rights of the Child (1989) state that children should be given relevant information, and have a right to express views and be involved in decisions about their future. Ideally, parents should be involved in, and consent to, any disclosure about their health status. In the absence of parental consent, it should not be assumed that nothing can be done. The local authority should start with consultation and planning with the child while waiting for the issue of parental consent to be resolved or over-ridden. Under the Children (Scotland) Act (1995), an uninfected child who is affected by HIV/AIDS in the family is defined as a "child in need" or "child affected by disability". Therefore, the whole spectrum of resources across all departments should be made available to assist the local authority in fulfilling its obligations.

Prospective families with blood-borne virus infection

Carer with blood-borne virus

A prospective carer with a blood-borne virus who wishes to foster or adopt a child has to be assessed in exactly the same way as any other family. If an applicant is believed to be at high risk of being infected with a blood-borne virus, consideration should be given to testing as part of the approval process. Where the prospective carer has been diagnosed with a blood-borne virus infection, a thorough medical assessment is necessary, in the same way as any carer who has a significant medical condition. Almost all infections with a blood-borne virus occur through four routes: sexual intercourse, sharing contaminated equipment (including needles), treatment with infected blood or blood products, and perinatal transmission. Within the household, normal contact and social activities pose little risk for blood-borne virus transmission (Friedland *et al*, 1990; Simonds and Chanock, 1993). However, stringent hygiene practices should be adopted universally. There is insufficient evidence to support the routine use of HAART after a possible non-occupational exposure to HIV, such as may be sustained during the care of a child (Centers for Disease Control and Prevention, 1998; 2001b).

The risk of transmission for HBV is much higher (Table 1), and infected healthcare workers have transmitted HBV to patients in clinical settings. The vaccine is safe and effective, and should be offered to other household members, if the carer is an infectious carrier of HBV infection. It may be prudent to offer that placement only to children and young people who have been immunised against HBV infection. In the event of any accident to a non-HBV immune child where there is break of skin or mucous membrane, the wound should be flushed with copious amounts of water. Urgent medical attention should be sought, with a view to passive and active immunisation with HB immunoglobulin and vaccine.

If clinically well, the carer with a blood-borne virus infection should be able to look after a child who is independent in daily activities. In the medical assessment, information is required on the stage of the carer's illness, its effect on mental and physical well-being, any medications prescribed and whether these are likely to jeopardise the care of the child. For example, tablets should be stored where they cannot be accidentally ingested by young children and needles should be discarded without risk of accidental needle stick injuries. Consideration should also be given to the life expectancy of the carer, as this will have an effect on a child who may have already experienced multiple losses and bereavement.

Child with a blood-borne virus

Due to the shortage of carers, a family already looking after a child with a blood-borne virus infection may be asked to take another (uninfected) child. Each case must be considered individually, and at all times, stringent hygiene practices must be emphasised. Whether or not this is advisable depends on the following factors which must be weighed up for each child:

- *Age and developmental status* Is there developmental delay or are there behavioural problems (e.g. biting, self-harm with cutting) which might put the uninfected child at greater risk of acquiring a blood-borne virus infection?
- *Health and emotional needs* Does the uninfected child also have a

health problem which might require hospital visits and emotional support?

- *Stage of illness of child with a blood-borne virus* Is it likely that the infected child has a high viral load, making him or her more infectious to the uninfected child? As a measure of the burden of care, is the infected child on multiple medications or in a terminal stage of illness?

If the child is an infectious HBV carrier, the family will already be immunised. The placement could be considered for an uninfected child already immunised against HBV infection.

Conclusion

Advances have been made in the care and management of HIV, HBV and HCV infection. To offer the best service to looked after and accommodated children, and their carers, all those working in this field should ensure that they are kept up to date with the latest good medical practice. This chapter has discussed some issues which might arise when making substitute care arrangements, but in no way suggests that children or families with a blood-borne virus infection should be treated differently.

References

AIDS Treatment Information Service website, *Guidelines for the use of antiretroviral agents in pediatric HIV infection*, www.aidsinfo.nih.gov

Bulterys M and Lepage P (1998) 'Mother-to-child transmission of HIV-1', *Current Opinion in Pediatrics*, 10, pp 143–50

Centers for Disease Control and Prevention (1994) 'Revised classification system for Human Immunodeficiency Virus infection in children less than 13 years of age', *Morbidity and Mortality Weekly Review*, 43/RR-12, pp 1–19

Centers for Disease Control and Prevention, US Public Health Service (1998) 'Management of possible sexual, injecting-drug-use, or other non-occupational exposure to HIV, including considerations related to anti-retroviral therapy', *Morbidity and Mortality Weekly Review*, 47/RR-17, pp 1–19

Centers for Disease Control and Prevention, US Public Health Service (2001a) 'Revised recommendations for HIV screening of pregnant women', *Morbidity and Mortality Weekly Review*, 50/RR-19, pp 59–86

Centers for Disease Control and Prevention (2001b) 'Updated US Public Health Service guidelines for the management of occupational exposures to HBV, HCV, and HIV and recommendations for post-exposure prophylaxis', *Morbidity and Mortality Weekly Review*, 50/RR-11, pp 00–00

Department of Health (1992) *Children and HIV: Guidance for local authorities*, London: HMSO

Department of Health (2001) *Prevalence of HIV and hepatitis infections in the United Kingdom*, Annual Report of the Unlinked Anonymous Prevalence Monitoring Programme, London: Department of Health

Department of Health (2002) *The National Strategy for Sexual Health and HIV – Implementation Action Plan*, London: Department of Health

Dupuy J M, Giraud P, Dupuy C, Drouet J and Hoofnagle J (1978) 'Hepatitis B in children: study of children born to chronic HBsAg carrier mothers', *Journal of Pediatrics*, 990, pp 200–04

The European Mode of Delivery Collaboration (1999) 'Elective caesarean-section versus vaginal delivery in prevention of vertical HIV-1 transmission: a randomised clinical trial', *The Lancet*, 353, pp 1035–39

The European Collaborative Study (2001) 'Fluctuations in symptoms in human immunodeficiency virus-infected children in the first 10 years of life', *Pediatrics*, 108, pp 116–22

European Paediatric Hepatitis C Network (2001) 'Effects of mode of delivery and infant feeding on the risk of mother-to-child transmission of hepatitis C virus', *British Journal of Obstetrics and Gynaecology*, 108, pp 371–77

Fowler M G, Simonds R J and Roongpisuthipong A (2000) 'Update on perinatal HIV transmission', *Pediatric Clinics of North America*, 47, pp 21–38

Friedland G, Kahl P and Saltzman B *et al* (1990) 'Additional evidence for lack of transmission of HIV infection by close interpersonal (casual) contact', *AIDS*, 4, pp 639–44

General Assembly of the United Nations (1989) *The Convention on the Rights of the Child*, www.unicef.org/crc/text.html

Grubman S, Gross E and Lerner-Weiss N *et al* (1995) 'Older children and adolescents living with perinatally acquired Human Immunodeficiency Virus infection', *Pediatrics*, 95, pp 657–63

International Perinatal HIV-1 Group (1999) 'The mode of delivery and the risk of vertical transmission of human immunodeficiency virus type 1', *New England Journal of Medicine*, 340, pp 977–87

Leroy V, Newell M-L and Dabis F *et al* (1998) 'International multicentre pooled analysis of late postnatal mother-to-child transmission of HIV-1 infection', *The Lancet*, 352, pp 597–600

Public Health Service Task Force (2003) 'Recommendations for use of antiretroviral drugs in pregnant HIV-1 infected women for maternal health and Interventions to reduce perinatal HIV-1 transmission in the United States', www.aidsinfo.nih.gov

Simonds R J and Chanock S (1993) 'Medical issues related to caring for Human Immunodeficiency Virus-infected children an and out of the home', *Pediatric Infectious Diseases Journal*, 12, pp 845–52

The Scottish Office (1992) *Children and HIV: Guidance for local authorities and voluntary organisations*, Edinburgh: The Scottish Office

Thorne C, Newell M-L and Peckham C S (1999) 'Clinical and psycho-social service needs of children and families affected by human immunodeficiency virus in Europe', *European Journal of Public Health*, 99, pp 8–14

Thorne C, Newell M-L and Botet F A *et al* (2002) 'Older children and adolescents surviving with vertically acquired HIV infection', *Journal of Acquired Immune Deficiency Syndromes*, 29, pp 396–401

The challenge for social work

7   Social work and parental substance misuse

Donald Forrester and Professor Judith Harwin

This chapter is intended to provide an introduction to the general topic of social work and parental substance misuse. It starts with definitions. You may be tempted to skip over this bit – but don't! How misuse is defined is important: there are a range of definitions and different definitions incorporate their own sets of values and implications for policy and practice. They also have a considerable impact on understanding the research literature. This is demonstrated in the second and third sections, which consider the extent of parental substance misuse in referrals to social services and evidence of the impact on children. Clearly, information on both these topics is essential for effective practice and service planning. But equally important is an understanding of the issues facing social workers in this field and the views of young people whose parents misuse substances. We draw on our own research to examine both these topics. We conclude with a discussion of the practice implications and suggest an agenda for addressing an issue that we consider to be amongst the largest and most serious facing children in Britain today.

Defining substance misuse: use, misuse and dependency

There are complicated debates about what exactly a "drug" is. For our purposes we are interested in illegal drugs and alcohol. The terms use, misuse, problem use, addiction and dependency are used throughout the literature, but there are significant differences in their meanings. The choice of terminology relates to different models for understanding drug and alcohol use, and it is important to have an appreciation of this. Some definitions that you may find useful (adapted from Alcohol Concern and Drugscope's websites – see end of chapter) are:

- Drug or alcohol *use* does not imply that drug-taking or drinking is wrong and the term is therefore useful if one wants to avoid being judgemental.
- *Abuse* or *misuse* implies that the use is harmful. They refer to use of a substance that is part of or associated with problematic or harmful behaviour. The same is true for *problem* drinking or drug-taking.
- *Physical dependence* is when there are withdrawal symptoms if a substance is not taken. There is a common misconception that physical dependence is all there is to *addiction*. In fact physical dependence is only one factor that defines addiction: others include the pattern of use and psychological feelings associated with not using, such as feeling a craving.

"Addiction" and "dependence" are words that are more common in a psychiatric or medical approach that sees misuse of substances as a disease. In contrast, the terms "misuse" and "problem use" tend to be associated with psychosocial approaches. These focus on the difficulties that use is causing rather than dependence per se and interventions may target more controlled substance use or reducing harm associated with misuse (Orford, 2001; Kroll and Taylor, 2003; and see Drugscope and Alcohol Concern websites). However, because many people who are physically addicted are "good enough" parents (Velleman and Orford, 1999; Klee *et al*, 2002), while large numbers of people who are not addicted have problems related to their substance use in caring for their children we favour the terms substance "misuse" or "problem use" .

How many children are affected?

Estimating how many children are harmed by parental substance misuse is extremely difficult. Misuse of alcohol or illegal drugs is something people tend to minimise or deny and, as a result, obtaining accurate figures is virtually impossible. Furthermore, there is no simple relationship between misuse and harm and it is therefore difficult to be sure of the relationship between the number of parents misusing substances and the number of children experiencing harm. Also, as noted above, different definitions lead to very different estimates of the extent of the problem.

Nonetheless, it is certainly clear that very substantial numbers of children are affected by parental misuse of substances. A recent authoritative report by the Advisory Council on the Misuse of Drugs (ACMD, 2003) estimated that between 250,000 and 350,000 children in Britain – or two to three per cent of all children – have a parent with a significant drug problem. There are various definitional limitations in using this figure, not the least of which is that more than half the parents did not have their children living with them. Nonetheless, it is likely that several hundred thousand children are affected by serious parental drug misuse.

If anything, estimating the numbers of children living with a parent with a drink problem is even harder, as only a small proportion of people with drink problems receive treatment. In these circumstances our "best guess", based on the range of estimates used by others (see Brisby *et al*, 1997; Cleaver *et al*, 1999), is that somewhere between 500,000 and 700,00 children are living with a parent with a drink problem (i.e. around four to six per cent of all children). It is possible that the numbers are considerably higher than this.

It is certainly clear that, whatever the variations produced by different definitions, parental misuse of drugs and/or alcohol is an extremely widespread phenomenon in Britain, affecting several hundred thousand children, and perhaps over one million, at any one time. But what are the issues for these children, and what sort of cases do social workers become involved in?

The effect of parental substance misuse on children

Drawing conclusions from the literature on the impact of parental substance misuse on children is very difficult, for three main reasons. Firstly, as discussed above, different definitions are used in different studies. Secondly, misuse of drugs or alcohol is correlated with other factors (such as poverty or depression) and it is therefore difficult to be sure what is causing particular outcomes for children (Deren, 1986). For example, people sometimes drink because they are depressed, but drinking also makes people depressed, so the relationship between the two is difficult to disentangle. The same can be said for a range of factors including poverty, relationship difficulties and even having children with behavioural difficulties. It is therefore important to be careful in considering research in this area. A correlation does not mean a cause, and substance misuse may just be one factor in a complicated family situation. Finally, getting access to a representative group of families in which there is substance misuse is virtually impossible, and therefore studies use a range of groups to explore the issues. Each of these samples has particular weaknesses and limitations.

Despite the difficulties in disentangling the inter-relationship between substance misuse and other factors, there are some relatively clear findings from the UK and US research, and below we outline some of the most important. Recently a number of excellent summaries have been published and for the interested reader more detailed findings can be found in: Velleman and Orford, 1999; Tunnard, 2002 a and b; ACMD, 2003; Kroll and Taylor, 2003; or.

- Maternal misuse of drugs or alcohol during pregnancy can have permanent harmful effects on babies. This is particularly true for heavy and "binge" use (ACMD, 2003; Prime Minister's Strategy Unit, 2003).
- Young babies are particularly vulnerable, and therefore at increased risk from neglect or assault (Falkov, 1995; Harwin and Forrester, 2002; Forrester and Harwin, forthcoming).
- Alcohol misuse is associated with increased risk of violence in the home (Velleman and Orford, 1999 and see Cleaver *et al*, 1999).
- Children of parents who drink are at increased risk of emotional and behavioural difficulties and poor school performance in childhood and of negative outcomes in adulthood. They appear to be over-represented in prison and psychiatric populations and are at increased risk of developing alcohol problems themselves (Velleman and Orford, 1999).
- There is much less evidence on the problems associated with parental drug misuse. However, it appears likely that the children are at increased risk of poor school performance and increased risk of crime, of coming into care and of developing drug problems themselves (ACMD, 2003).
- The children of parents who misuse alcohol or drugs commonly report disrupted family life, exposure to drinking or drug-taking, having to take on caring responsibilities, fearfulness for their parent's welfare,

shame or stigma related to their parent's behaviour, fear of either their parent or the effect of misuse on their parent and isolation in dealing with the problem (ACMD, 2003; Kroll and Taylor, 2003).

- A fairly high proportion of child deaths and serious injuries involve parental substance misuse (Reder *et al*, 1993; Falkov, 1995; Wilczynski, 1997; Reder and Duncan, 1999).
- Substance misuse has been found to be related to physical, sexual and emotional abuse and related to neglect. In large-scale prospective studies it has been found to be the joint largest predictor of abuse or neglect, roughly trebling the chance of maltreatment (Kelleher *et al*, 1994; Chaffin *et al*, 1996).

A note of caution is needed in reading these findings. As noted earlier, large numbers of children are affected by parental misuse of drugs and alcohol and by no means all of them have the negative outcomes outlined above. Yet it is clear that parental substance misuse is associated with a range of serious difficulties and risks for children.

Parental substance misuse and social work

As might be expected, given these findings, a very substantial proportion of social work cases involve substance misuse. Department of Health funded studies during the 1990s found around 20 to 25 per cent of child protection cases involved parental substance misuse. In individual local authorities far higher rates have been found – with 60 or 70 per cent of cases said to involve parental substance misuse in some local surveys. In our own recent Department of Health funded study of court care plans for 100 children and their outcomes, we found that parental substance misuse was a "major factor" that played a central part in the care application for 40 per cent (23) of families, involving a total of 44 children (Harwin *et al*, 2003). Indeed it was the single most common parental difficulty in the study and the numbers would have been even larger if we had simply counted the number of families where substance misuse was mentioned in the court report. This reflects a general finding in the literature that the more serious the level of concern the higher the proportion of cases that involve parental substance misuse (Forrester, 2001).

In the light of this profile, it is perhaps surprising that until recently there had been no large-scale study exploring parental substance misuse in social work caseloads. Our own study (Harwin and Forrester, 2002; Forrester and Harwin, forthcoming) attempted to begin to address this gap. In the next section we firstly describe the sample and then we draw out the findings that might be of most interest.

The nature of substance misuse in social work cases

Our study looked at all children allocated a social worker in four London local authorities over an average 12 months. The most common reasons for children to be allocated a social worker were because they are "in need", at risk of abuse or neglect or because they have come into the care of the local authority. We used a very wide definition of substance misuse as we wanted to describe the whole range of situations that social workers were confronted with. We therefore included a case in the substance misuse sample if any professional expressed concern about parental substance use. Long-term cases were chosen to enable follow-up of the sample.

A total of 290 families were allocated a social worker during the period of the study. Substance misuse was an actual or alleged concern in 100 of these families (with 183 children) (i.e. 34 per cent), making it the most common parental difficulty in allocated cases. The figures below relate to the 100 families where parental substance misuse (or PSM) was identified.

There was a fairly even spread between alcohol and drug misuse. Forty-one families were affected solely by alcohol misuse, 32 families were affected solely by drug misuse and 27 families were affected by both. An unexpected finding was that crack/cocaine misuse was consistently identified at similar levels to heroin misuse in all four local authorities. While the proportion of cases involving substance misuse was close to one-third for both inner and outer London authorities, 70 per cent of cases involving drug misuse came from inner London authorities while 66 per cent of those involving alcohol misuse were in outer London authorities. This finding surprised us as we had expected to find more substance misuse in the inner London authorities. It would appear to suggest that substance misuse is a common issue for social workers even in local authorities with very different social and economic profiles.

The families in the PSM sample were more vulnerable on a variety of measures even when compared to other families who were allocated a social worker: the children were younger (45 per cent of all those under five were in the PSM sample) and the parents also had more individual difficulties identified on files. In particular, they were more than twice as likely to have been in care or known to social services as a child, 16 times as likely to have a criminal record and four times as likely to perpetrate domestic violence.

The families were also vulnerable socially: 82 per cent had no employed adult (compared to 65 per cent in non-PSM families); they were almost twice as likely to be in temporary accommodation and more than three times as likely to have housing difficulties. This pattern of vulnerability was heightened by the fact that 59 per cent of the PSM sample were single-parent families, and in the vast majority of these (52) there was concern about this single carer misusing. Overall, only 27 families had any adult in the household who did not misuse substances and there were only 16 in which the main carer was not considered to be misusing. As discussed in Chapter 10 on approaches to assessment, access to a supportive adult is a well-established protective factor (Velleman and Orford, 1999). So the fact that most cases were single-parent families, in which misuse by the carer was the main concern, highlights how vulnerable the children in the sample were.

The pattern of child care concerns had a clear relationship to the substances misused. Neglect was a unifying theme: whatever substance was misused, children appeared to be at risk of neglect. Alcohol misuse was strongly associated with violence in the home, with parental intoxication while in charge of children and with concerns about the emotional welfare of the children. Drug misuse was strongly associated with potential harm to newborn babies. In a small number of families children had suffered particularly serious harm (e.g. life-threatening assaults or serious disordered behaviour by parents). Alcohol misuse was a feature in all of these cases, and domestic violence and non-co-operation with social workers were common.

This profile of families with severe individual and social difficulties was reflected in the fact that PSM cases accounted for 62 per cent of all children subject to care proceedings when allocated to a social worker and 40 per cent of those placed on the Child Protection Register. Only 25 per cent of children allocated as "children in need" and, remarkably, only two per cent of children accommodated under s.20 Children Act 1989, had parental substance misuse identified. Drug misuse was strongly associated with care proceedings (41 per cent of all such cases) while alcohol misuse was associated with child protection cases (31 per cent).

The racial and ethnic profile of the PSM and non-PSM samples were broadly similar. One difference was that white children and black children of mixed parentage were somewhat more common in the PSM sample. More noteworthy was the fact that 17 per cent of the non-PSM children were black African and none of the PSM sample were. This was related to a more general finding that parents who were black or Asian first generation immigrants were considerably less likely to be in the PSM sample. This is probably partly related to lower levels of substance misuse within black and Asian communities (ACMD, 2003; Alcohol Concern, 2003; Prime Minister's Strategy Unit, 2003). Another factor may be that black and Asian families, particularly where the parents were first generation immigrants, were more likely to be referred for other reasons to social services. While this included some cases where the focus was on cultural differences in parenting practices, there appeared to be a complex mixture of factors associated with the involvement of social services in these families. Certainly, the upshot was that three-quarters of the parents in the substance misuse sample were white British, compared to half of those in the other 190 families.

Our study of care plans: what the children said

In our care plan study for the Department of Health we interviewed 26 of the children aged seven and above about their experiences in care over the two years since the care order. Parental substance misuse was a very common issue within this group of children. It had been a major factor in the families of 16 of the children and had been an issue for a further five. The following quotes are all from children affected by parental substance misuse. Listening to them highlights the complex and difficult decisions that social workers have to make in planning for children when parents misuse substances. As such it provides an important complement to the findings noted above.

Trying to do justice to the children's strong attachments to their parents was particularly difficult in the substance misuse cases, especially when considering the merits and drawbacks of early rehabilitation after the care order was made. The children, and in particular those of primary school age, often appeared very strongly attached to their parents even when there was ample information suggesting serious neglect and other problems. A typical quote comes from this 11-year-old girl, who had experienced serious neglect while in her drug-using mother's care:

> *She is brilliant, she is the best a mum can be . . . She is really nice and she is kind, she is loving, sharing and she is caring, I am going to write a book about her, she is the best mum in the world.*

In another case, a ten-year-old girl described a mother, from whom she had been removed several times due to severe alcohol problem, as follows:

> *[My mum is] Very, very, very important to me. [She is] Excellent ha. She is really nice to me, she only really tells me off if I do something really naughty, like if I swear or something like that. If I run around the house or break something she doesn't really tell me off.*

Older children tended to have a more complex picture of their parents, which often recognised both the negative side of their parents' behaviour as well as the positive aspects of their relationship. This more balanced attitude towards parents was particularly common amongst older children whose placements had been successful and it often correlated with good welfare outcomes. For instance one 14-year-old boy who made outstanding progress in a kinship placement described his relationship with his mother in the following way:

> *My birth mum . . . she is quite annoying at the moment. She, like, makes loads of lies up, but you can't just say I don't love my mum anymore, I do. She is an important part of my life.*

The complex emotional bonds between the children and their birth parents were a particular feature of the substance misuse cases. It seems likely that they contributed to the tendency, noted below, for social workers to try rehabilitation in circumstances that appeared unpromising when considered objectively. Usually the decision to try to return children home was agreed with, or even suggested by, the children's guardian or independent experts and then ratified by the court. In the light of this it is important to listen to what the children said about failed attempts to return them to their mothers.

One 11-year-old girl provides a vivid picture of the emotional anguish associated with this:

It was just bad. I couldn't talk to [Mum] then, when I was there I would just talk to her and it would keep going through my mind, I would pretend like friends. I would talk to my teddy bears or something [about] . . . why I was down and everything and what had been going on. So I used to just talk to them.

Was there anyone else you could talk to?

My brother, but he didn't listen he was too upset, because we used to cry and that when she was drinking.

So do you think it was a good idea for them to try to move you home?

Yes, it was at the time when she was sober, but not at the time when she was drinking.

Do you think the plan now – that you see a lot of her, but you don't go to live with her – do you think that is a good plan?

Yes because, no I am not saying that I don't want to go back to her, I would love to go back to her, I would be jumping up and down, but I think it is a good idea, yes, because she drinks.

Ultimately, listening to the children highlights the complex dilemmas social workers and other professionals are often faced with. On the one hand, there were children speaking movingly of their love for their parents and their yearning to return to them. On the other hand, there were equally moving accounts of the emotional damage of failed attempts at rehabilitation. In the light of the children's desire to return home, it is most understandable that workers tried to reunite children with their parents. However, it is perhaps precisely when emotions are running high that it is particularly important to step back and try to judge the risks of a breakdown as objectively as possible. Our evidence, and that from the USA, suggests that social workers were tending to try to return children to parents with an alcohol problem even when there was little evidence to indicate that a positive outcome was likely. Listening to the views of the children sheds light on why workers did this, but equally it highlights the consequences for children if the attempted return fails.

Key issues and findings

The first important finding was that substance misuse was a key feature in social work with children and families. This will not surprise most social workers, but it is worth highlighting because while workers tend to recognise the central importance of drugs and alcohol in social work this is not reflected in the broader research and policy literature. This neglect of parental substance misuse has also been largely mirrored in the development of policy and guidance for child care social work, with little mention of substance misuse in any detail. For instance, in the new social work degree, all courses have to teach social workers about mental health and disability but there is no such requirement for substance misuse. Our research highlights the importance of far more attention being given to substance misuse in the research literature and in policy and practice development.

This general neglect of substance misuse may have contributed to our second finding: social workers were often isolated and ill-prepared when working with substance misuse. They were isolated because in 71 per cent of families at allocation there was no substance misuse professional involved. Thus social workers were usually dealing with these issues themselves. Yet most of the workers were newly qualified and said that they had had little or no training on their social work courses about substance misuse. And this was reflected in their conceptual frameworks. Most did not have much understanding of the nature of or ways of helping with substance misuse. This is particularly important because research suggests that many interventions around substance misuse can successfully be undertaken by non-specialists (Heather *et al*, 1996; Moyer *et al*, 2002; McCambridge and Strang, forthcoming).

Our third important finding was that overall the alcohol-related cases raised more concerns than the drug cases. At the simplest level, there were more cases involving alcohol than drugs: 68 of the 100 families were affected by alcohol misuse. However, our reasons for greater concern ran deeper than this. Children were far more likely to have already experienced harm at the point of allocation if their parents misused alcohol and, worryingly, the harm was often serious in nature. By contrast, most children affected by parental drug misuse were identified at an early stage and strong and co-ordinated protective action was often taken before harm had set in. This helps explain why the children in the drug misuse subsample were also younger than those affected by alcohol misuse and this was an advantage in planning alternative care. Finally, examination of previous social work involvement also exposed a worrying picture of the way in which alcohol misuse was managed. We found that a minority of cases raised serious concerns about previous social work involvement. These included:

- families with a history of more than ten previous referrals;
- families where other professionals made complaints about social services' interventions/actions;
- a small number of families where children suffered serious harm shortly after a previous case closure.

Alcohol misuse was very strongly over-represented in all these categories. This suggested an association between alcohol misuse and difficulties in previous social work involvement.

In our study of court care plans and their outcomes referred to earlier, we also had greater concerns in relation to alcohol misuse. The plans for children affected by drug misuse always involved placement out of home (usually adoption or kinship care). By contrast, home placement was the most common plan when alcohol misuse was concerned, often justified on the basis of the strength of the child's attachment to the mother and her stated commitment to overcoming her misuse. These placement plans were far more likely to break down than those involving drugs. Indeed, parental alcohol misuse was one of the strongest correlates of placement break-down, only just falling short of statistical significance. This has also been found in the US research where cases involving alcohol misuse were given more attempts at rehabilitation but were less likely to result in successful rehabilitation than any other type of case (Murphy *et al*, 1991).

In short, alcohol misuse in both our studies was correlated with poorer care planning and this appears to be supported by the US evidence quoted above. Why should this be so? One factor may be that social workers treat alcohol misuse less seriously than drug misuse and this may lead them to underestimate the risks to children from parental alcohol misuse. Forrester (2000), for instance, found that most social workers rated drug misuse as "very concerning", but alcohol misuse as only "moderately concerning", when it was present in families on the Child Protection Register. This in turn may reflect our culture's general acceptance of alcohol, and most workers' direct experience of using it: in short, professional attitudes may be distorted by societal attitudes which lead to over-optimism about the impact of parental alcohol misuse. Conversely there are many negative stereotypes associated with drug use that may be influencing decisions.

Alternatively, social worker judgements may reflect a genuine differ-ence. Perhaps the cases involving drug misuse *were* more serious than those involving alcohol misuse. It is difficult to provide strong evidence in relation to this. (To do so one would have to allow some of the babies at high risk to be cared for by their drug-using parents to see what would happen!) However, we could not find any cases in which the social work decision to remove children appeared excessive in relation to drug misuse. On the contrary the behaviour of the parents, including virtually abandon-ing their babies at hospital, often left workers with little choice.

It would therefore appear that the strong reaction to drug misuse may well be justified – to at least some degree. The reasons for this are not clear. Heavy use of heroin and crack/cocaine may have a more serious impact on parenting than alcohol, but this cannot be considered in isolation. The fact that drugs are illegal also has a major influence – in two important ways. Firstly, it makes the use, purchase and financing of heavy drug use far more difficult and this often pushes parents into criminality, with associated problems for families. Secondly, making a substance illegal alters the profile of those who use it. The overall numbers tend to decline and this means that a higher proportion of users will have a serious problem (Royal College of Psychiatrists, 2000). For instance, if alcohol was made illegal most people would stop drinking, but people with a drink problem would be far more likely to devote themselves to getting alcohol. In other words, the fact that drugs are illegal means that a higher *proportion* of drug users will have a serious problem than if drug use was legal.

What our research, and that of others noted above, suggests is that, whatever the reasons, social work responses to alcohol misuse tend to be over optimistic. Cases are closed when families are doing worse than non-alcohol misusing families; parents are given more chances at rehabilitation despite less likelihood of success; more complaints come in from other agencies about non-response by workers; more children are injured shortly after closure; and more families have histories of more than ten referrals without an allocation. This presents a general picture of under-response to alcohol misuse that has clear implications for policy and practice.

Conclusions

Our findings have some very clear and unequivocal messages for policy and practice. First, substance misuse is a major problem for social services. Insofar as cases tend to be at the sharp end (children on child protection registers and going for care proceedings), the costs to social services are high: these cases involve complex management and inter-agency liaison and they are financially expensive. More importantly, this study highlights the very vulnerable situation that so many of these children are in. Despite the numbers of cases involved and the difficulties raised by staff in care planning and case management, the problem is seriously neglected. There is an urgent need to remedy this situation because of the widespread harm that parental substance misuse can bring to many children.

What needs to be done? First, more information is needed on the nature and extent of substance misuse in social services cases and on social workers' response to the problem. Our sample was based on inner and outer London and while these results might well apply to other inner city and suburban areas, they may not be applicable in rural areas. Second, social workers require far more training in recognition, assessment of harm and above all, in making links between children's difficulties and the nature and severity of parental substance misuse. Social workers also need training, supervision and guidance on engaging and working with parents whose use of drugs or alcohol is causing problems. They need help in setting goals, evaluating intervention and making care plans that will stick. This last point is important because our study for the Department of Health found a clear association between successful implementation of court care plans and good child placement outcomes. Thirdly, our two studies taken together send out a strong message about the response to alcohol misuse. Training should explore attitudes to alcohol misuse and help workers acquire the knowledge and skills to underpin effective intervention and to make realistic judgements about prognosis to counter the misplaced optimism that was evident too often. Last, but by no means least, social workers need skills in direct work with children as well as parents. Too often, as other studies have shown (see Kroll and Taylor, 2003), the child gets left out. This is a large agenda. That is because dealing with parental misuse of drugs and alcohol is one of the most important challenges facing policy-makers, senior managers and practitioners today.

Websites of interest:

Alcohol Concern: www.alcoholconcern.org.uk

Drugscope: www.drugscope.org.uk

References

ACMD (2003) *Hidden Harm: Responding to the needs of children of problem drug users*, Report of an inquiry by the Advisory Council on the Misuse of Drugs, London: Home Office

Alcohol Concern (2003) 'Alcohol drinking among Black and minority ethnic communities (BME) in the United Kingdom', in Alcohol Concern's *Quarterly Information and Research Bulletin*, Spring 2003, www.alcoholconcern.org.uk/files/20030819_150600_Ethnic%20minorities.pdf

Brisby T, Baker S and Hedderwick T (1997) *Under the Influence: Coping with parents who drink too much*, A report on the needs of the children of problem drinkers, London: Alcohol Concern

Chaffin M, Kelleher K and Hollenberg H (1996) 'Onset of physical abuse and neglect: psychiatric, substance abuse and social risk factors from prospective community data', *Child Abuse and Neglect*, 20:3, pp 191–203

Cleaver H, Unell I and Aldgate J (1999) *Children's Needs – Parenting Capacity: The impact of parental mental illness, problem alcohol and drug use and domestic violence on children's development*, London: The Stationery Office

Deren S (1986) 'Children of substance abusers: a review of the literature', *Journal of Substance Abuse Treatment*, 3, pp 77–94

Falkov A (1995) *Study of Working Together 'Part 8' Reports – Fatal child abuse and parental psychiatric disorder: an analysis of 100 area Child Protection Committee case reviews*, Department of Health, ACPC Series, London: HMSO

Forrester D (2000) 'Parental substance misuse and child protection in a British sample', *Child Abuse Review*, 9, pp 235–46

Forrester D (2001) 'Prevalence of parental substance misuse in Britain', *Children Law UK Newsletter*, pp 4–5

Forrester D and Harwin J (forthcoming) *Parents who Misuse Drugs and Alcohol: Effective interventions in social work and child protection*, Chichester: John Wiley & Sons

Harwin, J and Forrester, D (2002) *Parental Substance Misuse and Child Welfare: A study of social work with families in which parents misuse drugs or alcohol*, Interim Report for the Nuffield Foundation, London

Harwin J, Owen M, Locke R and Forrester D (2003) *Making Care Orders Work*, London: The Stationery Office

Heather N, Rollnick S, Bell A and Richmond R (1996) 'Effects of brief counselling among male heavy drinkers identified on general hospital wards', *Drug and Alcohol Review*, 15, pp 29–38

Kelleher K, Chaffin M, Hollenberg J and Fischer E (1994) 'Alcohol and drug disorders among physically abusive and neglectful parents in a community based sample', *American Journal of Public Health*, 84, pp 1586–90

Klee H, Jackson M and Lewis S (eds) (2002) *Drug Misuse and Motherhood*, London: Routledge

Kroll B and Taylor A (2003) *Parental Substance Misuse and Child Welfare*, London: Jessica Kingsley Publishers

McCambridge J and Strang J (forthcoming) 'The efficacy of single session motivational interviewing in reducing drug consumption and perceptions of drug-related risk and harm among young people: results from a multi-site cluster randomised trial', *Addiction*

Moyer A, Finney J W, Swearingen C E and Vergun P (2002) 'Brief interventions for alcohol problems: a meta analytic review of controlled investigations in treatment-seeking and non-treatment-seeking populations', *Addiction*, 97, pp 279–92

Murphy J M, Jellinek M Quinn D, Smith G, Poitrast F G and Goshko M (1991) 'Substance abuse and serious child mistreatment: Prevalence, risk and outcome in a court sample', *Child Abuse and Neglect*, 15, pp 197–211

Orford J (2001) *Excessive Appetites: A psychological view of addictions*, Second Edition, Chichester: John Wiley & Sons

Prime Minister's Strategy Unit (PMSU) (2003) *Alcohol Harm Reduction Project, Interim Analytical Report*, available at http://www.pm.gov.uk/files/pdf/SU%20interim_report2.pdf

Reder P and Duncan S (1999) *Lost Innocents: A follow-up study of fatal child abuse*, London: Routledge

Reder P, Duncan S and Gray M (1993) *Beyond Blame: Child abuse tragedies revisited*, London: Routledge

Royal College of Psychiatrists (2000) *Drugs: Dilemmas and choices*, London: Gaskell

Tunnard J (2002a) *Parental Drug Misuse: A review of impact and intervention studies*, Dartington: Research in Practice

Tunnard J (2002b) *Parental Problem Drinking and its Impact on Children*, Dartington: Research in Practice

Velleman R and Orford J (1999) *Risk and Resilience: Adults who were the children of problem drinkers*, Amsterdam: OPA

Wilczynski A (1997) *Child Homicide*, London: Greenwich Medical Media

8 The interface between substance misuse and child care social work services: Can workers co-operate?

Joy Barlow

Recognising the problem

As other contributors have stated, research, media reports and public concern all point to an increasing awareness of problems faced by children who are affected by their parents' drug misuse. The difficulties of children of alcohol-misusing parents have been better documented over the years, but those affected by drug misuse are also now becoming a significant feature of policy and practice initiatives:

> *The future well-being of a large number of children now being born into drug-misusing households is of serious concern, and ensuring their better protection must be a priority.* (The Scottish Child Protection Audit and Review, 2002, 8.48)

Meeting the needs of this vulnerable group, and promoting the capacity of their parents and others to look after them in the context of the family and its wider environment, is far from straightforward. It is complicated by under-recognition and under-identification of the causes of their difficulties, and by the patchy accessibility of services.

An essential need for collaboration

Parental substance misuse is a growing concern across a number of disciplines and has implications that are medical, political, social and psychological. Ensuring the welfare and protection of children as noted above requires better communication and collaboration between agencies as many Inquiry reports have stated. Spotting danger signs (Barnard, 1999, pp 1109–11), carrying out reliable assessments, keeping each other informed, and responding in a manner that provides both for the safety of the child and for continuing, constructive support of the family, cannot successfully be achieved without close co-operation between all services involved. Making such a response is particularly undermined when the linkages between child welfare and drug problem services are insufficiently co-ordinated (Azzi-Lessing and Olsen, 1996, pp 15–23).

There has previously been a lack of an effective interface between agencies involved in this field, and this has created a barrier to successful intervention on behalf of, and with, for example, drug misusing parents (Mountenay, 1998). Research (McKeller and Coggans, 1997) indicates some of the ingredients of this failure by different services to act together. For example, social work staff may have limited knowledge and therefore uncertainty about how to respond appropriately to the needs of substance-misusing parents. They may have skills for assessing child care cases, but feel de-skilled when faced with drug and alcohol issues. This can be exacerbated by lack of training and clear agency policies and procedures. The result can be that social workers either ignore substance misuse or over-react to it.

Similarly, substance misuse workers may feel de-skilled when faced with child care issues. Historically, substance misuse services have been adult focused, and have considered passing on information as a breach of confidentiality which is potentially damaging to their relationship with the client. Health service staff tend to focus solely on health issues and also have difficulties about breaking confidentiality, to the detriment of good joint working. All professionals may be unclear as to the full range of duties and options in working with this client group.

The policy context

Over the past five years, there have been a number of developments in government strategies, policies and programmes that aim to tackle substance misuse, reduce social exclusion and poverty and improve child health.

In Scotland, the children of substance misusers, particularly those whose parents are drug misusers, have been specifically identified in relation to these aims in *Getting Our Priorities Right* (Scottish Executive, 2003). Further, all Drug Action Teams and Area Child

Protection Committees are now required to have in place local policies to support substance-misusing parents and their children, in line with the national guidance referred to above. The *National Plan for Action on Alcohol Problems* (Scottish Executive, 2002) and the subsequent Alcohol Problems Support and Treatment Services framework, also cover the needs of children affected by their own or other people's alcohol problems.

In England, the policy context is less robust. In the updated Drug Strategy, there is a lack of attention to the children of drug misusers. This may indicate that, at a strategic level, neither the number of children nor the extent of their needs has yet been fully recognised (Advisory Council on the Misuse of Drugs, 2003 7.3, 7.43). Also, in England, the National Treatment Agency has identified that only a very small proportion of current drug misuse treatment budgets is being used directly to help the children of drug misusers. The development of an Alcohol Strategy is currently being undertaken in England which, it is hoped, will include recommendations for the welfare and protection of children and families.

However, across the UK, securing the well-being of children, protecting them from all forms of harm and ensuring that their developmental needs are responded to appropriately, are equally priority areas of government policy (Helliwell, 2000). The recent report, *Hidden Harm*, by the Advisory Council on the Misuse of Drugs (2003) has made an important contribution to the recognition of the needs of children of drug misusers.

There may be the opportunity to develop more services for children affected by substance misuse through the recently published Green Paper in England, *Children at Risk* (DfES, 2003). Its aim is to develop policies that improve the life chances of children and young people aged 0–19 years, who are at risk of a wide range of negative outcomes. Although the Green Paper omits any mention of *Hidden Harm*, it is clear that the negative outcomes it lists (including educational under-achievement, offending, victimisation and poor mental health) may also be areas of risk for children of substance misusers.

The extent and nature of support offered to families

After considerable experience in setting up, developing and managing specific provision for substance dependent women and their children in the non-statutory sector, I carried out a study in Scotland (Barlow, 2001) to determine the nature and extent of support that was available generally for families affected by substance misuse. The evidence from professionals involved indicated that agencies found it difficult to work together in this area. The study examined the reasons for this, identified where change was necessary, and considered implications for staff training and development.

The study looked at agencies in five Scottish local authority areas that were involved in either the drugs or child care fields, and therefore came into contact with substance-misusing parents and their children. A considerable amount of work with these parents and children was being undertaken by both drugs and child care social workers. However, it was patchy, inconsistent and did not reflect the size or importance of the problem.

There were instances of some very resource-intensive work, and it was generally agreed that, if delivered in a consistent fashion, this could bear fruit in terms of keeping families intact. There was more opportunity for therapeutic family work in drugs agencies where this work is prioritised and workers have a remit for this. In such agencies, work with both parents and children was carried out in a more holistic and therapeutic environment. By contrast, social workers described more practical support being offered and demonstrated the priority they give to crisis intervention work. There was a lack of resources or support to enable them to engage in preventive work. Responses also showed that social workers were undertaking work for which they had not received adequate training. Drugs workers were similarly disadvantaged and were also doing work that was not within their formal remit.

The author concluded that work with substance-misusing parents about child care issues is taking place by default, and there still remain a significant number of drug and alcohol agency workers who see their role primarily with the adult clients (even though many of these were parents). Professionals involved in the study agreed that inter-agency preventive work with families, backed up by multi-disciplinary training, was the way forward, but very few could give examples of this happening. Similarly, while staff in all agencies prioritised the need for help in working with substance misusers and their children, there appeared to be a lack of policy and practice impetus to effect this, and staff identified the need for further help.

Barriers to collaboration within and between agencies

The necessity for collaboration between services has been stressed in a number of government documents, e.g. *Getting Our Priorities Right* (Scottish Executive, 2003) in which a major section is dedicated to 'Building strong inter-agency partnerships'. These guidelines also indicate some of the difficulties that stand in the way of partnership and co-ordination of policy and services. These include:

- uncertainty about roles and responsibilities of other agencies and professionals;
- different perceptions of issues such as confidentiality, and unwillingness to share information;
- poor or no access to information technology and incompatibility between different agency IT systems;
- professional or agency protectionism;
- perceived inconsistency between legislation and professional guidance applying to different agencies;
- pre- and post-qualifying training restricted to limited professional perspectives;
- lack of understanding of the legal process;
- different funding streams.
  (Scottish Executive, 2003, p 60)

The continuing lack of a partnership perspective and collaborative work is illustrated in my study (Barlow, 2001) which found:

- evidence of a lack of guidelines or their use *within* agencies, and an even greater need of agreed protocols for assessment *between* agencies;
- no co-ordination across agencies and a wide variety of support offered

by substance misuse agencies and child and family workers. Such co-ordination is necessary to ensure that *all* the essential types of work are covered.

Assessment

One of the major obstacles in putting policies into practice, illustrated by my study, was the lack of a co-ordinated, comprehensive and inter-disciplinary approach to assessment.

It is impossible to say with any certainty that appropriate assessments were being made in relation to children growing up with problem drug using parents. (Barlow, 2001, p 93)

The approach to assessment recommended by numerous government documents is that it should be interdisciplinary and also one of prevention rather than of crisis intervention. The Barlow study showed a clear need for agencies to have a common assessment tool which would indicate the required prevention strategies.

Confidentiality

A further difficulty in the list of barriers to working together mentioned above is confidentiality. Decisions about when to involve other agencies, when to break confidentiality, when to report concerns are difficult and complex. Various factors have to be taken into account, from the specific areas of assessment (e.g. the degree of risk exhibited by parental substance misuse), to the legal framework (including the Human Rights Act 2000 and the Data Protection Act 1998).

Both *Hidden Harm* and *Getting Our Priorities Right* indicate that the risk of harm to a child will always over-ride a professional or agency requirement to keep information confidential (Scottish Executive, 2003, p 43). All service providers have a responsibility to act to make sure that a child whose safety or welfare may be at risk is protected from harm. Parents should always be made aware of this. Specific protocols for the sharing of information and training in such mechanisms are a pre-requisite of any inter-agency collaboration to safeguard the welfare and protection of children living in vulnerable situations.

Training

The Barlow study further noted the lack of training, both within disciplines and across them, for work with families affected by substance misuse. This conclusion had been foreshadowed by other sources.

In 1990, the Advisory Council on the Misuse of Drugs drew up a report addressed specifically to the training needs of workers across a wide range of professions concerned in some way with drug misuse (Advisory Council on the Misuse of Drugs, 1990). This noted the limited provision of such training, the reasons why training has not been more fully developed, and the urgent need to ensure that appropriate levels of training are available to those expected to provide help to drug misusers. Nine years later, a document from the Department of Health stated:

Professionals who work primarily with children may need training to recognise and identify parents' problems and the effect these may have on children. Equally, training for professionals working with adults should cover the impact that parental problems may have on children. Joint training between adults and children staff can be useful. (Cleaver *et al*, 1999, p 11)

Finally, in 2003, *Hidden Harm* is still recommending training of all disciplines involved with families and substance misuse as a necessary part of joint work. It contains references and recommendations supporting training for those in health, education and social care (Advisory Council on the Misuse of Drugs, 2003: Chapters 7, 4, 8, 15, 39; and Recommendations 23, 27 and 31).

Practical recommendations for change

Support for drug misusers and their children

My study indicated a need for greater agreement between services about the types of work which should form a common "curriculum" for substance-misusing parents and their children, and which service should offer what. Recommendations from this study are now supported by those in *Hidden Harm*, particularly regarding collaboration between services, joint use of a common assessment tool, agreements on inter-agency information sharing, and joint action plans for individual cases.

Recommendations from the study included the following:

- *A common assessment framework* should be developed by agencies working in the same areas, supported by agreed protocols (SCODA, 1997, 6).
- *Adult-focused work with clients should broaden out* to encompass clients' role as parents, and the question of parenting capacity to become part of the common assessment framework.
- *Child protection procedures and training on these* should include issues of parental substance misuse and assessment of parenting capacity.
- *Children of drug and alcohol misusers should be considered as children in need*, and a continuum of assessment should reveal the extent of risk. By recognising such children as being in need, services can be developed to provide preventive interventions that may reduce risk. (Those universal services already developed, described in *Hidden Harm* [Ch. 6] such as 'Sure Start', would also provide more preventive work.)
- *Interventions should be developed of a longer-term, preventive nature*, recognising the need for the flexibility required to contain the risks of drug and alcohol misuse as a potential chronic, relapsing condition (McLellan *et al*, 1998, 53f).
- *Service provision* should be planned on a collaborative, cohesive basis to avoid duplication and disparity. Key aims and objectives for work with families should be established at the outset on an inter-disciplinary basis (Marsh *et al*, 1237f).
- *Interventions based on parenting skills, parent drug and alcohol misuse and family management* should be developed as a matter of course within drug agencies (Catalano *et al*, 1999, p. 241). Children's service plans should provide vehicles for the resourcing of such support.

Staff training and development

The following recommendations from the study focus on joint training by the agencies involved as an important pre-requisite for successful collaboration:

- Joint commissioning and planning of services should facilitate a multi-disciplinary approach to service provision and training.

- Social workers and drug/alcohol agency workers should be trained in identification, assessment and intervention skills for working with substance misusers and their children.
- Service training audits should include the issue of working with substance misusers and their children. Training on identification and assessment should be made available, even where agency priorities are identified as other than those associated with this topic. It may well be that children's needs are going unrecognised because staff lack training in these areas.
- Greater attention must be given in policy and practice implementation to recognising the needs of children within drug and alcohol services. Training should be established to assist that recognition.
- Agencies should recognise the importance of bringing drug and alcohol misuse issues into the areas of core training on child development, family work and communicating with children.
- The implementation of government guidelines on inter-agency work with drug misusers and their children must be adequately resourced, and a training programme developed for their "roll-out" to health boards, local authorities and non-statutory agencies. Such training should be planned and executed on multi-disciplinary lines, and include:
  - identification of problems associated with parental drug misuse and parenting capacity;
  - identification of the specific needs of children;
  - common assessment frameworks for need and risk;
  - integration with risk assessment and child protection procedures;
  - interventions for change and long-term support.

- Consideration should be given to the status of inter-agency guidelines and in particular to the weight of priority given to training in the areas covered by them. The bodies responsible for social work and social care training should consider the core competencies in relation to this area of work for the registration of social care staff. Priority of core competencies in this regard would have an efficacious impact on the priority of training.

Again, this is supported in *Hidden Harm* (Home Office, 2003) and broadened to cover the whole of the UK:

Social care staff can only be expected to act effectively in the interests of the children of problem drug users if they are properly trained . . . It is to these Councils (Social Care Councils) that we look to ensure that all future social care workers who are working with children and families are suitably trained regarding the impact of problem drug use on children, how such children and their families can be assessed and what practical steps can be taken to help them. (7.39)

Fostering and adoption

The number of children of problem drug users who are currently being adopted is small. The majority in residential or foster care will return home. However, the British Association for Adoption and Fostering (BAAF), in evidence to the Prevention Working Group of the Advisory Council on the Misuse of Drugs, voiced their belief that the assessment of the capacity for recovery of parents with a significant drug problem is sometimes unrealistically optimistic:

The need for a comprehensive and careful assessment of the child's needs and of the home and parental circumstances cannot be underestimated. (Advisory Council on the Misuse of Drugs, 2003, 7.43)

The report considers that, of the options available, fostering offers the greatest potential for development; but it points to the need to increase both the flexibility of arrangements and the intensity of support for foster carers – how they are trained, financially resourced and supported by health, education and social services (7.44).

The training of foster carers is important if they are to be viewed as part of the holistic response to the needs of children affected by substance misuse. Such training should include factual information about drug and alcohol misuse, attitudinal work, and help with understanding the complex nature of substance dependency and its effect on parenting capacity. Foster carers should also be helped to understand the potential impact on children of growing up in drug- and alcohol-misusing households.

Recent progress

Since the days of William Hogarth's etching of *Gin Lane*, society has been concerned about the effects of parental intoxication on the welfare and safety of children. It is clear to us all that the children of substance misusers are at risk of a range of adverse outcomes (McKeganey, 2002). Yet the goal of child safety cannot be met in isolation; nor can parents' needs be met without simultaneously dealing with those of their children. By viewing the family as the unit of attention, all agencies working with substance misusers and their children should have as their goal the support of the family as caregivers. This requires the collaboration described in this chapter.

In recent months there has been substantial progress in some areas of Scotland and England towards meeting the deficits indicated by Barlow (2001). Child protection procedures are now taking account of parental substance misuse and the potential consequent for physical and emotional neglect of children. Procedures and protocols are in some instances being adopted across disciplines, and inter-agency training on these procedures is increasingly taking place.

In 2001, the Scottish Executive established STRADA (Scottish Training in Drugs and Alcohol), a training agency for professional groups across Scotland on drugs and alcohol misuse and related issues. That year, it conducted a training needs analysis in which children, young people, parenting, women and pregnant substance misusers were identified as major specific training issues by all respondents. Modules have been specifically devised in response to these findings (Advisory Council on the Misuse of Drugs, 2003, p 69). A module entitled 'Children and families affected by drug and alcohol misuse' has been delivered to multi-disciplinary groups across Scotland since April 2002. In some areas it is being used to assist the implementation of *Getting Our Priorities Right*. Feedback is largely very positive, with learning objectives being met for all participants, and competency in identification and assessment being enhanced. It is hoped that STRADA's work over the next three years will include practice-based, skill-development workshops, and that these will assist the growth of new interventions in work with families affected by drug and alcohol misuse.

However, such changes do not take place overnight, and much work is still required if interagency practices are to be adopted in every area rather than in a few.

Levels of joint work between the services appeared to vary widely and is just one aspect of an overall impression of inconsistency, with no clear geographic pattern of either service provision or regular inter-agency working. (Advisory Council on the Misuse of Drugs, 2003, 4.20)

Policy statements and guidelines from central government have pointed to the need for and the way to collaboration between agencies, and to joint training as an important factor in implementing this. Some areas and authorities have begun to act to fulfil these aims. It remains for all agencies across the UK to take up that challenge.

References

Advisory Council on the Misuse of Drugs (1990) *Problem Drug Use: A review of training*, London: Home Office

Advisory Council on the Misuse of Drugs (2003) *Hidden Harm: Responding to the needs of children of problem drug users*, London: Home Office

Azzi-Lessing L and Olsen L J (1996) 'Substance abuse-affected families in the child welfare system: new challenges, new alliances', *Social Work*, 41, pp 15–23

Barlow J (2001) 'The nature and extent of support for problem drug users who are parents and for their children and the implications for training', MSc Dissertation, Edinburgh University Library

Barnard M (1999) 'Forbidden questions: drug dependent parents and the welfare of their children', in *Addiction*, 94:8, pp 1109–11

Catalano R F, Gainey R, Fleming C B, Haggerty K and Johnson N O (1999) 'An experimental intervention with families of substance abusers: one year follow-up of the focus on family project', *Addiction*, 94:2, pp 241–54

Cleaver H, Unell I and Aldgate J (1999) *'Children's Needs – Parenting capacity'*, London: Department of Health

Department for Education and Skills (2003) *Children at Risk*, Green Paper, London: DfES

Helliwell K (2000) 'Introduction', in Harbin F and Murphy M (eds), *Substance Misuse and Child Care: How to understand, assist and intervene when drugs affect parenting*, Lyme Regis: Russell House Publishing

Horn W F (1994) 'Implications for policy-making', in Besharow D (ed), *When Drug Addicts Have Children*, Washington DC: Child Welfare League of America, American Enterprise Institute

McKeganey N (2002) 'Meeting the needs of drug-using parents', Unpublished paper given at National Conference of the North East Scotland Child Protection Committee

Marsh J C, D'Aunno T A and Smith B D (2000) 'Increasing access and providing social services to improved drug abuse treatment for women with children', *Addiction*, 95:8, pp 1237–47

McLellan A T, Hagan T A, Levine M, Gould F, Meys K and Mountenay J (1998) 'Children of drug-using parents', *Highlight No. 163*, London: National Children's Bureau

Mountenay J (1998) 'Children of drug-using parents', *Highlight No. 163*, London: National Children's Bureau

McKellar S and Coggans N (1997) 'Responding to family problems: alcohol and substance misuse', *Children & Society*, 11:1, pp 53–9

SCODA (Standing Conference On Drug Abuse) (1997) *Drug-using Parents: Policy guidelines for inter agency working*, SCODA – Local Government Forum, Local Government Association

Scottish Executive (2002) *National Plan for Action on Alcohol Problems*, Edinburgh: The Scottish Executive

Scottish Executive (2002) *It's Everyone's Job to Make Sure I'm Alright*, Report of the Child Protection Audit and Review, Edinburgh: The Stationery Office

Scottish Executive (2003) *Getting Our Priorities Right – Good practice guidance for working with children and families affected by substance misuse*, Edinburgh: The Stationery Office

9 The needs of black and dual heritage children affected by parental substance misuse

Sara Mayer

As therapists/workers/parents we must remember that we are the custodians of the health, education and well-being of this and future generations of Black children. (Jocelyn Emama Maximé in Varma, 1993)

The STARS Project

When you come to STARS you can tell all of your problems to your STARS worker. When you tell your worker all your problems you will feel much better. (Child aged 11, STARS)

The Children's Society, a voluntary organisation of the Church of England, is an innovative national children's charity working directly with 50,000 children and teenagers in 90 towns and cities, in partnership with communities, schools and families. It tackles bullying, exclusion, youth justice, drug and alcohol misuse and supports young carers, the young homeless, child refugees and children and young people with disabilities.

The Children's Society STARS Project (Support, Therapeutic, Advocacy and Research Studies) is a stand-alone project for children offering support, therapy, advocacy and research services to children affected by substance misuse by their parents or other adults. It works with children from the age of three upwards across the City of Nottingham and is funded by The Children's Society, Nottingham City Social Services Department, Nottingham City Drug Action Team and Nottingham City Children's Fund.

How did STARS begin?

It helps to talk when you have a naughty mummy who smokes drugs. (Child aged 10, talking about STARS)

I came to The Children's Society with an interest in families affected by substance misuse having worked in a family rehabilitation centre for such families, and in a local authority as a social worker and Team Manager within Children in Need teams. These experiences made me acutely aware of the need for more preventive services. The concept of STARS emerged from consultation work I undertook with professionals focusing upon gaps in local service provision. It was also informed by a piece of work that The Children's Society had previously undertaken with some children in the north of the city. Both these projects clearly identified drug misuse as an issue of increasing concern. After looking at some of the few research reports on this topic (Velleman, 1992; Laybourn *et al*, 1996), it became clear that little research had been done, particularly in terms of assessing interventions for children affected by this. Further, services for these children were few and far between and often family rather than child centred.

The circumstances of the children and young people attending STARS are all different. Some live with parents who "use", others with parents who "did use". Some are privately fostered, others are looked after by the local authority either in residential or foster care. A few might be living at home subject to care orders made under the Children Act 1989. Often children are cared for by family members or friends. Some have circumstances that are ever-changing.

> *Coming to STARS has helped me not to get into trouble. It is really difficult being away from home.* (Young person aged 13, STARS)

Referrals

Initially, our referrals came from a range of sources including schools, the Youth Offending Team and other voluntary projects. The majority are now from child care social workers, following a targeted mailout in October 2002. We have received several self-referrals from children and young people and continue to have a mix of referral sources including social workers, criminal justice workers and some parents. In February 2004, 24 per cent of our referrals were from parents or carers. The Project accepts referrals only when the referring person has sought permission from the child and the parent (where possible). This is in line with good practice, which is at the core of the Project, throughout the process of our involvement with a child. So far, STARS has had only three parents or carers refuse to give consent for the Project to begin work with their child. This clearly challenges the many pervasive myths about the resistance of substance-misusing parents to seeking help and support for their children.

Children attend the Project for as long as they need to. Some come to just a few sessions, the majority for between six and nine months. There are a few who require intervention which lasts over a year. Sessions are usually held on a fortnightly basis, although if concerns are high, or if children are very young, we may hold weekly sessions. The Project tends to lessen the frequency of sessions towards the end of a piece of work, as a way of supporting the child in moving on from the Project.

Links with other professionals

The Project works closely with other professionals – our workers attend core group meetings, child protection conferences and reviews, looked after children reviews and strategy meetings as required. Their role at these meetings tends to be focused upon advocacy and sometimes means that individuals or organisations are challenged. However, this has not been as problematic as we might have initially imagined. Once other professionals are able to observe the relationship that STARS workers have with the children, the value of the work being done and the impact upon the child, this tends to resolve any unease in working together. The Project has also tried not to be too "precious" about confidentiality, ensuring that it has sought the views of children and young people wherever possible, ready to be shared at meetings and reviews.

Having a multi-agency steering group and the involvement of other professionals from the beginning of the Project have also been useful ways of building and maintaining links. Where we believe that the Project has yet to engage with specific agencies or groups, targeted mail shots have been found to be an effective method of raising awareness of and referrals to the Project.

Therapeutic interventions

Before I came to STARS I had no one to talk to about stuff to do with drugs at my house. Even though my mum doesn't take drugs anymore,

I was still worried that when she was stressed she would start taking drugs again. I would search in the bin to see if she had used anything to take drugs like cans with holes in. (Child aged 10, STARS)

The therapeutic work that children undertake with their STARS worker is largely decided by the children themselves. The Project takes the view that if work is to be therapeutic, then the child has to want to engage with it on some level. There are moments within the therapeutic process, however, when a new theme is identified either by the worker or during the supervision process. In such a situation, the worker may introduce this theme into the work, but if the child or young person does not wish to explore it, then it will not be pursued.

The therapeutic process involves using a variety of interventions and techniques – every piece of work undertaken at STARS has been unique and centred around the individual child. We have quite simply found that different techniques work with different children. Remaining child centred is important, no matter what. Often the family's circumstances are fascinating, tragic, chaotic and demonstrate high levels of need. The worker must, however, remain clear that the child is experiencing this and focus upon the impact upon him or her, and be prepared to advocate for the child no matter how difficult that may be. Our role as advocates can cause pain for others. A parent who hears their child's worker read out at a review that the child wants the parent to 'stop using brown', can be moved to tears by this, as can workers. If we want to effect change rather than collude with the embarrassment that pervades our society about substance misuse, we must be prepared to ensure that children's voices are heard. Promoting the child's voice can require a great deal of courage. There are many people who find children's own messages painful and even distracting. If it is hard for adults to hear, then what must it be like to be the child – a child able to move adults to extreme discomfort or sadness just by describing their own situation?

The needs of the children attending STARS have been diverse and consequently themes covered by workers have been wide ranging. Some children have experienced severe abuse, sometimes on many levels, and need to work through what this means as part of the overall impact of their parents' substance misuse. Some children and young people are seeking a way of "letting go" or moving on – perhaps when a parent has misused in the past and the child is finding it hard to believe that the future might be a positive one.

The most popular themes chosen by children include:

- how I can learn not to get so angry;
- how I can chill out and relax;
- sexual, emotional and physical abuse;
- drugs and alcohol;
- living with parents who use drugs or alcohol;
- playing truant or missing school;
- bullying;
- what happens if I have problems at a later stage?;
- I want to stand on my own two feet;
- what my worries are.

I still love mum and did not want to leave her, but she could not care for me. (Child aged 14, STARS)

She used to say I put you into this world and I can take you out again. (Young person aged 14, STARS)

Children from minority ethnic communities

Racism denigrates and dehumanises communities leading to lowering of individual's self-esteem, sense of worthlessness and depression. (Fernando (1988) in Dwivendi, 2002)

Shaikh and Naz (2000) cite the experience of racism as a significant risk factor in respect of alcohol misuse. They describe "internalised racism" as increasing the likelihood of suffering mental distress and substance misuse, including excess drinking. Children who are of minority ethnic status and affected by parental substance misuse (Velleman, 1992; Laybourn *et al*, 1996) may be at a disproportionately high risk of becoming problematic substance misusers. The importance of culturally sensitive interventions with this group must therefore be recognised as a priority area for service development.

Since its launch in January 2002, the Project has worked with over 160 children and young people. About 24 per cent of these children and young people are from minority ethnic groups. Some key themes have been identified in its work with this group of children and young people:

- children having unclear ethnic origins;
- differing ethnic identities within sibling groups when considering permanent placements;
- stereotypes of racial groups: the attribution to one ethnic group within a family of the role of "perpetrator";
- issues of ethnic identity within family placement;
- experiences of racism and violence amongst black and dual heritage children and young people affected by parental substance misuse.

Case studies are used throughout this chapter, as a means of highlighting the difficult circumstances frequently faced by this group of children and young people and the professionals working with them. All names and ages of the children and unusual circumstances have been changed in order to respect the importance of confidentiality in the Project's work.

Children having unclear ethnic origins

I liked looking at my skin colour [at STARS], but I'm shy to talk to other people about it. (Child aged 9, STARS)

Several children attending the Project are of mixed ethnicity and unaware of their exact ethnic heritage. This is particularly the case for children and young people whose parents may have led "chaotic" lifestyles – sometimes synonymous with problematic substance misuse – and have limited recollection of their sexual partners. Further, some children attending STARS are thought to have been conceived as a result of prostitution and therefore are unlikely to have any more than scant information about their own heritage.

Case study

Carolyn is 12 and has been abandoned by her mother, almost certainly because of her mother's chaotic substance misuse and its impact upon her lifestyle. Carolyn is cared for temporarily within her white family.

Carolyn is of mixed ethnicity – her mother is white north European and her father is thought to be of Japanese origin. In the beginning of her work at STARS, Carolyn appeared to reject any suggestion that she is of mixed ethnic origin. Carolyn's worker decided to take a directive approach to the therapeutic work they had embarked upon. She introduced themes of culture and identity into Carolyn's sessions, via the use of the skin tone paints we have at STARS. Carolyn was surprised to learn that her skin tone was much darker than she had previously perceived during sessions focusing upon ethnic identity and began to realise that she was different from both her sibling and carers in respect of ethnic origin. Carolyn now loves to wear the kimonos in the STARS dressing up box, seemingly to explore her new-found identity. She readily depicts herself as a child of mixed ethnicity in her artwork at STARS.

Any potential carers for Carolyn need to have a clear understanding of the therapeutic journey she has embarked upon, during which she has made sense of her ethnic background. This needs to be reinforced by future carers who must crucially be able to accept her own ways of interpreting her ethnic identity. This includes Carolyn's creation of a father figure, a very positive role model, whom she has named and developed within her play. In addition to this, carers would require at least some understanding of the lifestyles of problematic substance misusers. This would enable them to offer her an explanation of the circumstances of her birth, why she is unlikely to meet her father, and how her mother came to be unable to care for her.

Carolyn's work at STARS has also covered issues around substance misuse. The themes that she has explored are:
- education around the general effects of substance misuse;
- education in more detail about her mother's substance of choice including its impact upon relationships and attachments;
- behaviour associated with the problematic use of substances and how it can lead to the separation of children from their parent(s).

These issues are ones that most of us are likely to be far from comfortable with. Carolyn will need carers who are able to avoid reinforcing stigma and offer her explanations that are as compassionate and non-judgemental as possible. Openness around substance misuse within her family will also be crucial to her – both in terms of understanding her past and being able to create a happy and healthy future as she matures.

Different ethnic identities within sibling groups and considerations for permanence

This is a problematic area in relation to permanence planning for children and young people affected by parental substance misuse. It is a common characteristic for the sibling groups we work with at the STARS Project to be made up of children from different ethnic origins. This can be compounded by the increasing social phenomenon of children and young people being bought up by lone parents or within step-families (Office of National Statistics, 2001).

When this group of children find themselves being looked after within public care with a view to permanence, or by relative carers, practitioners can be faced with some challenging dilemmas, likely to be focused upon the appropriate placement of children in these sibling groups.

Case study

Ayesha is ten years old. She is white British and her siblings Jonte, aged seven and Sherry, aged five, are of white British and black African-Caribbean parentage. Their mother is currently serving a ten-year prison sentence. The plan for the children is to find a permanent placement for all of them, preferably together.

Ayesha's father, Gary, has recently come forward as a carer for all three children, having had some sporadic contact with Ayesha over the last three years. He lives in an area predominantly populated by people of white British descent. Gary and his new partner know little about African-Caribbean culture, but are committed to learning about this and supporting Jonte and Sherry in all of their needs.

Sherry and Jonte's paternal grandparents have also come forward as carers, but do not believe they could appropriately meet Ayesha's needs. Their son visits his parents' home frequently and thinks he may eventually be able to take on the full-time care of Sherry and Jonte in the future, with his parents' support. He has always maintained contact with his children and has a notably close bond with them.

Scenarios like this are far from uncommon amongst the children of problematic substance misusers. Research undertaken by Harbin and Murphy (2000) clearly illustrates that this group of children has an increased risk of being subject to child protection registration, public care, child care proceedings and adoption. Yet, decision-making around the needs of sibling groups such as that above can really become a "catch 22" situation.

From a child-centred perspective, some key considerations include the following.
- Is there a way of keeping this sibling group together while ensuring that their identity and cultural needs are met?
- Can white carers really meet the needs of mixed ethnicity children?
- Should the ideal of keeping the sibling group together outweigh the need to place Sherry, Jonte and Ayesha in culturally appropriate placements?
- How would Sherry and Jonte react to being placed in a black family when they have been raised, until recently, by a white carer?
- Do Sherry and Jonte's family have negative views about mixed ethnicity children?
- If the group is split amongst their respective families, can the families maintain contact in a meaningful way, also ensuring that the siblings are raised to respect their differences?

In cases such as these, it is inherently difficult to make the right decision for children and young people. Often one child's needs may be compromised by meeting the needs of his or her siblings. From the STARS Project perspective, however, the key to promoting emotional health and well-being is to listen to children as much as possible, work with them to ensure decisions are explained and recorded fully, and for children to revisit if and when they wish to do so. Finally, practitioners must ensure that work is undertaken with children around these issues – it is too simplistic to argue that work focused upon minority ethnic issues needs to be undertaken by experts. All therapists, counsellors and family workers should be competent in exploring these fundamental issues with children, young people and their families. Projects working with this group of children around other issues must ensure that they can work effectively around ethnicity as an integral part of their work, as opposed to being an "add on" or a theme that is simply referred to during therapy.

Racial stereotypes: the attribution to one racial group within a family of the role of "perpetrator"

Can you get drugs addicted from your mum? (Child aged 7, STARS)

Practitioners within STARS have recognised that, while some children and young people are more likely to misuse substances themselves, this group can also be prone to becoming dedicated to an anti-drug or alcohol stance. This issue becomes even more complicated in respect of mixed ethnicity children, where one parent is a substance misuser and the other is not. These children can understandably develop a skewed and stereo-typical view of the racial group from which their substance misusing parent originates. They may believe that this group is more likely to use substances per se, and to live a lifestyle which is often associated with misuse. These views are arguably backed up by stereotypes that prevail in British society – those of the white working-class heroin user, the young black crack user, or the thirty-something "ladette" British woman who binge drinks at the weekend.

The stigma that exists within our society about substance misuse leads to experiences of shame and anger by those who love and care for substance misusers, as well as those who themselves misuse. Often, relatives of a substance misuser have experienced many heartbreaking events, arousing the shame or anger outlined above or in some cases, the more extreme feelings aroused by bereavement (Sims, 2002). Mixed ethnicity children can face an even more difficult set of circumstances. One member of their family may be portrayed as the "perpetrator" – responsible for all the negative aspects of substance misuse, with another as the "rescuer" – having to pick up the pieces following the impact of the misuse. For children placed with relative carers, or friends of the family, these dynamics can become distinctly pertinent. In addition, the possibility of having to keep their parent's substance misuse secret (Barnard and Barlow, 2003) could be potentially damaging for children in exploring their feelings towards their parent(s).

Case study

Jacob, aged 11, has a mother who is white/African-Caribbean and a father who is white British. Jacob and his siblings have been in and out of care since he was seven, due to neglect, significant and often chaotic poly drug use, and concerns about dealing from the family home. Jacob has been raised in an area in which prostitution, drug dealing and gun crime are rife. Although Jacob's father occasionally uses drugs, it is his mother who is a problematic heroin and crack user.

Jacob, referred to STARS while living in a foster placement, caused much concern at the Project. His mother's frequent involvement in dealing and prostitution and her own heavy use, reinforced by similar activities in his local community amongst other black people, had led Jacob to begin to stereotype this ethnic group. He believed that all mixed heritage or black adults became drug dealers, pimps or prostitutes and had guns. The focus of therapeutic work with Jacob included: racial stereotypes, looking at the inevitability Jacob perceived of himself conforming to these stereotypes in the future, as well as terminology around themes of "race". Jacob presented, believing it was inevitable that he would become a drug dealer as a young adult. The work enabled Jacob to challenge his own beliefs and to begin to feel positive about his culture and ethnic identity.

This highlights the importance of training and ongoing support for substitute carers. In scenarios such as this, it is also imperative for substitute carers and therapists or counsellors to work closely together. While we do not offer a specific service to substitute carers, we would liaise as closely as possible with them to ensure that they are aware of key issues for the child. Challenging children and young people with deep-rooted beliefs is likely to require great care, backed up with love and understanding, as well as the positive reinforcement of the themes explored in therapeutic sessions.

Issues of racial identity within relative placements

The phenomenon of children affected by problematic substance misuse being placed permanently with family members is far from insignificant. This is reflected by the children and young people we work with at the Project: at times, as many as one-third of our current client group of children have been placed with family members. This is an area which has been overlooked by research:

> Little is known about the circumstances of the many children who have been separated from their parents and live with other relatives or friends, or have been fostered, adopted or accommodated in residential care. (Advisory Council on the Misuse of Drugs, 2003)

Case study

Janie is eight years old. Her father is white Irish and her mother is of African origin. Two years ago she was placed with her grandmother Edie, who wished to care for her on a permanent basis but is unsure whether she can continue to do so. She is finding it difficult to cope with Janie's increasingly challenging behaviour and the very visible racial difference that exists between them. Although only eight, Janie was given considerably more freedom and fewer boundaries when cared for by her parents than Edie allows.

This case demonstrates the need for preparatory work with substitute carers before such placements begin. The impact of parental substance misuse upon children's development can result in angry, challenging and rebellious children unused to boundaries. This, combined with ethnic differences within the relative placements, can create almost impossible situations for children and their carers. If careful consideration is not given to all of the child's needs and the work required to be undertaken with the family, incorporating issues around differences, then such placements may inevitably be over before they begin.

Placements with relatives can be seen as a "happy ending" for children and young people. In reality these placements are likely to require a great deal of forethought and the support of all concerned. Family members can feel desperately sad, and perhaps even guilty, that their kin have experienced neglect or abuse at the hands of a parent and relative of theirs who is a substance misuser. They may be keen to help the child out of loyalty, guilt, compassion or fear of the care system. If, however, the carer is to successfully raise a well-adjusted young person, happy and healthy in all areas of development, they must have some key qualities. These include:

- an understanding of the impact of parental substance misuse upon children's development, including behaviours;
- the ability to positively embrace the child's ethnic identity and heritage in a child-centred way;
- the wisdom to put aside grievances with family members, especially the child's parents or previous carers, and to ensure that any grievances they might have do not (inadvertently) turn into negative messages about the child's own heritage;
- the understanding that the child may well require support and thera-peutic input in respect of their heritage, possibly outside the family;
- the commitment to talk openly about substance misuse within the family setting, while maintaining respect for the child's parents or previous carers.

Experiences of racism and violence amongst black and dual heritage children and young people affected by parental substance misuse

STARS helps you, so don't give up. (Young person aged 14, STARS)

The majority of the children and young people the STARS Project has worked with have experienced bullying. Many of these children are perhaps visibly different from their peers. Some children of problematic substance misusers will have experienced neglect (Kroll and Taylor, 2003) and this can be obvious to their peers in respect of poor clothing, nutrition or hygiene.

Velleman (1992), Laybourn *et al* (1996) and the *Hidden Harm* Report (Advisory Council on the Misuse of Drugs, 2003) cite social isolation as a key factor for this group of children and young people. We have witnessed the enormous emotional burden carried by this group of children and young people, which on occasions can be physically manifested, with children presenting as much older than their chronological age. To be the child of a problematic substance misuser is to be different. It may result in isolation from peers and, potentially, the inability to interact on a similar level in a variety of situations.

If, however, the child or young person in question is also black, or black of mixed ethnicity or from a minority ethnic group within their community, their chances of experiencing bigotry, harassment, racism and further bullying are likely to increase. Many children of black or mixed heritage attending STARS have experienced significant bullying, often of an extreme nature. One child we worked with was attacked by a local white drug dealer because his parent owed the dealer money. He was threatened with a weapon and the drug dealer stole his pocket money. Another has experienced significant bullying by a peer. This has been a major obstacle in her therapeutic work and, at times, has effectively disabled her from looking at the themes around having a parent who misuses substances. It is difficult to doubt that the racial differences between the perpetrators and their victims outlined above played a part in these traumatic experiences:

Racism . . . may leave children and their families feeling hopeless when they experience bullying and racial abuse. (Dwivedi, 2002)

The needs of black or mixed ethnicity children affected by parental substance misuse therefore require careful consideration by all significant adults in these children's lives. Foster and relative carers, as well as prospective adopters, clearly require an understanding of the impact of racism and oppression upon an already marginalised group of children and young people. In particular, it may be the case that therapeutic work with this group may take longer to begin, due to issues of trust and experiences of racism. Consequently this may lengthen the child's therapeutic journey.

Conclusion

In order to be heard, there must be a listener. (Cattanach, 2002)

The needs of black and mixed ethnicity children and young people affected by parental substance misuse, who find themselves in substitute family care, may well be far more complex than they initially appear. Practitioners making decisions about, or working therapeutically with, this group should avoid any temptation to view issues of "race" and the impact of parental substance use as separate phenomena. For this group of children, the two may be inextricably linked and must be assessed, addressed therapeutically and planned for as such. If practitioners and substitute carers are to carry out their professional and moral responsibilities on behalf of this group of children and young people, they must ensure that they are equipped with a thorough understanding of their potential needs. Without this knowledge base, this group of children and young people is unlikely to reach their full potential:

> *Tell children that they need to tell someone, whether its school, or STARS, or social workers. There is people they can talk to, not just those. So tell children to get help.* (Young person aged 14, STARS)

References

Advisory Council on the Misuse of Drugs (2003) *Hidden Harm – Responding to the needs of children of problem drug users,* London: Home Office

Barnard M and Barlow J (2003) 'Discovering parental drug dependence: silence and disclosure', *Children & Society,* 17, pp 45–56

Cattanach A (ed) (2003) *The Story So Far: Play therapy narratives,* London: Jessica Kingsley Publishers

Dwivedi K (ed) (2002, 2nd edn) *Meeting the Needs of Ethnic Minority Children – A handbook for professionals,* London: Jessica Kingsley publishers

Fernando S (1988) *Race and Culture in Psychiatry,* London: Croom Helm

Harbin F and Murphy M (ed) (2000) *Substance Misuse and Child Care: How to understand, assist and intervene when drugs affect parenting,* Lyme Regis: Russell House Publishing

Kroll A and Taylor B (2003) *Parental Substance Misuse and Child Welfare,* London: Jessica Kingsley Publishers

Laybourn A, Brown J and Hill M (1996) *Hurting on the Inside: Children's experiences of parental alcohol misuse*, Aldershot: Avebury

Office of National Statistics (2001) *Census 2001: National Report for England and Wales*, London: HMSO

Shaikh Z and Naz F (2000) *A Cultural Cocktail: Asian women and alcohol misuse*, London: EACH

Sims H (2002) *Families in Focus – England*, London: ADFAM

Varma V (ed) (1993) *How and Why Children Hate: A study of conscious and unconscious sources*, London: Jessica Kingsley Publishers

Velleman R (1992) *Counselling for Alcohol Problems*, London: Sage

Resources for children and young people, parents, carers, therapists, counsellors, social workers

Akin T *et al* (1990) *The Best Self-Esteem Activities: For elementary grades*, Torrance, California: Innerchoice Publishing
A book containing a number of activities aimed at teaching life skills, promoting confidence and encouraging personal and social responsibility.

Cohen J (1995) *Life Files – Drugs*, London: Evans Brothers Limited
An educative book looking at the effects of drugs – legal and illegal, legal matters relating to them and how schools should be dealing with drug-related issues.

Feelings T (1991) *Tommy Traveller in The World of Black History*, New York: Black Butterfly Children's Books
A cartoon-style book which explains about African-American history to a young boy who discovers a private library of books on the subject.

Green J (2001) *How do I Feel about . . . Dealing with Racism*, London: Franklin Watts
Contains photographs, cartoon strips and easy-to-read text to support young readers in learning more about racism and strategies for dealing with it.

Heegard M (1991) *When Someone has a very Serious Illness: Children can learn to cope with loss and change*, Minneapolis: Woodland Press
A workbook containing various exercises which enable children to discuss their feelings around these issues.

Heegard M (1991) *When Something Terrible Happens: Children can learn to cope with grief*, Minneapolis: Woodland Press
Another workbook containing exercises which enable children to discuss their feelings around these issues.

Hoffman M and Northway J (1991) *Nancy No-Size*: London: Little Mammoth
A storybook for young children focusing upon themes of difference.

Johnson J (1996) *How do I Feel about . . . Bullies and Gangs*, London: Franklin Watts
Contains photographs, cartoon strips and easy-to-read text to support young readers in learning more about bullying and strategies for dealing with it.

Johnson J (1999) *How do I Feel about . . . Being Angry*, London: Franklin Watts
As above, but also dealing with how to cope with anger.

Parnell K (2002) *Street Smart: A teenager's guide to being sussed and safe*, London: Piccadilly Press
Focused upon safety, this book offers practical guidelines, tips and advice on how to handle different situations aimed at promoting safe, independent living for teenagers.

Perkins U (1989) *Afrocentric Self Inventory Workbook for African American Youth ages 12–15*, Chicago: Third World Press
A workbook for African-American young people aimed at helping to better understand their potential, culture and heritage.

Shah I (1998) *The Lion who Saw Himself in the Water*, Cambridge: Hoopoe Books
Based upon ancient stories from the East, this book can be used with young children to enable them to overcome fears that may be caused by events they may not understand.

Terzian A *(1993) The Kid's Multicultural Art Book*, Vermont: Williamson Publishing
Outlines arts and crafts experiences from around the world. Using the book, children can make ceremonial art to display and artifacts to wear and use, plus pointers to encourage to check out each artifact's significance.

Striker S and Kimmel E (1978) *The Anti-Colouring Book*, London: Scholastic Children's Books
Contains a variety of pictures that can be used by children of all ages in exploring their life experiences, hopes, beliefs and feelings.

Vigna J (1990) *My Big Sister takes Drugs*, Illinois: Albert Whiteman Prairie
A storybook for fairly young children.

Vigna, J (1988) *I Wish Daddy didn't Drink so much*, Illinois: Albert Whiteman Prairie
A storybook for fairly young children.

For information about The Children's Society, visit: www.childrenssociety.org.uk

To contact The Children's Society STARS Project:
Telephone: 0115 9422974
e-mail: STARS-Project@childrenssociety.org.uk

The following helplines can also provide advice and support:

ADFAM   www.adfam.org.uk 020 7928 8898
FRANK   frank@talktofrank.com 0800 77 66 00

ADFAM hosts a website that contains lots of useful information – a data base of family services and a bulletin board where families can exchange views and information.

FRANK is a campaign run by the Home Office and the Department of Health, which seeks to offer honest information about drugs to both young people and their parents. FRANK offers a free, 24-hour, confidential helpline, and a website to provide facts and advice to those in need, those who might be curious about drugs and their consequences or anyone seeking more information on drugs.

10 Social work assessments with parents who misuse drugs or alcohol

Donald Forrester

As identified in Chapter 7, most social workers have little training in working with substance misuse. This being so, this chapter outlines research and theories that may be useful to workers undertaking an assessment. An attempt has been made to concentrate on key findings or theories that may be of most use to practitioners, rather than reviewing the full range of research evidence in this area. (Some excellent recent research reviews have already done this, for instance, Cleaver *et al*, 1999; Velleman and Orford, 1999 and Kroll and Taylor, 2003.)

This chapter has two main sections. The first section provides a brief review of the research evidence in relation to parental substance misuse, the main risks that parental substance misuse poses for children and a model for thinking about risk and resilience in relation to long-term emotional welfare. The second section considers what information social workers should collect and how they can deal with problems around parental denial or minimisation of misuse.

However, before considering these areas it is important that anyone doing an assessment starts by looking at their own values. Understanding our own values and emotions is a first step in any assessment, and it is vital in assessments where substance misuse is an issue. We all have experiences of substance use by ourselves or people we know. These may be negative (for instance, if we have experienced the harmful effects of misuse in our own lives) or positive (for instance, if we drink or take drugs ourselves and do not consider it to have been harmful). Either way they have the potential to distort the assessment. In addition, our society is permeated with folklore about drugs and alcohol, much of which is inaccurate or only applies to some drinkers or drug users.

Fortunately, social workers do not have to have a detailed knowledge of different theories of misuse or addiction – but they do need to realise

163

that they are dealing with some complex issues that are full of value judgements. There are two steps that are important in responding to this. Firstly, they should have a critical awareness of their own values and emotions in relation to use of alcohol and drugs. This includes any views on the nature of "addiction", "misuse" and so on. It is important to then step back and make sure that these feelings and perceptions do not unfairly distort the assessment, for instance, by stereotyping parents in a negative or discriminatory way or by failing to see real risks. Secondly, the best way of doing this is to focus on the actual or likely effect on the child. Returning to focus on the child is a recurring theme within this chapter. It is the heart of a good assessment and particularly useful when considering the impact of parental substance misuse.

What information do you need?: the research evidence

The first step in focusing on the child is to try to specify what the concerns are for their welfare: in other words *what* are they at risk of? Specifying this is necessary both to assess the level of risk and to plan interventions that reduce it. Broadly speaking in relation to substance misuse there are two types of risk: short-term risk of serious injury and longer-term risk of emotional or behavioural difficulties.

In the whole population serious injuries to children are fairly rare. However, they are not all that rare in social work caseloads – and significant numbers involve parental misuse of drugs or alcohol (Forrester, forthcoming; Forrester and Harwin, forthcoming). There are problems in finding research that social workers can learn lessons from in this area, and in practice most of the useful information on cases of serious harm comes from retrospective studies of child deaths or serious injuries. From a research point of view this has serious limitations. Most importantly, looking back at correlations can be misleading. As Calder (2003) points out, a high proportion of people die in bed, but this does not mean that you should sleep on the floor! Nonetheless, social workers need some indication of key factors to consider in attempting to protect vulnerable children. Situations where there may be risk of serious injury are:
• the presence of young babies – particularly where there are indications of the parent having problems in caring for the child and/or themselves

(Kearney and Ibbetson, 1991; Reder *et al*, 1993; Falkov, 1995; Reder and Duncan, 1999);

- families where there are high levels of repeated violence, particularly where this involves alcohol misuse (Cleaver *et al*, 1999; Forrester and Harwin, forthcoming; Forrester, forthcoming);
- dual diagnosis of substance misuse and mental illness, particularly when associated with violence (Falkov, 1995; Wilczynski, 1997).

The presence of one or more of the above suggests that a child may be at serious risk. The circumstances of individual cases will vary, but these factors suggest the potential for serious harm and appropriate protective action may be needed.

In addition, inadequately secured drugs are responsible for a number of child deaths each year. This includes drugs or drug-taking equipment stored where children can reach them. Of particular concern is methadone which is sometimes not stored properly (for instance, in the fridge without child locks), but is potentially lethal when taken by a child. This is an important issue to consider in an assessment of immediate risk, but is usually resolvable in partnership with the parent/s.

In general, there is much stronger research evidence on the longer-term impact of alcohol misuse on children. Broadly speaking, if parents misuse alcohol their children are at increased risk of doing poorly in school, having behavioural difficulties and of having low self-esteem or other emotional difficulties (Cleaver *et al*, 1999; Velleman and Orford, 1999; Kroll and Taylor, 2003). Because parental drug misuse is a much more recent phenomenon, there is less evidence about the effects that it may have on children; however, research suggests that some of the effects may be similar (Advisory Council on the Misuse of Drugs, 2003).

This paints a fairly bleak picture of the impact of parental substance misuse on children. Certainly, substance misuse is associated with some very serious negative outcomes for children, but it is important to consider two important issues before jumping to conclusions. Firstly, as with the relationship between dying and being in bed, a correlation between parental substance misuse and difficulties for children does not mean that one causes the other. Misuse of alcohol and of drugs is associated with poverty, with relationship difficulties, with parents having had childhood difficulties and with other factors that may explain or contribute to the correlation (Deren, 1986). In other words, it may not simply be the substance misuse that is causing the difficulties. Secondly, there is only limited evidence that childhood difficulties persist into adulthood. For instance, some research suggests that if the substance misuse stops then the children's difficulties disappear fairly rapidly. Certainly while some adult children of problem drinkers have difficulties, most probably do not (see Velleman and Orford, 1999).

Velleman and Orford (1999) undertook an extensive review of the literature on the impact of a parental drink problem on children as well as a large-scale study of the views of young adults who had lived in such homes. Their work was specifically designed to consider the issues noted above, namely, what the causes of difficulties for the children of problem drinkers were and what factors were associated with these difficulties continuing into adulthood. In doing so they developed a framework for thinking about the impact of alcohol misuse that can help in both assessing risk and in thinking about interventions. There is no equivalent work in relation to drug misuse; however, it is likely that the broad structure of their model can be applied to the long-term risks of neglect or emotional harm as a result of parental drug misuse.

Velleman and Orford suggest that there is a fairly strong association between parental alcohol misuse and family disruption, and between family disruption and problems in childhood, and between problems in childhood and problems as an adult. Each of these can be thought of as a link in a chain between parental drinking and problems to adulthood. However, between each link a substantial proportion of children manage to achieve better outcomes. For instance, often parental drinking is not associated with family disruption. In many disrupted families children appear to avoid developing difficulties, and even where children have had difficulties in childhood, significant numbers avoid them in adult-hood. As a result, most children living with a parent with a drink problem do not experience difficulties as adults. Furthermore, by looking at the factors associated with children avoiding moving on to the next "link" we can identify protective factors (i.e. things that are associated with children doing well in difficult circumstances).

Perhaps the most important relationship identified by Velleman and

Orford was that where alcohol misuse was not associated with family disruption (as could be the case), it did not result in children having difficulties. "Family disruption" was a composite measure of arguments (including violence), the quality of relationships within the family and the extent of positive or negative experiences in childhood. The relationship between parental alcohol misuse and difficulties in childhood was entirely related to the presence of family disruption caused by the misuse. In other words, it is not the presence or extent of parental substance misuse that is the key issue to assess – it is the extent to which the misuse impacts on the child's life. This may sound obvious, but it is not uncommon for researchers, social workers and other professionals to become overly focused on the extent of substance misuse rather than on the impact that it is having on family functioning, relationships within the family and the experience for the child. Once again, a key lesson from this research is the importance of focusing on the child's welfare, not the substance misuse alone.

While it is useful to have the importance of family disruption highlighted, in practice almost all of the families that social workers deal with have at least some degree of family disruption. However, an important finding from a variety of studies is that, even where there is family disruption, there are a range of factors that are associated with children being less likely to develop difficulties in childhood. These are often referred to as "protective factors". In this respect it is useful to include research on how children survive well in other potentially difficult circumstances (such as having a parent with a mental illness), as it seems likely that many of these protective factors will also work in relation to parental substance misuse. Some of the most important protective factors that mediate between family difficulties and having problems in adulthood are outlined in Figure 1. The factors in the diagram are drawn from Velleman and Orford's review of research on alcohol misuse and a more general summary of risk and resilience factors undertaken for the Scottish Office (Newman and Blackburn, 2002).

Finally, Velleman and Orford make the important point that the relationship between childhood emotional and behavioural difficulties, and problems of adjustment in adulthood, is not as strong as might be thought. Many people who have had difficulties in childhood overcome

Figure 1

A model for assessing the effect of parental substance misuse
(A diagram representing the ideas of Velleman and Orford, 1999)

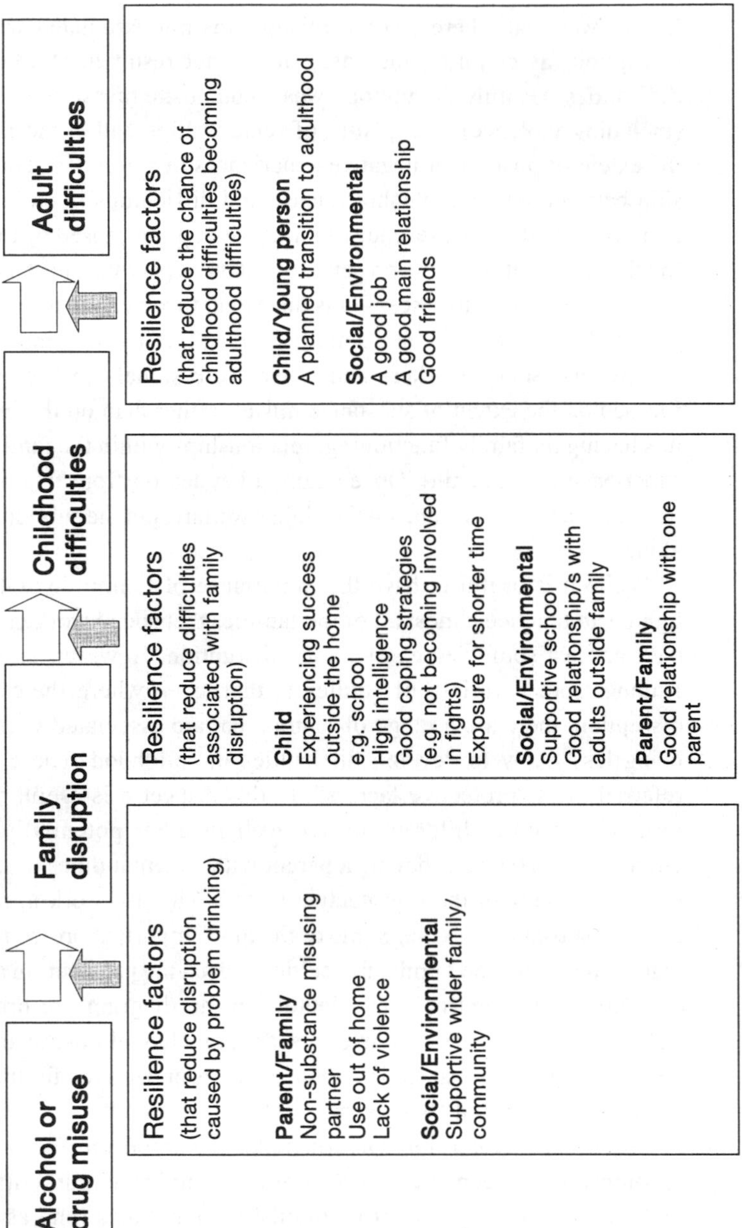

Alcohol or drug misuse → **Family disruption** → **Childhood difficulties** → **Adult difficulties**

Resilience factors
(that reduce disruption caused by problem drinking)

Parent/Family
Non-substance misusing partner
Use out of home
Lack of violence

Social/Environmental
Supportive wider family/community

Resilience factors
(that reduce difficulties associated with family disruption)

Child
Experiencing success outside the home
e.g. school
High intelligence
Good coping strategies
(e.g. not becoming involved in fights)
Exposure for shorter time

Social/Environmental
Supportive school
Good relationship/s with adults outside family

Parent/Family
Good relationship with one parent

Resilience factors
(that reduce the chance of childhood difficulties becoming adulthood difficulties)

Child/Young person
A planned transition to adulthood

Social/Environmental
A good job
A good main relationship
Good friends

them as adults. (Conversely, significant numbers of people who did not have any difficulties as children unfortunately develop them in adulthood.) An important finding from Velleman and Orford's work was that young people who had made planned transitions to adulthood tended to be happier. This was particularly true for women, and it had an independent effect even when childhood difficulties were taken into account. In other words, young people who left home later, who took their time before settling down with a partner, who avoided having children too early and who planned their career or job were more likely to overcome difficulties in childhood. Velleman and Orford also found that having a satisfying primary relationship, a job that one enjoyed and a group of friends that one liked were important in helping people overcome difficulties in childhood caused by parental drinking. These findings highlight the importance of support that helps young people in the crucial 14 to 24 age group in planning the transition to adulthood. It also emphasises once again the importance of effective leaving care provision.

The Department of Health Assessment Framework provides the recommended national guidance for social workers undertaking an assessment (Department of Health, 2000). It suggests that assessments need to look at three areas: social and environmental factors, characteristics and needs of the child and the capacity of parents to provide for their child's needs. The "risk and resilience" approach suggested here works well with the assessment framework. As can be seen in Figure 1, risk and resilience factors can also be grouped into those relating to the child, those relating to the parent or family and those in the wider environment. (Though this is not true at every stage because, for instance, it is not the child's responsibility to prevent their parent's drinking causing family disruption and the parent's behaviour is not as important once the child has grown up. It is nonetheless true overall that factors can be grouped into these three areas.) Perhaps more importantly, the resilience approach emphasises considering changes over time and thinking about the implications of the current situation for future outcomes. Crucially, risk and resilience factors are based on research evidence. They are therefore an important way to ensure that social work assessments are evidence based. In other words, it is a way of going beyond collecting evidence and moving towards analysing that evidence – something that social workers are often criticised for not doing enough (Department of Health, 2000).

Gathering the information

The research evidence reviewed so far highlights key factors to consider in an assessment and attempts to provide a framework for considering both risk and resilience issues. In this section more practical considerations around what information to collect and the process of collecting it are considered.

The first and still perhaps the most useful assessment guidance in relation to substance misuse is the SCODA (now Drugscope) guidance (see end of chapter) (LGDF/SCODA, 1999 or Kroll and Taylor, 2003). These guidelines were drawn up by professionals who worked with adult drug misusers. As such they are particularly good for highlighting issues that child care professionals might miss, for instance, the importance of drug storage, the impact on general lifestyle and how money is raised for drug use. Another strength is that they are very specific about the areas to be considered. This can be particularly useful for practitioners not experienced in working with drug misuse. Furthermore, while the guidelines were developed in relation to drug misuse they can be adapted with fairly little difficulty to assessing alcohol misuse. The SCODA guidelines have therefore made a major contribution to developing practice in this area.

Having said that, the guidelines are not without limitations. Kroll and Taylor (2003) identify two that are particularly significant. Firstly, they are relatively adult centred. There is no mention of the child's view, let alone some of the complexities of obtaining this view. Furthermore, issues around child development, attachment and resilience in the child are not considered in sufficient depth. Kroll and Taylor's book provides an important contribution to considering some of these complexities in the assessment process. Secondly, Kroll and Taylor point out that the SCODA guidelines do not consider the difficulties in collecting the information outlined. In our research we found that the biggest problems social workers described were *how* they could collect the information they needed for an assessment, rather than what information to collect (Forrester and Harwin, forthcoming). Of the many issues that came up, the most common was dealing with parental "denial" or "minimisation" of their substance misuse. More than almost any other issue that social workers deal with (except perhaps sexual abuse), substance misuse can be hidden. It tends not to occur in the presence of the worker and parents have considerable control over when, where and how much they use. Even when under the influence of drugs or alcohol, behaviour can be moderated to disguise the impact of use should the parent meet the worker when intoxicated. As a result, parents are often able to hide the presence and impact of substance misuse, and social workers can struggle with assessments in such circumstances.

Dealing with denial

Seen from the parent's point of view, minimising or denying substance misuse is very understandable. People who misuse substances often feel ashamed of their misuse and a general tendency to minimise or keep secret the presence or extent of use is well documented. This is not a reaction that is unique to substance misuse: most of us tend to keep quiet about or deny things we are ashamed of, sometimes even denying to *ourselves* the extent, nature or impact of our behaviour. However, this reaction is likely to be even greater in relation to social work assessments. While a parent might be prepared to talk to an anonymous counsellor or a trusted friend, talking to a social worker has the additional dangers of the possibility of children being removed or placed on the child protection register. For the social worker, the parent's denial can appear to be an insurmountable barrier, and the worker can often feel stuck and unsure how to undertake an assessment with a parent who does not appear willing to tell the worker the truth about their drinking or drug-taking. There are various ways in which this problem can be approached, but perhaps the most important is to consider ways in which the parent might be encouraged to feel they can talk about their substance misuse.

The issue of dealing with "denial" is not confined to social work. In fact, it is a central issue in the field of substance misuse treatment. Of particular relevance in this respect is motivational interviewing (MI). Motivational interviewing was developed specifically in response to problems of denial or minimisation (Miller and Rollnick, 2002). Miller and Rollnick marshal a range of evidence that suggests that "denial" is not an inherent component of addiction, more a product of a confrontational style of interaction. There is strong evidence for this, but on reflection it is common sense. Imagine you are talking to someone about a bad habit *you* have. If that person is very confrontational and tries to force you to acknowledge the terrible nature of your bad habit, you will probably be defensive and minimise or deny the extent of what you do or its negative impact. On the other hand, if they take a more sympathetic approach and appear interested in hearing what you have to say without judging you, you will feel more able to talk to them. Miller and Rollnick review a range of evidence that suggests that good, empathic listening is associated with better outcomes and that challenging and judgemental counselling is counter-productive. They then go on to suggest a number of ways in which sympathetic listening can be combined with helping people to explore the negative side of their substance misuse, making plans for doing something about it and instilling hope that things can change for the better. It is a really excellent book that anyone interested in working with substance misuse should study.

For the social worker doing an assessment, these findings are very important. They emphasise the central importance of the skills of empathic listening that have long been recognised to be at the heart of good social work practice. Often we forget these skills when confronted by a parent misusing substances and it is useful to be reminded that they are still central to good assessment work. But sensitive listening does not resolve the problem of denial for social workers. While it may help in facilitating getting information from a parent, this will not always be the case. Therefore social workers have to know how to gather information to confirm or confute the parent's account, irrespective of whether they are able to engage the parent.

There are four assessment principles that workers might find useful in dealing with this difficulty. The first and most important is, once again, to focus on the child. Too often workers become overly concerned about positive tests for drugs or alcohol, or about what the indicators of use or misuse are. In fact, there is no simple relationship between what is taken, how much is taken, the behaviour of the carer and the effect on the child. Most people know from personal experience that some people will become aggressive after even a small amount to drink, while others seem able to drink great quantities without a huge impact on their social behaviour. This variation holds true to some extent for all drugs. This can be still further complicated by whether the substance use takes place when the child is awake and by whether the person was responsible for the child at the time. So information on pattern of use is of limited utility in making an assessment.

What *is* important is how the substance misuse impacts on the parenting of the child. And this is where focusing on the child is crucially important. The child's progress is the best indicator of the parenting they have received. Of course this is not an absolute rule; some children develop Attention Deficit Hyperactivity Disorder (ADHD) or other difficulties independently of the care they receive, and children are born with different temperaments and abilities. However, the fundamental place to start the assessment is how the child is progressing and trying to understand the reasons for any difficulties that they may have. Even with an unborn child, the assessment should focus on the potential impact of substance use on the child, rather than the substance use itself. Furthermore, this focus allows the principles of motivational interviewing to be used most effectively. By focusing on the child, social workers make it clear why they are there, that they are not bringing their own values to stereotype or judge the parent, but they can highlight potential difficulties that substance use may cause for parents in relation to child care.

A second assessment principle is that the adults' management of their own lives is a good indicator of their ability to look after a child. This is true in relation to bigger issues, such as holding down a job, keeping a tenancy and the pattern of relationships within their lives. It is also true in relation to the minutiae of everyday living, such as whether they keep appointments, whether they look after their own health and so on. Of course it is important to be aware of one's own values in making such judgements. Many of us sometimes miss appointments, have housing difficulties and complicated relationships – at least at some point in our lives. The measure here is whether the parents are causing themselves harm through their failure to manage their own lives. If they are, then this indicates concern about their ability to manage their child's life.

A third key assessment principle is that the best predictor of future behaviour is past behaviour. If the social sciences teach us anything it is this, a fact Munro has emphasised in her recent work on child protection decision-making (Munro, 2002). In practice, this means that an accurate chronology should be collected and a full social history should be a central aspect of any assessment. However, while this should start with the collection and collation of information from social work files, the preparation of a chronology should, where possible, include the parent (and if they are old enough the children). Too often chronologies are prepared by social workers without engaging the family in the process. This is not ideal because the parent can often shed important light on the records held by social services. A more accurate chronology is therefore often produced when the work is undertaken with the client. And just as important is the fact that preparing a chronology together provides an opportunity to empower the parent and to establish a foundation for working together.

The fourth assessment principle is that information from a variety of sources is better than information from one. This is a commonplace within child protection work, but it is worth emphasising once again. Gathering information from the professionals from different agencies who are familiar with children and their families is obviously crucial. Another important source of information can be members of the wider family. There can be confidentiality issues in obtaining information from these sources. However, often parents will give their permission, and where they do not, this can be over-ridden where concerns are sufficiently serious. The family network, and particularly grandparents, often take on a caring role in relation to children of parents who misuse drugs or alcohol. Including them in the assessment is important because, as noted earlier, they can provide both valuable sources of strength and support for children as well as vital evidence for the assessment.

Conclusion

This chapter has reviewed research evidence, expert guidance and practice wisdom of relevance to assessing children whose parents misuse substances. The intention has been to highlight the types of concerns associated with parental substance misuse, to consider factors that increase or decrease the likelihood of poor outcomes for children, and to suggest some practical ways of approaching common difficulties in collecting the information required for a thorough assessment. A recurring theme has been the importance of focusing on the child not on the substance misuse.

While it is hoped that the above may be helpful, it seems prudent to end on a note of caution. Assessments of risk focus on the future and the future is not entirely predictable. This makes the assessment task both difficult and stressful. Yet if there is one thing that both research findings and practice experience agree upon, it is that parental misuse of drugs or alcohol puts children at increased risk of harm. Accurate assessments are the starting point for putting in effective services to help families and, where this is not sufficient, for taking protective action to ensure that children are safe. While the assessment task can be very challenging, when done well it can be the first step in transforming vulnerable children's lives for the better. For this reason it is vital that social workers, and those who train and manage them, ensure that they are adequately prepared for the challenge.

References

Advisory Council on the Misuse of Drugs (2003) *Hidden Harm: Responding to the needs of children of problem drug users*, London: Home Office

Calder M C (2003) 'The assessment framework: a critique and reformulation', in Calder M C and Hackett S, *Assessment in Child Care: Using and developing frameworks for practice*, Lyme Regis: Russell House Publications

Cleaver H, Unell I and Aldgate J (1999) *Children's Needs – Parenting Capacity: The impact of parental mental illness, problem alcohol and drug use and domestic violence on children's development*, London: The Stationery Office

Department of Health (2000) *Framework for the Assessment of Children in Need and their Families*, London: The Stationery Office

Deren S (1986) 'Children of substance abusers: a review of the literature', *Journal of Substance Abuse Treatment*, 3, pp 77–94

Falkov A (1995) *Study of Working Together 'Part 8' Reports. Fatal Child Abuse and Parental Psychiatric Disorder: An Analysis of 100 Area Child Protection Committee Case Reviews*, DoH, ACPC Series, London: HMSO

Forrester D (forthcoming) *What Happens to Closed Social Services Referrals? A study of patterns of re-referral over two years*, PhD, Brunel University

Forrester D and Harwin J (forthcoming) *Parents who Misuse Drugs and Alcohol: Effective interventions in social work and child protection*, Chichester: John Wiley & Sons

Kearney P and Ibbetson M (1991) 'Opiate dependent women and their babies: a study of the multi-disciplinary work of a hospital and a local authority', *British Journal of Social Work*, 21, pp 105–26

Kroll B and Taylor A (2003) *Parental Substance Misuse and Child Welfare*, London: Jessica Kingsley Publishers

LGDF/SCODA (1999) *Drug-using Parents: Policy guidelines for inter-agency working*, London: LGA/Drugscope

Miller W R and Rollnick S (2002 *2nd edn*) *Motivational Interviewing: Preparing people for change*, New York: Guilford Press

Munro E (2002) *Effective child protection*, London: Sage

Newman T and Blackburn S (2002) *Interchange 78 – Transitions in the Lives of Children and Young People: Resilience factors*, Report for Scottish Office by Barnardo's Scotland, www.scotland.gov.uk/library5/education/ic78-00.asp

Reder P, Duncan S and Gray M (1993) *Beyond Blame: Child abuse tragedies revisited*, London: Routledge

Reder P and Duncan S (1999) *Lost Innocents: A follow-up study of fatal child abuse*, London: Routledge

Velleman R and Orford J (1999) *Risk and Resilience: Adults who were the children of problem drinkers*, Amsterdam: OPA

Wilczynski A (1997) *Child Homicide*, London: Greenwich Medical Media

The Standing Conference on Drug Abuse (SCODA): Guidelines for professionals assessing risk when working with drug-using parents

(SCODA is now DrugScope)

Parental drug use

1. Is there a drug-free parent, supportive partner or relative?
2. Is the drug use by the parent: Experimental? Recreational? Chaotic? Dependent?
3. Does the user move between categories at different times? Does the drug use also involve alcohol?
4. Are levels of child care different when a parent is using drugs and when not using?
5. Is there evidence of co-existence of mental health problems alongside the drug use? If there is, do the drugs cause these problems, or have these problems led to the drug use?

Accommodation and the home environment

6. Is the accommodation adequate for children?
7. Are the parents ensuring that the rent and bills are paid?
8. Does the family remain in one area or move frequently; if the latter, why?
9. Are other drug users sharing the accommodation? If they are, are relationships with them harmonious, or is there conflict?
10. Is the family living in a drug-using community?
11. If parents are using drugs, do children witness the taking of the drugs, or other substances?
12. Could other aspects of the drug use constitute a risk to children (e.g. conflict with or between dealers, exposure to criminal activities related to drug use)?

Provision of basic needs

13. Is there adequate food, clothing and warmth for the children?
14. Are the children attending school regularly?
15. Are children engaged in age-appropriate activities?

16. Are the children's emotional needs being adequately met?
17. Are there any indications that any of the children are taking on a parenting role within the family (e.g. caring for other children, excessive household responsibilities, etc.)?

Procurement of drugs

18. Are the children left alone while their parents are procuring drugs?
19. Because of their parent's drug use, are the children being taken to places where they could be "at risk"?
20. How much are the drugs costing?
21. How is the money obtained?
22. Is this causing financial problems?
23. Are the premises being used to sell drugs?
24. Are the parents allowing their premises to be used by other drug users?

Health risks

25. If drugs and/or injecting equipment are kept on the premises, are they kept securely?
26. Are the children aware of where the drugs are kept?
27. If parents are intravenous drug users:
    do they share injecting equipment?
    do they use a needle exchange scheme?
    how do they dispose of the syringes?
    are parents aware of the health risks of injecting or using drugs?
28. If parents are on a substitute prescribing programme, such as methadone:
    are parents aware of the dangers of children accessing this medication?
    do they take adequate precautions to ensure this does not happen?
29. Are parents aware of, and in touch with, local specialist agencies who can advise on such issues as needle exchanges, substitute prescribing programmes, detox *and* rehabilitation facilities? If they are in touch with agencies, how regular is the contact?

Family social network and support systems

30. Do parents and children associate primarily with:
    other drug users?
    non-users?
    both?
31. Are relatives aware of the drug use? Are they supportive?
32. Will parents accept help from the relatives and other professional or non-statutory agencies?
33. The degree of social isolation should be considered particularly for those parents living in remote areas where resources may not be available and they may experience social stigmatisation.

Parents' perception of the situation

34. Do the parents see their drug use as harmful to themselves or to their children?
35. Do the parents place their own needs before the needs of the children?
36. Are the parents aware of the legislative and procedural context applying to their circumstances (e.g. child protection procedures, statutory powers)?

The views of those affected

11 Listening to what children have to say

Valerie Corbett

Introduction

Aberlour Child Care Trust is a Scottish charity, with 42 projects throughout Scotland. We work with and for children, young people and families who need additional support to promote their development and well-being. One area of work is with children and families affected by drugs and alcohol, providing residential rehabilitation services to mothers and their children, and community outreach services working with parents and children in their own homes.

An important principle of our work is to keep children and young people at the "centre" and give them a voice, so that they do not remain "invisible". We try to give them opportunities to speak more openly about their experiences, including having dedicated children and young people's workers. Having time for yourself is very important, especially when you can choose what to do and can count on it happening. We were reminded of this when a three-year-old child politely knocked on the playroom door and asked the worker to write down her appointment time as she had things to say and do.

In order to grasp the impact of problematic parental substance use one needs to appreciate that not all parents are "bad" parents. Often the child's own experience of being parented is more significant than the substance use alone. However, children and young people living with problematic parental substance use, particularly drugs, can be emotionally and physically disadvantaged. Life is characterised by inconsistency, lack of boundaries, lack of routines, caring for the parent and siblings as well as variable levels of physical care and emotional support. Living on their wits and nerves is an enormous pressure to place on these children and young people.

There is variation in the impact of parental substance use depending upon age and the level of external and family support available to children and young people. Not all parents "fail" their children intentionally.

Helping and supporting families and children means acknowledging what has been good as well as bad in their family. The children's resilience can be remarkable. We have long recognised the need of children and young people to thrive and develop, including being like everyone else and doing everyday things. From our experience we know that they will, and do, have common experiences within their families. But they are also different and require to be fully heard, if their own individual needs are to be met.

Being a parent using drugs

To put the comments of the children and young people in context, the following quotations from parents show that their anxieties can mirror those of their children. Confidentiality is important because of the fear of being judged and losing your child. They want to keep their children safe and protect them from drug use, recognising that this gets more difficult as the children get older and feel the impact differently:

> *I always loved them, I always gave them my love but how can you give them your love, it's false love when you are stoned, when you have the hit . . . you're 'oh, my wee darling', play with them for five, ten minutes then it's . . . you're fed up, that's truthful.*

> *We knew we needed help but we didn't want to bring an outside party in, we didn't want to let anyone know. We were frightened – the fear factor, there seems to be a fear factor attached to social work, 'don't tell a social worker anything – they'll take your weans away'.*

> *I've never taken anything in front of them. We were always in the kitchen but as I've said, he knew wrong was getting done. As far as he was concerned we were in the kitchen taking our medicine. He knew you're in there doing what you're doing.*

What children and young people have to say

The following has been taken from what children and young people have said when using our services, as well as from the Aberlour Report *Keeping it Quiet* (McGuire, 2002), the result of a collaboration between statutory and voluntary organisations in Glasgow. It documents the needs of children and families affected by parental drug use through interviews with parents, relatives and young people. Given the nature of substance misuse and the perceived need to "keep it quiet", the comments below reflect the views of younger children, where parental consent was given. Where no age is given, they are from young people aged 16 years and older who were able to make their own decisions about being interviewed.

Finding out

I don't know, it just came to the time that I was getting older, and that was just me getting to notice the way she looked and I knew she looked different everyday when I came in from school . . . And I just noticed straight away and I said to her, 'Are you on anything? Are you taking anything?' And she always used to say 'no', and I'd believe her because I was still young. But then it just got to an age when I knew she was taking them.

Wouldn't talk about it, it's not really something you'd talk to your ma and da about.

The carer role

I've been her mother figure for a couple of years, 'cos I'd always make her dinner and she'd come to me and say, 'Can I stay out 'til 10 o'clock' or 'Will you sign my punishment exercise?'

Protecting siblings

I said to my ma, millions of times, I don't care what you do, I don't care how you do it , as long as they don't see it, nothing, I don't care.

Being let down

I asked her, 'what's the big deal of taking it, what do you get out of it?' and she says, I can't remember what she says, I think she just ignored me.

Carrying on

But I thought, this is life, get on with it!

What I like about the Residential Project

Going out to the library and swimming. (Nine-year-old)

Coming into the project I was shy and happy because I knew that my mum couldn't take drugs. (Nine-year-old)

My friends could come and play, I could go out and play. (Six-year-old)

My mum taking me up to the dome room to play the computer and watch. (Six-year-old)

Fear of being removed from parents

I could just imagine if there was any sort of drug ones [drug workers] brought into our house years ago, we might no have been here now; well, I'd be old enough now, but I could imagine . . . I always thought be quiet so nobody finds out.

I would have hated to have been taken off my mum, I would have rather stayed here to look after her.

Being accepted

They don't say anything about addicts when I'm there 'cos they know my mum's an addict and it might upset me!

Taking friends home

Some time you feel that you canny offer them a drink 'cos you know they would nae want to drink out of our cups. But the pals I would take in the house I would make sure that they dinnae feel that about me 'cos I would only take certain people in.

Support and comfort from friends

Aye, 'cos you've got someone to talk about it with, instead of you just keeping it all into yourself, like I could always talk to them about it, like if I keep it all bottled myself, then one day I'll just like all build up in myself and I'll just end up taking it out on the wrong person and start doing something. Like start fighting with them or something, but that's how you are better off just letting it all out and telling somebody. And that's how I told my friend.

What I would change if I had a magic wand

For everything to be made of chocolate. (Nine-year-old)

My friends could come and play and I could go out to play. (Six-year-old)

My mum taking me and watching me play the computer. (Six-year-old)

To go to the beach for a picnic with my sister. (Six-year-old)

A Barbie bike. (Five-year-old)

Bullying

See at school, see if your pals know that your ma's on drugs you get called a junkie, that's what happened to me at school, but I used to no let it bother me.

Treated differently

'Cos you would feel embarrassed that your teachers would know, and giving you sympathy anda' that . . . I would nae like it.

Protecting parents and siblings

I just knew to keep it quiet.

Embarrassment

It would disgust me, I wouldn't know what to say and my pals would laugh, 'What are you doing talking to him?' [to parent] and I'd be like I don't even know him.

Others not knowing

'Cos, I always had the best of gear and was always bigger than everyone else my age.

Having few boundaries

I just done what I like and that was it. Maybe that's what kept me away from thinking about it, but I done what I liked played the computer, watched videos 'cos that's all I've done all my life since I was old enough to play a computer.

Resilience

I don't think that it has actually affected me at all, but other people I'm sure it did affect them.

Don't get me wrong, my ma's got a drug habit we did nae get all the clothes that we wanted and all the things what we wanted but we got what we needed. We got fed every day, breakfast, supper, everything. We got all that.

Parents getting off drugs

Before it would have been embarrassing, my mum wouldn't have had enough money to get all the things that I would need to have a sleepover so I wouldn't have had it. Plus I wouldn't have had a good birthday but I know 'cos I've got all my friends around me and my mum is better now, I'm going to have a really good birthday.

My voice

Before I came to the Aberlour Project I wanted my mum to be sober. The drinking became too much for her as she became ill a lot and ended up in hospital very often, as much as two or three weeks at a time. And every time she went into the hospital I was afraid she wouldn't come home. My younger sister was a bit too small to really understand what was going on with our mum. It came to the crunch and luckily she found the Project was the answer to all our problems or most of them.

I felt happy that we were going to move to a new home but I miss my friends. In the Project we were better behaved than we used to be and my mum is looking better than she used to, and now I feel I speak to her more and she listens to me a lot more than she used to listen to me.

The Project has helped my family to be a family again and it's also fun in here. And if I could help other children I would say, 'There's help for everyone'. (Ten-year-old)

Reference

McGuire M (2002) *Keeping it Quiet: Children and families in Great Govan affected by parental drug use*, Stirling: Aberlour Child Care Trust

12 Telling it like it is

Rena Phillips

Our knowledge and understanding of substitute family care has been greatly enhanced through listening to the voices and expertise of adopters and foster carers. Yet, little attention has been given to their experiences of caring for children placed from a substance-misusing background. It is therefore important to obtain some insight into their observations, thoughts and feelings on the subject. This chapter records some of these.

I made contact with families through Adoption UK, a UK-wide self-help group supporting prospective and established adopters, long-term foster carers and their families. One of the services on offer is a Members' Experience Resource Bank (formerly ERBIE, now PAL [Parents Are Linked]) – a contact database of over 800 families willing to speak to others about specific aspects of long-term placements. With the help of PAL's Co-ordinator, we identified approximately 100 families with children affected by parental substance misuse. I sent a letter to 30 of these families, requesting contributions to the book, with suggested guidelines, but encouraging them to tell their story "as it is".

Eighteen families responded to the letter, some putting pen to paper, with some writing quite extensively and others very briefly. I also had some quite lengthy phone conversations with parents on the ups and downs of meeting the specific needs of their children. In this chapter, extracts from some of the contributions have been assembled around the topics of information the families had on substance misuse, the challenges and positives of caring for their children, and post-placement support. In view of the sometimes difficult and demanding issues involved in contact with birth parents, the chapter that follows describes more fully the experience of one family. Another chapter describes the experiences of an adoptee, as told in her own words. It is important to acknowledge that for some contributors this was at a cost as it reawakened unresolved and painful feelings. As one adoptive parent put it:

Well, that's all I can think of today. I am quite tired from writing some of this and my husband and I have put all this behind us and have grown together as a family. But it has been cathartic for me, so thank you for that!

While these are individual accounts from a very small number of families, they give a glimpse of the reality of those directly involved in caring for children affected by parental substance misuse. We thank them for their generosity in sharing their experiences. We need to continue to hear what they are saying to us.

Information on substance misuse

We did not receive any specific training on drugs or alcohol in our preparation. We did, however, receive a lot of input about child behaviours that are difficult to manage – the emphasis was from the angle relating to children who have been damaged emotionally after multiple family placements. We attended a parenting session facilitated by the social services medical adviser that briefly went through how children can be damaged in uterus, but quite honestly I could have given a better talk. All the doctor said was that we really do not know how drug or alcohol-affected children turn out, or what they are like to bring up, or any useful management strategies or things to look out for as they are growing up or what in general terms are good ideas in looking after such children. She commented that we need more research.

We were only told that the mother and father were alcoholics, that was all – the rest was confidential. We had no medical information on our daughter before we made our decision to become her parents, merely that her social worker said she was fine. To have a really good understanding about how drugs and alcohol and the birth parents' lifestyle affects the unborn child, you need to have three hour-long sessions given by someone who has a thorough medical and social background in this area. I did not meet anyone in our adoption process who had this information and could give it in a meaningful way. There is no ongoing training.

When I questioned our daughter's social worker about her medical or developmental milestones, he became aggressive, bamboozled us with stories of how her foster carers loved her dearly, and in a very thinly veiled threat told us there were plenty of other prospective adoptive couples who would want this beautiful baby. We were emotionally blackmailed, and we knew it, and if we wanted to be parents after all the heartache we had had, we could do nothing about it.

I thank goodness that I am a trained nurse and health visitor and have cared for many many patients on the wards with drug- or alcohol-related illnesses. At least I felt I knew the fullest implications of how drugs or alcohol and lifestyle issues can affect the unborn child and what this could mean for our daughter in the long term. (The L Family)

Our son David is now three years old and was placed with us at just ten months. He was featured in the under-fives section of the adoption listings and we felt an instant affinity with him. His profile was explicit about his having been born heroin-addicted and we were not put off in any way by this. This is possibly because we knew one or two people who had been addicted to heroin and who had managed to kick the habit. As a result we knew quite clearly what our attitudes to addiction were. Addiction wasn't something we saw as "bad" and "being weak willed" – we saw it as another chronic illness which required its own treatment. We have never judged David's birth mother for her drug addiction; rather, we feel enormous compassion for her.

We did as much of our own research as we could before we met David's social workers. Our social worker gave us excerpts from Bruised Before Birth, *which was a harrowing read and we looked on the web for anything we could find. We spoke to personal friends, and friends of friends who were GPs and had spoken to paediatricians for us. We also spoke to the local authority's medical adviser under whose care he had been. I suppose what was the most frustrating, but in a sense the most positive conclusion we reached, was that there was simply no conclusive evidence of the impact on a child born to a heroin-addicted birth mother.* (The M Family)

We received little or no information about this topic at all. In fairness to the adoption agency, ten years ago the knowledge relating to Foetal Alcohol Syndrome/Foetal Alcohol Effects was very scant in this country. We subsequently picked up what we could from libraries, the internet, etc. Support groups for FAS/FAE do now exist which is heartening for those parents, adoptive or otherwise, who will come across the problem in the future. However, when you are without the necessary knowledge/support, it leaves you wondering whether you are handling situations correctly and you often end up doubting your ability to be a parent. (The S Family)

We never received any information at all concerning drugs or alcohol prior to our daughter's adoption other than being asked if we thought we could cope with it! The quality of information given to prospective adopters in my area on this subject is poor to say the least. Perhaps we need to organise drug and alcohol awareness sessions as part of the assessment process. It is all very well and good parents saying they think they can cope with these damaged children, but the reality is very taxing and difficult.

Our daughters are now at High School where there is lots of information on drink and drugs and young people. We regularly discuss these topics as well as lifestyle choices, especially why a 12/13-year-old child would wish to get pregnant. (The B Family)

The best ideas and information I have obtained have been from parents/ professionals talking about an actual child/children they have or know. This is because they show how different the varieties of outcomes can be, and give practical advice on how to solve particular problems they have come up against rather than give you frightening generalisations about an anonymous group of children. (The H Family)

Challenges and positives

Their mother had been a heroin addict for 14 years. The children when placed, then aged 23 months, three years, six years and eight years, were severely neglected and had scabies, impetigo and head lice. They had never been to school and were allowed to run wild. The youngest had been able to change her own nappy since the age of 18 months. When social services had become involved the parents had taken them and gone "on the run" living in a tent in deep snow. The children only had the clothes they wore and no underwear. They had no belongings of any kind as all money had been spent on drugs. These four children arrived to stay for a weekend and have never left. (The C Family)

He has a very high threshold to pain. The sorts of bumps and falls which cause most children to cry do not result in tears. I sometimes wonder whether this is to do with the amount of pain he experienced during heroin withdrawal. And he, like other adopted children, will have to decide whether he tells others his life story because he will no doubt experience prejudice around the heroin addiction. This is something we are already helping him with by telling him that his story is his private story, and for now it's just for the family. Other than that I can't think of anything that I would link specifically to his experience of heroin, although that is probably because we have found so little about what the specific problems might be. He is also still very young.

We already speak to our son about his being born heroin-addicted and that because he was sick and couldn't keep his body temperature up he had to lie on a heat pad. Interestingly this makes great sense to him as he is still a cold child and needs three times as many clothes on at anytime as his elder sister. We have also told him that he lost his sucking instinct and had to be taught how to suckle again because he was in a lot of pain. He says, 'my tummy mummy was an addict and I was cold', which at just turned three is not bad. We haven't found any age-appropriate information about substance misuse to help him and will keep looking. (The M Family)

I think the one main thing we can connect to substance misuse with our daughter is the fact that she doesn't appreciate that having a glass of wine with your evening meal doesn't constitute a person getting drunk and losing control. (The B Family)

I am writing to you now because we have, so far, had no major problems with our children and I wondered if you wanted this sort of contribution too. We adopted four siblings three years ago. The oldest two had lived with their parents while they were drugs users (heroin definitely and possibly some others). The younger two were both born addicted to heroin – the youngest was born approximately six weeks early and with multiple addictions. The two born addicted are actually the more "normal" of the four, educationally and socially, whereas the other two may be suffering as a result of how long they were in the system (they were seven and five when they came).

I would have been glad to read that there was a possibility that the children would have no lasting side-effects of their addictions, but I don't know how common that is – nor can I be sure that it is going to be true forever, as they are only four and five years old now! (The W Family)

"L" came to us in September 1984, when she was eight months old. I was a foster carer and L was an emergency placement – it was 7 pm. Her mother could not be found and her nine-year-old sister was with her. L arrived in the clothes she was wearing and no bottle or food with her.

From the outset I struggled to find out what she would drink or eat – all she would take was a bottle of tea (with milk and sugar in it). She only weighed 9 lbs when she came to us. I later found out that she was 6 lbs at birth. It was difficult to care for her as she did not like to be held or cuddled and did not cry but whined. When the information came from the social work department about the mother, I was told she was an alcoholic.

As L grew, and even after a few weeks with me, I realised that there was something very different about her to the others I had fostered. She did not respond to any stimulation. All she wanted to do was bounce up and down when you held her and she could and would not sit on your knee, so even feeding her a bottle was difficult.

Food was always a problem as L would not try new things, so it was constant trial and error. She would eat well enough of what she liked, but it was not always a very good diet. As a toddler she was very hyperactive and did not sleep well and this was a long-term problem. One of the other things that amazed me was if she fell or bumped her head she never cried or even stopped to rub where she had hurt.

Until she was two-and-a-half years old we, that is the social work department and myself, worked with L's mum to try and rehabilitate her but nothing worked. During all of this time I often mentioned to the social worker her behaviour, with which I was sometimes so exhausted and frustrated that I would be in tears. But their comments were that she was cute and they had no answers.

At night she did not sleep well, as I have mentioned, and even gates on her bedroom did not protect her as she climbed over everything even though she was very small for her age. I would be wakened by a noise and on some occasions find her walking along the tops of furniture and even wardrobes.

When L was two-and-a-half years old the plan was for adoption. When I took her for the pre-adoption medical this is when I got the reason for the behaviour and lack of learning, as they told me she had Foetal Alcohol Syndrome. I did not even know what that was, but I found out that it had been diagnosed at birth. (The Mc Family)

Our eldest daughter is fairly well grounded with typical teenage views on smoking, drinking and drug-taking. At the moment she is anti everything, but we do expect her to maybe try alcohol at parties. She is well aware that her birth mother's problems arise from her long-term drug misuse and has no intentions of letting history repeat itself. However, she has a major hang-up when it comes to taking oral medication. She can just about cope with medicine but has a severe mental block when it comes to tablets/capsules. If she takes anything it has to be in either liquid or soluble form. (The B Family)

Becky is eight years old. She was placed with me for adoption at 21 months of age with a diagnosis of Fetal Alcohol Syndrome and was given a gloomy prognosis as regards learning difficulties. I read various things including Fantastic Antoine Succeeds – Experiences in educating children with fetal alcohol syndrome *(Kleinfeld and Westcott, 1993) and would recommend this and its follow up* Fantastic Antoine Grows Up – Adolescents and adults with fetal alcohol syndrome *(Kleinfeld et al, 2000) to anyone with a child with FAS, as these are full of examples of the different levels these children can reach, written by birth and adoptive parents. They also give plenty of useful advice by professionals on teaching techniques, etc.*

Becky wears hearing aids, had a cleft-palate (now repaired) and wears glasses. She is slightly short for her age and is extremely thin (just under two-and-a-half stone in weight) in spite of a really healthy appetite. She has problems with her teeth.

I first realised how difficult Becky found it to control herself in certain situations when I couldn't get her to stop looking out of her bedroom window at night. She had a slightly raised bed with a cupboard underneath which was under the window. She used to stand on this and bend back slats on her blinds to see out – these were invariably broken. After trying all sorts of ways to stop her doing this (no sweets, removal of treats, a "reward system" – stars given for no damage) I gave up and moved the bed so she couldn't reach the window. Her reaction to this was to leap on me and kiss and hug me with gratitude 'You're so clever! Now I won't be able to break the blinds! Thank you! Thank you!' I think this was when I really understood how hard she found it to control what was "compulsive" or "repetitive" behaviour.

Becky has some insight into the fact that she is different and can sometimes offer suggestions as to how her problems can be dealt with. On occasions these are brilliant and I encourage her to think of answers, but sometimes they are not appropriate, e.g. 'Tape my eyes shut and then I won't keep pulling faces at so-and-so!' She needs to be taught social behaviour that other children instinctively know. She is friendly, amusing, a great mimic and is faster than anyone at running on all fours, like Mowgli in The Jungle Book. *She has many friends.*

Becky has low self-esteem in spite of all our efforts to make it not so, and when she started to say that she was weird we made her a book about alcohol, FAS and her life story. It was very basic, but now she understands how she is, it's not her fault, and I think she is happier and I would recommend doing this as soon as you feel a child has the ability to understand. (The H Family)

Her foster carer who had her from day five, after Lucy spent time in a Special Care Baby Unit, is absolutely certain that 'she was not right' as a newborn. She was delayed in her milestones until she was eight months old, when she finally began to catch up. She also reported that she was awful to feed because she was so easily distracted from the task of sucking her milk from the bottle – anything would disturb her, from someone walking by to a door movement. For each feed there had to be total silence and then she could be disturbed by the foster carer moving her arm or changing position, and she would then refuse to take any more milk.

Lucy was very difficult to settle for a sleep and didn't seem to be able to respond to her own sleepiness/tiredness. Once asleep she slept for far too long, not waking for a feed as a newborn even up to to seven hours later. The foster carer's diligent care was without question platinum standard and we are grateful beyond words for her input into our daughter in her first year of life. It is well documented that careful and attentive nurturing during the first year of life can repair some of the damage to the nervous system caused by drugs and alcohol.

The effects of alcohol exposure in the uterus that I feel are manifest in our daughter, now 21 months, are that she is very very petite/slight and is in all honesty "failing to thrive" however much food I try and put into her – she is so skinny you can see her ribs! She really can go for days without wanting food and some days she point blank refuses food; this is taking into account the usual issues with feeding a toddler. She needs lots of sleep and will sleep for 12 hours a night and then four to five hours in the day if I let her – which I don't because I feel she has other needs during the day like stimulation and play. She does not have the typical facial features [that other children with FAS have].

Lucy appears to have made a good recovery from her damaging intra-uterine experience, but she is very flighty and difficult to settle or relax into a cuddle. She finds it difficult to enjoy comfort and does a lot of "gaze avert" – are these attachment/bonding issues? To date I really do not think she is delayed in her social development or milestones. She copies and mimics and remembers and is learning something new each day as is age appropriate. I am absolutely thrilled!

One of the difficulties I have is that my husband will not see that our daughter may have problems related to alcohol misuse. All he sees is a

197

beautiful little girl who is his beautiful daughter; he adores her and, of course, I am so pleased that this is the case. So I find that I almost have to not talk about our daughter's possible problems until they rear their head. At least I know that there may be things to look out for in the future and we can work them out together as they come. Perhaps my husband is right – we should just enjoy what we have at the moment, as all appears well, and not worry about things that may/may not happen in the future!
(The L Family)

To summarise, the effects of drugs and alcohol on a child are extremely varied, and very difficult to predict, even by experts. Rachel was expected to have minimal special needs and Ben major problems, but the reality was quite different. A doctor can give you a likely outcome (if you can find one brave enough to give you any kind of prognosis, however guarded), but because of the nature of brain damage nothing is for certain.
(The H Family)

Support services

What has helped most with David thus far? Other adoptive parents who understand the experience of adoption, and, even if they don't have a child born drug-addicted, have the ability to be open-minded about what it means for us and for him. Again, this is true of adoption as a whole, but we are very careful who we tell about David's story, because we don't want them to judge him for his birth mother's illness and behaviour. Identification always helps, by which I mean other people identifying with our experience and really hearing what we have to say. Teachers who take your lead in how to behave with your child and don't try to "normalise" him – 'Oh all children do that' – when you know it's different. Time makes a big difference – having time to prepare him for change and taking time to go through the feelings and behaviour that result from that change. In fact, I think time and understanding are the two critical ones.

We haven't had to seek post-adoption support, but if we do, I would hope we would be met by non-judgemental professionals with a true understanding of adoption and the specifics of children born to substance-misusing birth mothers. I would hope that we would be provided with explanations and diagnoses on the basis of validated research. I would like to think that we would be given a strategy for helping David achieve his full potential as well as access to appropriate psychiatric or other help. Obviously it would be great if it could be funded, at least in part, by the government or local authority, since these children's adverse experiences were known to everyone from the outset, but this may be wishful thinking. Support groups for children and adopters experiencing problems as a direct result of ante-natal substance misuse would also be excellent.

We took the decision to adopt David very soon after he was placed with us and have never regretted it – he is absolutely gorgeous. He continues to meet all his milestones and we, and he, learn more every day about how we can help him be true to himself and his experience. (The M Family)

What is needed for these children and their adoptive families and foster carers is believing what they say about the difficulties they face, help and support to live and deal with the problems and admitting that the children or young people have problems. I was lucky in that I knew I could parent as I had already brought up a family of three children through some difficult circumstances and they are all well-balanced people and parents themselves. I also believe there should be adoption allowances or facilities available to fund respite care, because the special needs of these children can destroy their family, as well as their own lives, and they cannot help themselves.

One of the other things I feel strongly about is don't just talk about anger management. The agencies involved have to start facing the real roots of the children's problems – attachment disorders, Foetal Alcohol Syndrome and the damage caused by drug misuse, as well as the damage done by neglect in early childhood.

L now wants to know about these things and hopefully I can help her as she says she does not like being angry. I think we as adoptive parents

have to remember that our adopted children come from somewhere and someone else, and we all like to know where and who that is.
(The Mc Family)

We were given no information at all to give to our daughter about substance misuse. This was never mentioned, we were merely told to buy books about adoption and introduce her to this concept early on. I have not given much thought to what could be an effective post-adoption support probably because I feel so bruised by social services in general.

I find picking through old copies of Adoption Today, *the magazine of Adoption UK, helpful. As different things crop up in our own family life, different articles in the magazine have different meanings for us, and they always have useful contact addresses or telephone numbers. Adoption UK Co-ordinators, or those on the PAL (Parents Are Linked) list are also very helpful and I have called other adoptive mothers who have adopted children with Foetal Alcohol Syndrome for advice about some everyday issues with our daughter. I am in touch with a Foetal Alcohol Society set up by a mother who had adopted a severely drug- and alcohol-affected daughter.* (The L Family)

We received no offer of post-adoption services from our agency, who are not local to us. We have therefore simply had to cope over the years by finding out what we can, when we can, and asking lots of questions. As already stated, we have been very instrumental in bringing our son's situation to the attention of as many people as is possible, not to give us an easier life but to enable all parties to understand and accept things.

Our local area also offered little post-adoption support, so in conjunction with other adoptive families we have set up our own independent organisation. We work in close association with the local authority and adoption agencies, and are now recognised by the former as their post-adoption support. All members of the group subscribe to Adoption UK *and last year eight couples, including ourselves, benefited from the Adoption UK training programme,* A Piece of Cake, *held over an eight-month period.* (The S Family)

Basically, children adopted from this kind of situation need substantial love, support and understanding which is sometimes difficult to give if the adoptive parents have not got sufficient support networks in place. It is vital to have good non-judgemental friends and family who accept that your children will take some time to work through their problems.

Issues are ongoing, but there really is light at the end of the tunnel. It is a very slow process, sometimes two steps forward and one step backwards, but with a little love and affection, adopted children can live a happy and fulfilled life. Both our daughters feel much better about themselves, realise that they should be treated properly by friends and family, and more importantly that they deserve to be loved. (The B Family)

References

Kleinfeld J and Wescott S (1993) *Fantastic Antoine Succeeds!: Experiences in Educating Children with Fetal Alcohol Syndrome*, University of Alaska Press. Available from Amazon.co.uk-Books.

Kleinfeld J, Morse B and Wescott S (2000) *Fantastic Antoine Grows Up: Adolescents and Adults with Fetal Alcohol Syndrome*, University of Alaska Press. Available from Amazon.co.uk-Books.

Adoption UK
Manor Farm
Appletree Road
Chipping Warden
Banbury
Oxfordshire OX17 1LH

Tel: 01295 660 121
Helpline: 0870 7700 450
Fax: 01295 660 123
Email: admin@adoptionuk.org.uk
Web: www.adoptionuk.org

13 Adoption with contact – the impact of drug use

Euan's adoptive parents

We are the adoptive parents of Euan, who first came to us aged 11, and is now almost 21. Both Euan's birth parents were drug users. Apart from periods in care, Euan had lived within a "drug-using" culture throughout his childhood before he was adopted. His mother, Bianca, had used a variety of drugs from her mid-teens, including heroin, though she said she had stopped while pregnant. His father, Huw, had used a variety of drugs recreationally throughout adulthood, though at present he mainly smokes cannabis. Euan had regular face-to-face contact with his birth parents, as well as with various other birth relatives throughout his time with us. He is currently living with Huw, though he keeps in contact with us. We experienced something of the effects of contact on Euan and us, and hope this account will be helpful to other adoptive parents.

Preparing for contact

During our home study, the issue of contact was raised and discussed, and different types of contact were explained to us. Since we were considered for an older child, we could see that this might have advantages, although we expected it to be difficult given the lifestyles of Euan's parents. When we were identified as a possible match for Euan, it was clear from the outset that face-to-face contact with Bianca and Huw was considered essential, and his maternal grandmother Anna also wished to maintain contact.

There were a number of issues to be considered. Bianca was HIV positive due to injecting drugs, and in poor health. How did we really feel about HIV and AIDS? We had to consider how we would work around Bianca's health and her chaotic drug use in terms of the possibility of cancelled contact, problems during contact visits, and that we would have to support Euan through his mother's terminal illness and death. In some ways, this strengthened our commitment to contact, as we felt it was important for Euan to be able to continue to see his mother for as long as possible.

Huw was a different kettle of fish. His relationship with Euan had been sporadic, punctuated by frequent absences when he travelled abroad. Many of these journeys seemed to be to places with a reputation for a relaxed attitude to drug use. In fact he was away in Goa for most of the introductions period. He was also involved in a new relationship with Beatrice, an old friend of his and Bianca's. Beatrice and her two children occupied a great deal of his time. Contact with Huw looked likely to take in Beatrice and her children, and together with the absences abroad, this looked tricky.

In addition, it was clear that the expectation was that, after an initial period, we would manage the contact ourselves, with Euan seeing each parent four times a year. Even this level of contact was a reduction on what Euan, Bianca and Huw had been accustomed to during his most recent foster placement, and was opposed particularly strongly by Huw. Meetings with Euan's foster carers offered us some perspective on how they had managed contact, and were very helpful in giving us some idea of the difficult areas as well as the positives.

Social services were insistent that we meet Bianca and Huw before introductions to Euan began, to be sure we could work with them. There were some difficulties arranging a meeting with Huw, given his other commitments. When we met in the social services offices, we had an amicable chat about his hopes for Euan and the difficulties that had led up to his being placed for adoption. We saw much to like about him, though we could see that he was unable to put Euan's needs before his own, but we felt much more positive about contact with him after the meeting. The fact that his girlfriend and her children seemed likely to join contact visits seemed a positive, as he would be less likely to behave inappropriately in that context.

A meeting with Bianca was harder to arrange as she was not feeling well – looking back, we suspect she was stalling. Finally, a date and time were set, and Euan's social worker went with us to Bianca's flat. All the curtains were drawn and it took repeated knocking to get an answer. It appeared that Bianca had forgotten to put her clock forward the previous

Sunday and was not expecting us for another hour. She was still in bed, and had not taken her medication (she took methadone regularly as a substitute for heroin). Eventually she agreed to let us in and we sat around her bed in the darkened flat and talked for a few minutes. Bianca shook (no medication) and cried throughout the conversation. Not a very positive start, but at least a sharp introduction to the likely realities of contact. We did get a very strong feel for Bianca's love of books and her intelligence and articulateness. Our over-riding feeling after this meeting was one of pity and some apprehension. Would we be able to manage?

First contact

The first contact visit took place during the introductions between Euan and us. Bianca had missed a visit to Euan at his foster carers due to being in hospital. I (adoptive mother) was asked to take Euan to see her in hospital, on our way back to his foster carers, after a weekend with us. It was a very brief visit, but I felt it went quite well. Bianca was much more "together" and on her best behaviour in the hospital environment. Subsequently, several contact visits took place in hospital or hospices. Bianca would often complain that the staff did not give her medication correctly – which usually meant 'not as often as I want'. Euan was all over the place, over-excited and finding it hard to concentrate on anything, but nothing too unusual in that, and to be fair he had an awful lot on his plate. He rode on the adjustable bed and chattered happily. A warning bell sounded in my head when Bianca started to discuss with Euan exactly how she had damaged her bracelet in bed with her then boyfriend and the precautions she had taken to avoid transmitting HIV. I began to see what social workers meant when they said that Euan's parents were 'very open' about matters better left in the domain of adults. As they had warned us, Euan knew a fair bit about sex and drugs and rock'n'roll! Euan's social worker felt strongly that Bianca should make at least one visit to our home, but Bianca objected. Apparently she could not manage her medication with a one-and-a-half hour journey to us.

Euan arrived in late May. His social worker was leaving to take up a new team leader post the day after Euan's arrival, and there would be a period before a replacement could be allocated. In the interim, Euan and our family would be supported by the social worker from the voluntary agency who did our home study, and by phone by a social worker from the local authority Family Placements Team in Euan's home town.

Euan's social worker's parting comment before leaving to sort out her desk was 'and don't leave it too long to arrange a contact visit'. A few days later, Huw contacted us to ask that Euan come to the birthday party of Beatrice's son. We were worried about this, as Euan's feet had hardly touched the ground, but felt perhaps we should agree as we had been told not to leave it too long. However, on contacting Family Placements, we were told 'Oh no, it's much too soon'. Luckily, they were prepared to intervene and explain this to Huw.

Happily, Euan's new social worker was appointed at about this time, and she helped us to draw up a plan for contact visits which would gradually reduce the level of contact for Bianca and Huw to the planned level of four visits with each per year. Initially this meant we were involved in contact visits about one weekend in three for a few months, which meant some juggling and rescheduling of our plans for the summer, but we felt it was a reasonable approach and we could see the light at the end of the tunnel in terms of being able to settle down to a regular pattern of visits which seemed sustainable

For the first of these visits, it was agreed that I would take Euan to Bianca's for lunch with her and her mother Anna, and then take him on to Huw's after lunch – Huw would bring him back home in the evening. This would have worked well but for the fact that Bianca seemed incapable of producing a grilled pork chop in under three hours. As a result, we were very late arriving at Huw's and (although we had phoned to warn him) he was extremely irate. As we hurried up the street towards his flat, he berated me at the top of his voice from the doorstep, to the entertainment of his neighbours. Things were not helped by the arrival of Beatrice and her children, and I was very aware of Euan's agitation. I agreed that, in view of the late start, he should return Euan rather later than planned. He was still very angry when he returned Euan, and had a long and rather one-sided "discussion" with my husband over a cup of tea. As a result of this, we decided that combined visits to Bianca and Huw on the same day were not going to be feasible, and we would have to move straight away to separate visits, although at that time it still seemed that combining

Bianca and Anna's visits would be workable and had advantages in view of Bianca's health and drug issues.

Future visits

Visits to Bianca initially seemed to settle down fairly well after this. We had been told not to leave Euan unsupervised with her for longer than 90 minutes. We had the impression that this was due to her drug use; in other words, if left too long unsupervised she might expose Euan to risk by using either her methadone or other street drugs. Later, we felt that it was also a matter of Bianca's ability to cope with noise and boisterous behaviour, and to say 'no' to unsuitable callers. However, because Anna was sharing the visits we felt it was OK to allow two to three hours before collecting him. This did not always work out – for example, on one occasion Anna quarrelled with Bianca and left the flat, so that Euan and Bianca were both at the end of their tether when I returned.

Working with Huw was turning out much more difficult than we expected. He continued to be very resentful of the reduced contact, and continually pressed us to be flexible and agree to more frequent contact and overnight visits. He had no scruples expressing these views forcefully to Euan or to us, and if there was an audience to witness the show, so much the better. Euan was becoming very distressed and difficult after visits as a result. Time to call in the cavalry, the Marlborough Family Service (a psychiatric service specialising in family therapy), which had worked with Euan and his parents before. We wrote to Euan's psychiatrist at the Marlborough, explaining the difficulties, and he had a phone conversation with us and a meeting with Huw and Beatrice before we had a full meeting of all the adults: the psychiatrist, ourselves, Bianca, Huw and two social workers (Euan's social worker and the social worker then supporting us, from the voluntary agency which had completed our home study). We still don't know how he did it, but after about an hour-and-a-half we seemed to have reached an understanding. The frequency of contact would stand, because Euan needed some time for family life with us and activities such as music groups. Two of Huw's visits would be overnights at his home, and the other two day-time visits to Euan at our home.

Getting to know Euan

As Euan settled with us, we began to learn more details about his early experiences. Sometimes he just seemed to remember some incident and want to talk about it. We learnt a great deal about Huw's drug use and rave lifestyle on his trips to Goa (Euan had been taken along on one of these trips). We found that one of Huw's "friends" had offered Euan (aged 8) an Ecstasy tablet at a party where Huw was DJ. We heard about Bianca's drugs, crime and prostitution lifestyle, and the day her boyfriend died of a heroin overdose while Euan was with her. Euan would sometimes act out injecting drugs or comment on his mother's drug use if she were late for a visit at Anna's, 'She must be well shot up'. Sometimes an event would trigger a vivid flashback. Once, on a family camping trip, a large beetle landed on Euan's leg. He became absolutely hysterical, babbling about cockroaches and a rat running over him in a flat and how Bianca had been 'out of it' on drugs at the time.

Looking with Euan at the photos he had brought with him, we occasionally found that he had not fully understood an event, and we were able to explain and reassure him from the information supplied by social services. For example, one photo showed him on a visit to Bianca in a drug rehabilitation centre. (We picked this up from clues in the picture and the information we had about dates of events.) He had not realised the purpose of Bianca's stay there. Visits to the doctor were very anxious times for him, stirring up questions about his mother's HIV.

A working arrangement

Following the meeting at the Marlborough Family Service, visits with Huw started to settle into a pattern, and Euan seemed to find them much easier. That's not to say there were no difficulties. Huw proved that his reputation for disorganisation was fully justified, frequently ringing to say he was just setting out at the time we had been expecting him to arrive, and on occasions forgetting that he was due to have a visit altogether. Just after Euan was legally adopted, Huw and Beatrice moved much further away from us. This involved some renegotiation: clearly simple overnights would not be sensible, so the overnight visits became a week or so in the summer holiday and three to four days over New Year.

Again, since Beatrice and her children would be involved, we felt OK about this arrangement. Shortly after this arrangement was put in place, we found that Huw began to "forget" either the March or the June visit to us, so that he had three contact visits a year. On occasion he would stay overnight with us when he visited or when he returned Euan, something that would have seemed inconceivable at the start.

Generally, I organised Bianca's contact and accompanied Euan, while my husband liaised with Huw. This seemed to work reasonably well, as I was still rather apprehensive of Huw, and I suspect he saw me as something of a pushover, whereas my husband seemed more able to stand his ground.

There were occasional tussles over issues like whether Euan should ride pillion on Huw's motorbike, which we were unhappy about. Huw was unwilling to use the underground as 'they use CCTV there'. We wondered what he could be doing to make him so apprehensive of being filmed! We knew (from Euan) that Huw had strong views on the legalisation of cannabis, and we gained the impression that Huw still smoked it occasionally, but we saw no indication that this was during contact visits. The impact was mainly confined to some fairly lively debates on legalisation within our family. Interestingly, while Euan was well aware that cannabis was illegal, he had apparently not realised that heroin was too.

As we got to know Bianca there were difficulties too. She was much less direct than Huw in her approach, and would often make comments which made me scratch my head, until I worked out that they were intended as subtle digs at me. Her attitude to drugs was somewhat inconsistent. Sometimes she would make a great show of hiding her medication so that Euan would not see it, at other times she would take medication with little or no precaution. While she was strong in her warnings on cocaine and heroin to Euan, she did not see cannabis use as any problem, though she seemed aware that she should not use it during visits.

Bianca was diagnosed with AIDS shortly after Euan's arrival, which meant another "hospital" contact visit. Our elder (birth) son Richard happened to be with me when I collected Euan. He had not previously met Bianca and was very shocked to discover how ill she looked as a result of heroin and AIDS, and we had several subsequent discussions on the effects of drug use as a result. Bianca seemed to regard the diagnosis as a useful tool in her attempts to get more frequent and longer visits, and overnights. We resisted overnight visits, as we were quite sure Bianca would use drugs and/or have undesirable friends around over such a period. I did begin to allow longer day-time visits, monitoring them to see how she and Euan coped, so that five hours became a norm whenever Bianca was well enough and at home. However, this meant I had to find an inexpensive way of occupying myself during this time – window shopping on a wet January day has very limited appeal after a while.

Bianca was also developing a habit of inviting other people over during Euan's visits. This was fine when it was her sister, for example, but there were a number of times when I would arrive to collect Euan and find a mysterious stranger (usually male) in the flat. Bianca never seemed to see any need to introduce them, and usually they also seemed to be unfamiliar to Euan and to have little interest in him. It may seem unfair to be making this point about Bianca's contact, when Huw had overnight visits at which other people might or might not be present. But Bianca was known to have a significant drug problem, and Huw's situation was rather more family oriented in that we judged from our acquaintance with Beatrice that she was unlikely to encourage dubious characters to visit or tolerate drug use while her children were there.

I had occasional worries about Bianca's mental health (which later turned out to be justified). She reported seeing things (such as insects jumping into her drink) which seemed to have no objective basis. However, these did not seem to be very serious or a threat to Euan over the short periods he was visiting. Later, I consulted with social services to check, but they took the same view.

It was no longer feasible for Anna to combine her visits with Bianca's, because of their frequent disagreements, so I had to try and gauge how long Bianca could cope with Euan on each visit. Anna's separate visits were relatively easy to manage, though of course they represented extra time commitments.

Why should they need support now?

This relatively stable period lasted for about 18 months, but unfortunately Bianca began to be increasingly belligerent in her demands for extended and overnight stays and her criticism of us. At one stage she threatened to take us to court for the "right" to overnight stays. The upshot of this threat was only a very conciliatory letter from her solicitor explaining how much Bianca wanted to work with us and withdrawing the demand for overnights. We got the impression that the solicitor had told her a few home truths about contact.

Despite her solicitor's assurances, Bianca's behaviour during contact visits became gradually more and more difficult. A drug dealer was phoned and asked to bring drugs to the flat during at least one visit, and on another a drug dealer called at the flat while Euan was there. It took careful listening to Euan after each visit to find out what was troubling him. Unknown strangers became more common, and on another occasion Bianca re-opened Euan's old ear-piercing using one of her earrings. Since many of these incidents were disclosed to us by Euan, because they were causing him some distress, it was difficult to know how to raise them with Bianca without betraying the confidence. My husband and I discussed whether to raise them with her, but decided on balance that it was better to keep a watching brief and allow Euan to confide events that upset him. In retrospect, this may not have been the best decision, but it seemed sensible then. At about this time, Bianca complained to Euan's former social worker that we had disciplined him for misbehaviour by withdrawing some small privileges. The social worker was very supportive of us, but it was becoming clear that matters had gone beyond minor indulgence of Euan (buying him extra treats and so on) and that Bianca was attempting to undermine our parenting.

It seemed clear that the difficulties and tensions were causing Euan increasing distress and I decided to ask for help. I felt that I needed to talk through the issues and get some advice on how to deal with them, and perhaps have another "adults' meeting" of the type that had been helpful at the start of contact. Unfortunately, the original social worker at Family Placements, who we were supposed to approach for support, was about to leave and we were told to liaise with another member of staff who had never met us or Euan. I was met with the comment that I had been coping OK until now, why should I suddenly need support? I arranged to have some individual sessions at the Marlborough Family Service to talk through the difficulties, but I was very disappointed by the social worker's unhelpful attitude to what I felt were serious emerging problems. As a result of my discussions at the Marlborough, it was agreed that I might draft a letter to Bianca with help from a psychotherapist there and the social worker at Family Placements.

Before this letter could be sent, I had the next contact visit with Bianca which was the most difficult yet. She had a new boyfriend, who was there when I arrived and clearly intended to stay throughout the visit. He told me in no uncertain terms to get out of the flat and that I could come back at 7 to collect Euan. When I collected him, the boyfriend appeared to me to be "under the influence", unsteady on his feet and having problems with his speech. (I later found out that he was addicted to a variety of drugs including cocaine.) Euan was in a very difficult mood, aggressive and unco-operative towards me and my husband, and this continued for many days. It emerged that Bianca and the boyfriend had been telling Euan that they would get married, and that Euan would soon be 16 and should leave home and come and live with them. This was a resurgence of an old fantasy of Bianca's, which had never before appeared to have much substance, but it now seemed that Euan was taking it seriously. A week or so after this visit, a used condom fell out of Euan's pocket at church. He gave various explanations, but they all involved how he had acquired it during the contact visit. I was very worried, given Bianca's HIV status.

I alerted Family Placements, asking that they consider social services support/supervision for future contact visits as I felt it was unreasonable to expect me to manage contact unsupported in these circumstances. The primary consideration on their side seemed to be financial: would I pay the fees at a contact centre (circa £70/hour) if they arranged it? Why not? Well if I wanted to pursue this, I would have to apply to the adoption panel for funding and they would probably ask why I shouldn't fund it. Alternatively, contact would have to be at the Marlborough during the school holidays because that would not cost social services anything. It seemed I would have to continue trying to manage contact myself.

I sent the agreed letter to Bianca voicing my concerns, including those about the last visit, and that we needed to look seriously at how contact was conducted. I felt visit activities needed to include me, at least for the present, and that I would like her to give me advance warning if other people were to share the contact, and let me know who they were. I suggested that it would be helpful if she made at least one visit to our home, to see it for herself. Predictably, the letter was very badly received. The boyfriend made several abusive and incoherent phone calls, instructing us on his views on child upbringing and demanding to speak to his "stepson". For a month or so, we had to remind the children not to answer the phone, in case it should be another call from the boyfriend. Over the Christmas period, we had a frantic phone call from Anna, begging us to keep Euan away from Bianca and her boyfriend. This confirmed my view that my worries were not unfounded.

I stuck to my guns in the face of considerable pressure from Bianca and Euan. The next few visits were calmer, if somewhat strained. I planned to withdraw gradually from the visits if matters improved, and over the next few this worked out so that I spent a little time at the start and end of a visit with Bianca and Euan, and allowed them gradually increasing amounts of time unsupervised, usually in a public place, in the middle of the visit. For example, we might go out for a pizza, or to the shops, and I would pop to the loo or go to another part of the shops for a while. Her boyfriend was absent, and I was told that they had split up just after Christmas. But I picked up clues that he was still around from time to time, and in many cases it was obvious that we had missed him by the skin of our teeth either at the start or the end of a visit. When he was around, Bianca was invariably short of money and consequently out of temper, and on at least one occasion I was summoned to collect Euan early because Bianca could not cope any more. One contact visit was cancelled because Bianca did not "feel well". This was so uncharacteristic that I suspect that the boyfriend had turned up and she did not feel she wanted to send him away.

After around a year of this, we were more or less back to the original arrangements of several hours of contact time. Things seemed to be going more smoothly again. As Euan was getting on for 16, on social services' advice I was starting to prepare him to make contact visits more independently. I would not always drop him off at Bianca's or collect him at the end of a contact visit, arranging to meet him at the station instead. I would normally see Bianca at one end or the other of a visit, and felt this allowed me to get a view on how she was and how she was coping and to provide Euan with some support, as visits to his mother were always very emotional times for him.

Crisis

Despite the contact dramas with Bianca, Euan had managed to get himself a very creditable set of GCSEs, and had made a reasonable start in the sixth form. However, he quickly began to find that at A level it is not possible to live by your wits with a bit of last-minute work, and he became somewhat despondent. I suspect from some of his teachers' comments, as well as conversations with us, that he was struggling with identity and birth/adoptive family issues. He was studying theology as one of his A levels and this seemed to stir up issues about Huw's lifestyle in his mind. He was also starting to have the usual teenage battles over activities/ freedom, and it is true that many of his friends had considerably more latitude than he. However, it seemed to us that Euan was very immature in many ways, and coped poorly when given more rope. On balance he seemed to need more guidance and structure than a typical 16/17-year-old. This brought us into conflict with Huw and Bianca, whose own teens had been characterised by almost no parental guidance. For example, at 15 Bianca was living in a squat and taking a variety of drugs, and by the same age Huw had been expelled from school and was by all accounts coming and going from home at will.

Matters were complicated by the fact that Bianca's life expectancy was now very short. Euan briefly planned to fulfil her old fantasy by going to live with her for however long she had left. We decided to allow a few days' stay with her over the Christmas period, and this persuaded him that this plan was not feasible. We then came under pressure from Huw as well as Bianca to increase the frequency of contact with Bianca to a long weekend every eight weeks. We did not feel we could commit to this, though we were prepared to consider overnights and, of course, more frequent day visits especially if Bianca's health deteriorated further. At about this time, Bianca suffered a brief episode of acute mental illness during a period of hospital treatment. These episodes were to recur for the rest of her life. Euan settled down a little after Christmas, though he was worried about Bianca's health. Then in February, a bombshell: Huw phoned to say that he was splitting up with Beatrice. Euan had always maintained that he would not live with Huw while he was with Beatrice (Euan and Beatrice did not get on particularly well), but this split seemed to spark off the idea of leaving again. Huw fuelled it with almost weekly phone calls promising electric guitars, disco equipment and a host of other promises irresistible to a teenager. Huw's motivation seems to have been fear of loneliness once Beatrice left. Euan spent his Easter contact visit firming up his plan to move to dad, and despite a brief respite when it seemed he was still undecided, he moved to live with Huw in May. Since his move, we keep in regular touch with him by phone and letter, and he phones occasionally and comes to see us fairly regularly. We have made it clear that he is welcome at home, though I in particular find it very hard to come to terms with him leaving. In a way, roles are now reversed and we could be said to have contact visits.

On reflection

I think it would have helped just to know that social services were aware that even if we coped well with contact most of the time, there would be times when we might need support. It would be helpful if provisions had been made for this at the planning stage, so that there was not the nagging worry that social services will raise "the budget" as an obstacle when help is needed urgently. There seemed to be very much an attitude of 'we'll help set it up, but then they must get on with it by themselves' on the part of some (not all) of the local authority social workers.

Most of the time, all that was needed was a listening ear and advice. Perhaps some of the problems would have been spotted earlier and dealt with more promptly if social services had contacted us periodically to see how things were going, rather than leaving the onus solely on us to get in touch. However, I think where there are so many difficulties around contact, it may be useful to bear in mind that sometimes advice is not enough, and social services' help with supervision of contact may be necessary at some stages. I do feel that the birth family could have had rather more help in understanding and coming to terms with the idea that adoption is different from a foster placement, and with adjusting to the new contact situation. To sum up, I think there needs to be an awareness among professionals that contact can be very difficult, and that it is not static – support needs may change as circumstances alter.

Sadly, Bianca killed herself about eight months after Euan left. I attended the funeral at Euan's request and with Anna's agreement, hoping to offer Euan some support as well as to pay my respects to Bianca. I found this very difficult – obviously I was in a somewhat awkward position as an outsider to the family, especially given my difficult relationship with Bianca. However, I found her family to be very kind and accepting and mostly very appreciative of our role with Euan. Meeting the wider family and hearing family anecdotes as one does at a funeral has helped me, I think, to understand Euan and his family background better. I continue to be in contact with Anna.

Huw's relationship with Euan has been stormy. Initially, he allowed him almost unlimited latitude, but quickly became irritated, and there are reports of periodic rows about money and chores. Similarly, Huw saw no problem with Euan experimenting with drugs and alcohol until this caused him inconvenience, at which point he declared Euan 'out of control' and threatened to throw him out. We heard about this from Anna, and were very worried because if Huw considered the situation out of control, that seemed to indicate very heavy use or addiction. Anna has occasionally commented on Euan's heavy drinking and evidence of quite heavy use of cannabis while on visits to her, but we have seen no real evidence of either when Euan visits us. Apparently Huw was almost continuously stoned when he and Euan took a cycling holiday in Holland. Euan was in a similar condition during his art class trip to Amsterdam, to the extent that he began to worry that he was going down the same path as Bianca. Apparently he resolved to stop, but Euan's good resolutions have a habit of being short lived, so we are not holding our breath!

We continue to try to offer Euan support and to hope that he will come through this difficult period relatively unscathed.

14 Living with children who think and feel with a different brain

Kate Cairns

Children who live with developmental injuries acquired before birth are often difficult for those around them to live with. These children, who experienced significant adversity as a foetus, may be subject to a range of disorders that are global in their effects and have an impact on every aspect of life. Such gross foetal adversity as maternal use of harmful substances can lead to critical alterations in brain development. If the baby is born with a brain already significantly different from the brain of uninjured infants, then key brain functions will be different for that child forever. It is those differences that have a profound impact on others, especially on those parenting the child.

Impact on the core assumptions of carers

There are certain core assumptions about ourselves and the world that have been identified as necessary for good mental health (Janoff-Bulmann, 1992). In order to maintain sound mental function we need, at some deep level, to believe that:

- the world is benign;
- the world is meaningful;
- the self is worthy.

These core assumptions, or cognitive schemas, generally persist in the face of a great deal of disconfirming evidence. But they do not always persist. If we are confronted with certain overwhelming experiences, our core assumptions about the world may shatter or dissolve and then we can develop mental health problems. My observation is that living with children who think and feel with a different brain can challenge the core assumptions of carers and therefore have an impact on their mental health. This chapter will offer some ideas about what the impact might be, and suggest measures to protect the health of carers. For if we do not look after the carers, they cannot look after the children.

The assumption that the world is benign

Every human being has been present at the birth of a baby, for here we all are. Each of us has our own history of a time we cannot ordinarily remember, and that time before our conscious memory is the period when patterns were being laid down in our brains and bodies that last us for the rest of our lives.

Beyond the givens of genetic inheritance, pre-birth experience and temperament, the principal shaper of these patterns for life is the nature and quality of our attachment experience in the early years. The dynamic quality of the complex dance that takes place between every baby and its carers sets the template in the brain for all our assumptions about the world and our place in it for the rest of our lives. The cells of our bodies and brains are sculpted, shaped and formed by our interactions with those on whom we depended as infants for our very lives.

Most people emerge from their early years with enough good experiences to allow them to form the kind of assumptions about the world that will be good for their mental health. They will find the world and other people interesting and attractive. Their general approach will be to move towards others, to be sociable, empathic and responsive to others. People who have been cared for well enough in their dependency have basic trust of self and others. They believe that the world is fundamentally benign.

Adults whose core assumption is that the world is benign and whose fundamental orientation is trust are generally the sort of people we would select to care for children, and rightly so. But there is a difficulty. Children who have been injured before birth often suffer from regulatory disorders, and have difficulty regulating their own inner state. This has profound effects on their ability to function, especially in relation to other people. And these difficulties present serious challenges to the core assumptions of secure, well-adjusted adults. What is often called challenging behaviour is, above all else, a challenge to the mental health and well-being of the adults who care for the child. The people who are most fitted to look after children are also those who are most vulnerable.

Pressure points

Regulating arousal

All babies are born lacking the ability to regulate their own levels of arousal. They rely on their carers to soothe them when they are distressed and at times to stimulate them when they need to connect to the world around them. When they receive reliable and consistent enough responses to their arousal needs, their developing brains grow the necessary mechanisms that will through life serve them as regulators of their inner state. But babies who have suffered injuries before birth may be unable to develop such regulatory structures even though they are provided with soothing and stimulation.

The process of developing such regulation relies on the fact that carers will feel stress when their baby is distressed. As they act to regulate their own stress through attending to the baby they also enable the baby to develop regulation of inner states. If the baby is unresponsive to soothing or stimulation carers will therefore be subject to unresolved stress. Unresolved stress destabilises us, and has an impact on our ability to perceive the world as benign.

The child who has not acquired patterns for regulation of arousal in their first year will continue to dysregulate to stress. They may be hyperaroused or they may dissociate and be "switched off". In either case they are very difficult to live with. They are likely to be predictably unpredictable in their responses, and the responses themselves are often incomprehensible to others. To live with such behaviour is intensely wearing. The long-term stress can have a significant effect on the health of carers.

Trust

Babies whose needs are being met reliably and consistently enough generally develop trust in their carers. And secure adults will also have a trusting approach to the world. Bring the two together and a delightful relationship of mutual trust and pleasure can grow.

Children who were injured before birth often cannot respond to the soothing and stimulation provided in the earliest weeks of life by their carers, however. They therefore have no template on which to build trust, which would grow out of the experience of being kept safely regulated. The child in whom arousal is unregulated is one whose most basic needs are not being met, even though the carers may be providing for those needs. And the child whose basic needs are not met is a child unable to develop trust.

When a secure adult finds that they are living with someone who does not respond with trust to trustworthy behaviour they become disorientated. Trust is so central to our mental stability that disrupted patterns of trust disrupt our basic sense of the order of the world. And the longer the disruption continues the more the basic assumption becomes out of kilter. Yet trustfulness, established in the earliest days of life, becomes a basic stance forever. So trustworthy adults who live with untrusting children will become increasingly disorientated in their dealings with the child as the years pass.

Affective attunement
When babies are not able to benefit from the soothing and stimulation provided by their carers, and do not develop trust, they are unable to engage in the beautiful dance of attunement. This will leave them without the means to develop certain key brain functions.

Linking inner states reliably with feelings and emotions depends on the interaction between the child and the carers that accompanies an attuned relationship. Affect, the bodily change that precedes emotion, is expressed on the face. Attuned babies are hungry for faces, and when they find one in their visual range they lock onto it and study it intently. Attuned adults put themselves within the visual field of the child, and take pleasure in the interaction this provokes. The movements and sounds that create the "conversation" or dance between adult and child create patterns in the developing brain that will allow the child to make sense of feelings.

Children who have not been able to benefit from this pattern of attunement are likely always to have difficulty in recognising and processing their own feelings. They will also be likely to have great difficulty with recognising and interpreting the feelings of others, so will struggle to develop empathy. People who cannot experience, express or regulate their own feelings and who do not experience empathy are often deeply disturbing for others to be with. They contradict core assumptions about the nature of human beings and the relationships between them.

Regulating impulse

Affective attunement is the key to the next stage of the attachment process – impulse regulation. Babies who turn to their carers for soothing when aroused, who expect their carers to be stimulating companions and enjoy that stimulation, who have developed fundamental trust in those on whom they depend, and who are beginning to recognise and appreciate feelings in themselves and in others, are ready to make use of their carers to build a template for regulating impulse. Children have many impulses, and not all of them are safe. This step in the attachment process is therefore vital to keep the child safe. It is also an essential step in the development of a moral presence in the world for the growing personality.

When injuries before birth prevent the child from benefiting from the earlier steps in the attachment process, they will also be unable to use their carers to build the patterns of regulation that will eventually enable them to regulate impulse themselves. Most children will have gained the beginning of impulse regulation during their second and third years. When children have not been able to build these templates for regulation of the self they will be likely to suffer continuing disorders of impulse regulation.

Such children are wearing to live with. They also become increasingly challenging to the core assumptions of secure adults as they grow older. It is tiring but not too challenging to be with a four-year-old who cannot manage their own impulses. By the time they are 14, however, it becomes apparent that being unable to regulate impulse also leads to being unable to be morally accountable. They genuinely cannot account for their own actions, since they have no brain pattern linking impulse to cognition. Children and young people who are morally unaccountable present profound challenges to the unarticulated basic assumptions of the adults around them.

Managing shame

Shame is the affect that brings about the transformation from external regulation of impulse, the carer taking responsibility for the actions of the child, to internal self-regulation. Infants who have travelled successfully through all the preceding stages of the attachment journey will find shame manageable even though it is an intensely uncomfortable affect. In the attuned relationship the child's experience of shame is that it is unpleasant but transient. The child does something inappropriate, the carer lets them know that this is not acceptable, the child feels shame which inhibits the behaviour, and the carer ensures that the attuned relationship is instantly restored. This brief negotiation, repeated many times a day in the life of a toddler, builds a template in the brain for the management of shame.

Clearly children who have not been able to benefit from the earlier stages of the attachment process will be equally prevented from acquiring management of shame. People who cannot manage the experience of shame are unable to take responsibility for their actions, may develop a range of protective behaviours such as blaming or perfectionism to attempt to regulate the discomfort, and may be unable to make choices.

All these phenomena are likely to cause disruption to the core assumptions of those around them. Assumptions laid down in our own infancy are the schemas through which we perceive the world. They are not ordinarily open to conscious consideration. So any experience that collapses such an assumption will create what Bateson (2000) described as a "Level 3 change", a change that deconstructs our sense of reality. Secure adults see the world as benign without usually being aware that they do so. But it is difficult to continue to see the world as benign when people we live with and love are living in a different moral universe.

The assumption that the world is meaningful

Children injured before birth often have difficulty with processing sensory information, with creating and understanding language, and with narrative memory. We need to be able to recognise, interpret, symbolise and remember our experience in order to make sense of the world. Secure adults, the people we rightly perceive as the most fitted to care for children, will have a core assumption that the world is meaningful. Living with children who cannot make sense of the world will challenge this assumption. Again we see the profound paradox that those most fitted to care for children are also those most vulnerable to traumatic stress injuries as a result of providing that care. Only when this is understood can we care properly for our carers.

Pressure points

Visual processing

Children whose ability to interpret visual signals is disordered will struggle with many aspects of day-to-day life. Other people are part of the visual world, and children with visual processing difficulties are likely to find it very difficult to read the non-verbal signals of others both in terms of facial expression and body language. Reading is a problem for people who cannot make sense of visual stimuli. Spatial awareness may be difficult, both in two dimensions – making sense of pictures, diagrams and maps – and in three dimensions – making sense of the solid environment.

Adults who are living with children, who are living with these impairments, are likely to find their core assumptions about the world of meaning under challenge. What sense can we make of a child who cannot make sense of the visual world we share? When we live with people with recognised visual impairments we know where we stand. But children with processing disorders often go unrecognised. Carers expect the child to be seeing what the carer is seeing. The child knows no other visual universe. Recognition of the struggle of the child is vital. The difficulties are transformed when we have access to the limitations with which the child is wrestling. Without that transformation, however, the carers are vulnerable to the collapse of core assumptions.

Auditory processing

Children who have problems with auditory processing will struggle to make sense of the spoken word, and may present as having variable or occasional hearing impairment. Adults find such children very frustrating. They may seem to be able to hear "when they want to", although the truth is they lose the ability to make sense of what they are hearing under certain defined conditions. They may, for instance, become unable to make sense of language when they are under stress. Or they may lose the capacity to process what they hear when they are relaxed and not under the influence of adrenaline. They may grasp just the beginning of what is said. Or they might process just a percentage of any sentence and try to guess the meaning from the context.

Again, dealing with children who have auditory processing difficulties is generally different from dealing with children who have recognised hearing impairments. Processing problems often go unrecognised, and even when they are known they produce behaviour that disrupts the perception of those around the child. Children who seem to understand or hear some things but not others are much more puzzling than children who consistently have impaired hearing.

Kinaesthetic processing

Some children who have been injured before birth cannot make sense of the messages of their own body. They may complain that their knee hurts when they have an ear infection. They may be very clumsy in relation to objects in the world around them. They may not know what it is to taste food or drink, or may develop strange or inappropriate behaviours in eating and drinking. Sometimes they develop an image of their own body as being grotesque or disproportionate. Often they have poor recognition of their own body temperature.

In general we do not recognise the extent to which our processing of sensory messages about the felt world outside and within the boundaries of our bodies are shaping our sense of the meaning of the world. But living with children who are not able to create a meaningful sensory geography of their personal space exposes and challenges those very basic assumptions.

Language

Children with residual impairment after pre-birth injuries are likely to struggle to use and understand language. This may be general, or it may involve specific difficulties in forming or understanding words or sentences. Some children, for example, have difficulty with accessing reliably the names of familiar objects, and may ask to be passed the peas when they mean marmalade. Others may form words in a partial way, such as "spital" for "hospital". Many will develop an appropriately complex vocabulary for "outside" words – tree, dog, run, perambulate – but a very limited language for inner state words – happy, sad, beautiful.

Secure adults make sense of the world through language and metaphor. Whole therapeutic systems have been built on the centrality of language. Children who find it difficult to process information and have difficulty forming and using language present a daily challenge to the inner world of their carers.

Memory

From about the age of 18 months we are forming an "autobiographic self" (Damasio, 1999). Within a short time this develops into our human capacity, and need, for narrative memory. Our lives are the stories we tell ourselves, and the meaning emerges from the narrative.

Children who cannot easily create and use language will struggle with memory. These are the children who have forgotten by the time they reach the top of the stairs what they were asked to do at the bottom, so wander off and do something else. At school they never have the right kit at the right time in the right place. They fail to bring home important information from their teachers. They cannot remember what they were asked to do for homework. They forget the names of people they should remember, forget to feed their pets, forget where things are kept. They are frustrating to live with, and, since they can see that other children behave differently, they frustrate themselves. Yet this is their normality, and they know no other way of being, so they perceive themselves, and are perceived by others, as inattentive or wilfully defiant or obstructive.

Living with people who are not forming narrative memory disrupts core assumptions about the world of meaning. Our sense of the benevolence of the world depends upon the possibility of reciprocal compassion and warmth. Our sense that the world is meaningful depends upon the possibility of a social construction of reality that can be matched against our inner world. Children living with developmental impairment create a shared space in which these usually unremarkable possibilities are absent.

The assumption that the self is worthy

We believe that we are worthy and the world reflects to us that we are right. We believe that we are worthy because the world reflects to us that we are. This intricate, ordinary dance of action and reaction and integration is disrupted by living with people who cannot hear the music.

Children who cannot make sense of their world cannot act as mirrors for ours. And children who cannot regulate their own impulses and reactions behave aggressively, or rudely, or they disconnect from us and ignore us, and day by day such treatment eats away at the self-esteem of those who care for them. Yet the children have no idea, locked as they are in their own painful struggle to stay alive in a hostile world, that they are doing any harm. Or if they do get a sense of this they are powerless to do anything about it, and their own fragile sense of self-worth is further eroded.

The sense of self-worth also largely depends on the assumption that the world is benevolent and meaningful. So the erosion of self-esteem is both a consequence of day-to-day life with a child who cannot reflect to us our worth to them, and a secondary effect of the dissolving of other core assumptions.

Stress disorders in carers

Carers whose core assumptions are affected by living with children bruised before birth are vulnerable to developing stress disorders. Such disorders can usually be prevented if people are fully informed about the causes of such disorders. They can then enhance their own resources and build resilience. This involves thorough self-awareness about their own strengths and weaknesses, a careful monitoring of their own health and resilience, the building of strong networks of support, the recognition of periods of particular vulnerability, and rapid treatment of any symptoms that do arise.

Strengths and weaknesses

Carers can make their own inventory of strengths and weaknesses, and can also draw on their support network to help them understand their own current position. It is important to recognise that strengths and weaknesses are always dynamic and always changing as circumstances alter and life stages progress.

It can be a salutary exercise to make a list of perceived strengths and weaknesses, and then to reflect on what circumstances would cause any listed strength to become an area of vulnerability and even a potential weakness. For example, a family with strong support from the next generation has great strength to offer a burdened child. But what would happen if the supportive elder became ill or died? That family may then be more vulnerable than a family that had never had such support.

Similarly, perceived weaknesses can become areas of resilience and ultimately strength. Families that have to battle through illness or disability, or process trauma, or deal with disadvantage, may be vulnerable at present, but will also be building patterns of resilience that will forever be a resource for all the family.

Signs and indicators of disorder

There are excellent self-test stress inventories available via the internet (www.isu.edu/~bhstamm/tests/satfat_english.htm) that carers can use to monitor their health and ensure that they take steps to deal with early signs of disorder. Looking after children who cannot help presenting a challenge to core assumptions may lead to different sorts of stress disorders in carers.

There is the general stress of caring for children with poor impulse control and limited understanding of the world, and then there is the traumatic stress that follows the dissolution or shattering of core assumptions. It is important for carers to be able to recognise the point at which general stress and strain are becoming injurious, leading to symptoms equivalent to those of post-traumatic stress disorder.

It is also vital that the support network is fully informed about stress disorders, since one consequence of developing disorder is that the individual loses the ability to perceive their own state accurately. People who are becoming disordered will be less able to assess their own needs, and less able to access their usual support structures. This quickly becomes a vicious spiral unless the support network is well informed and willing to intervene to protect the carers from harm.

Signs and indicators of possible developing disorder include:

- altered mood regulation: irritability, tearfulness, fearfulness;
- altered state regulation: sleep, appetite, ability to relax;
- altered social interaction: withdrawal, conflict, lack of interest;
- altered physiology: stress illnesses, loss of concentration;
- increased use of mood altering substances or activities;
- decreased use of support networks and healing activities.

Building networks of support

Carers need both formal and informal networks of support in order to care effectively for children who are thinking and feeling with a different brain.

Formal networks need to include an element of supervision as well as support. Carers should know that if they become affected by stress disorder they will lose accuracy in their own perception. At that point they need a trusted professional to guide them through the journey to recovered balance and equanimity. It is not enough to rely on demand-led services when a key indicator of disorder is the loss of ability to perceive the need.

Informal networks need to be understood as the prime resource to sustain the health of carers, and to be consciously monitored and maintained to this end. Carers may feel uncomfortable with this approach to their most intimate and loving relationships, but without such conscious management of the human environment, carers will be very vulnerable to injurious stress.

Periods of vulnerability

No matter how secure and stable, every individual and every family will have times when they are vulnerable. It is important that carers keep in their consciousness the level of personal and family vulnerability, and have strategies in mind to respond to periods of increased risk.

Some risk factors are obvious – illness and death of family members or close friends, moving house, moving job, relationship difficulties, financial difficulties, floods, fires, accidents. Others are less obvious or more idiosyncratic: changes in religious or spiritual belief or practice, changes in sexuality or sexual practice, changes in the experience of employment such as new management, the death of pets, the loss of physical or sensory abilities with ageing, and so on.

Preventing disorder and treating symptoms

The individual

There are steps that each individual carer can take to prevent the development of stress disorders. These would include:

- education and training about caring for children who think and feel with a different brain;
- education and training about prevention and treatment of disorders;
- maintaining personal resources and building resilience:
  - physical activities and hobbies
  - emotional support – close confiding relationships
  - intellectual interests – reading, study, mental exercises
  - spiritual practices – religion, art, music, connection to nature
  - social networks – extended family, friends, interest groups,
- monitoring stress levels and taking action if stress is becoming injurious;
- seeking and using professional supervision and support.

There are also steps that individuals can take to ensure that they recover from disorder if they do become symptomatic. These would include:

- recognising and acknowledging need for therapeutic help;
- finding and using appropriate therapy:
  - physical therapies to enhance relaxation and regulation of arousal
  - emotional processing therapy, such as psychoanalytic psychotherapy
  - cognitive restructuring therapy, such as cognitive analytic therapy
  - maintenance or reinstatement of spiritual practices
  - maintenance or reinstatement of social life
- keeping a record of recovery and enhanced resilience that follows;
- seeking and using professional supervision and support throughout.

The family

The family as a whole can take steps to prevent and treat stress disorders. These would include:

- providing and maintaining a relaxing environment;
- taking notice of the stress status of family members;
- helping anyone in the family who is becoming stressed to recognise and dealing with their condition;
- seeking and using professional supervision and support from people skilled in family work or group work.

The professional network

Professionals providing support and supervision to families and individuals caring for children who live with acquired impairments need to be fully informed about the implications of the work. Agencies must take responsibility for their contribution to the health and well-being of people who may be subject to stress injuries as a result of the care they provide for children who think and feel with a different brain. Supervision as well as support is vital, as people who are becoming disordered as a result of injurious stress will become less able to make use of support networks.

The professional task would include:

- providing support;
- encouraging peer support;
- providing supervision;
- assessing need, and recognising changing needs over time;
- providing access to appropriate therapy.

Wider society

It is the wider social order that determines the way that injured children are cared for, and it is important that there is a widening understanding of the implications of such injuries for the children and for the families that care for them. In particular, it is vital that a true understanding of the nature and extent of stress injuries and recovery from them grows in society. These are not new phenomena, but our understanding of them is growing all the time. In the past many people suffered, often in silence, from the consequences of stress injuries. Now we know how to prevent, recognise and treat such injuries. Yet there is till stigma attached to such suffering. Education to raise public awareness and understanding will do much to ensure that those who care for our most vulnerable children are able to stay healthy and resilient.

In conclusion

Children who live with impairments acquired before birth bring many gifts into the families that care for them. They are invariably interesting people. If we engage with them in their struggle to make sense of the world and to manage their own responses to it, we will find that our own understanding of the world and of other people grows and deepens. Moreover, although impairments acquired before birth are persistent, the grace and courage with which children will attempt to adapt to their own limitations and live in a world that is often puzzling and overwhelming for them is remarkable and inspiring.

The children bring gifts, and they also bring challenges. Sometimes those challenges will stretch carers and they will be able to grow and develop new understanding and new skills that will enhance their lives. Sometimes the challenges will be overwhelming. It is the responsibility of the whole social network to ensure that care families are given every opportunity to benefit from the experience of caring, and are helped to recover whenever they do become overwhelmed.

References

Bateson G (2000) *Steps to an Ecology of Mind*, Chicago: The University of Chicago Press

Damasio A (1999) *The Feeling of What Happens: Body, emotion and the making of consciousness*, London: Heineman

Frankl V (1997) *Man's Search for Ultimate Meaning*, New York: Plenum Press

Hobson R (1985) *Forms of Feeling: The heart of psychotherapy*, London: Tavistock Publications

Janoff-Bulmann R (1992) *Shattered Assumptions: Towards a new psychology of trauma*, London: The Free Press

Kaufman G (1992) *Shame: The power of caring*, Vermont: Schenkman Books

15 **Going right back to go forwards**

Louise

There are so many things that I would like to say about my adoption from a child's point of view . . . I hear so many adult adoptee stories but I very rarely hear anything from a young adult's point of view. It is difficult for me, as it was a very painful period in my life, and I feel that I am coming through it now, or understanding it more, I should say.

Before my adoption

I have always known I was adopted, I think one of the first words I said was "'dopted" as well as "burn", but I will explain that later. I was put in my adoptive placement when I was 17 months old and the paperwork went through when I was 23 months old.

Before that, there were about six different homes and a lot of moving about. My birth mother Tanya was working at and running an exotic dance club, and my birth father Steven was unfortunately in prison on drugs charges. It was not the best situation for a child, and I guess it was at this point that I got used to being unsettled.

While Tanya was out in the evenings, I would stay round various friends of hers, where I would remain until the early hours of the morning when she finished work, and then collected me. I am not sure what exactly happened in my early years, but as an adult and having done some digging there are many stories that have come to light – not many good ones, I hasten to add. Most of them are to do with drugs and prostitution and me being in the middle of it all. There was a "burn" on my back when I arrived at my new home and it was only about two years ago that I found out how it happened. Everyone was drunk and someone put a cigarette out on me. Other stories have come to light, all along the same theme as I said before, me in the back of dark dingy nightclubs and Tanya out in the front taking her clothes off round a pole.

I don't think that there were any suggestions that I was born addicted to drugs, but I definitely had them around me. It was mainly pot and speed, but there was always other stuff – LSD, heroin and opium – floating around. I was told once that my nappy had been used to smuggle drugs into prison for my father and that Tanya had grassed my father up, hence he was in prison. She did not even tell him that she had me adopted, but then she did not tell her own family that she had had me until I was about three, and already adopted.

I am 24 now and have spent the last seven years trying to find out who I would have become if circumstances were natural and I have come to the conclusion that sometimes it's nice not to know some things. Well, you know what they say: curiosity killed the cat!! Well, this is a little snippet of what went on before I was adopted, you can imagine the rest.

Childhood

I had a very happy childhood so far as it went. As I said earlier, 'curiosity killed the cat' and I can't leave things alone. The pain and suffering caused all around me by the quest of my wanting to know the truth still staggers me.

I suppose it all started to go wrong at the last bit of primary school where you feel different at the best of times, but when you are "different" it makes it twice as bad. That's when I started to search for who I might have been and what a rollercoaster my life has been since then. I have ended up in many ways the same as Tanya, with a strong character and a good head on my shoulders and a love of the good times, but with my adoptive mother's values of peace and integrity, and a family to be proud of. This is quite strange as they are worlds and lives apart, so different you would not believe. One is a dancer who smokes dope and the other is as straight as a pin. And I am in the middle.

It's been quite a muddle that I have been trying to sort out myself, as all the psychiatrists and social workers I have seen over the years just do not understand. I am not different, I did not want to see shrinks to sort out my problems. I was just an average teenager growing up not knowing my roots – although I knew a lot about them I needed something tangible to put it together. The problem was mainly that I wanted to know about my adoption and by your professional standards, because I was under age, I could not know. Don't get me wrong – my adoptive parents fully supported my quest for knowledge and without them, and years of digging by my mother, I wouldn't have known as much as I do. My mother had been finding out bits and pieces of information for years and we pieced them together. She found the name of the social worker that had handled my adoption, and that she was still working in the same place.

I don't know whether finding out everything so young, and always knowing that I was adopted, helped or hindered me. It definitely gave me a thirst for knowledge of what I could not obtain, but I think every circumstance is different. I know that I have brothers that I met a few years ago and am no longer in contact with as Tanya did not agree with me meeting them. Tanya had four children and gave them all up – like I describe later she was a very confused person. My birth father has since died.

Teenage years

I have blocked a lot of the teenage years out, as there were some painful times. I stayed short term in the house of a friend of my adoptive parents as everyone was hoping for a reconciliation. After that I went to boarding school for a little while and then into care. I was placed with a foster family which had two daughters that I didn't hit it off with. I just felt I needed my space. I was 13, I think, and was told to be in early and had £3.50 pocket money a week. I was only there for a few months when it was decided that I was "too old" for their family and I had to move on. I never seemed to settle and as an adult it is hard for me to settle now. I always want to be on the move at certain times of the year – especially in the spring, when it was the time of my placement with my parents, after Tanya finally relinquished me.

I was about 14 years old when it was decided (after I refused to go back home) that I would go into boarding at my school for a "cooling off" period, to see whether I would settle down again, but sadly I did not. I think this was down to the fact that as a child I had never settled and that carried on for many years. In many ways, I think if I had not been sent to the school that I did go to, things wouldn't have turned out the same. The reason I say this is that the school I was at, which was a private girls' school, and also a music school, gave me a very good grounding. So I came out of school after reluctantly sitting my GCSEs and actually passing them – more's the surprise considering what I was going through at the time.

From my boarding school I went into my second foster placement where my foster mother Rachel gave me a key and told me to ring if I was not coming home, or was not in for dinner to let her know, that it was my responsibility to go to school and basically to get on with it. This was the best thing I think she could have done, in fact the only thing she could have done given the circumstances. It was also one of the worst, as it allowed me to go out into the world when I was feeling very lost.

I really don't know if it was my adoption that caused me to go off the rails, or so much of the WRONG support that I received, together with all that had happened. Out of all the people whom I spoke to, the only ones that made sense were the ones who had the insight to listen instead of asking textbook questions and making studies of what I do, what pictures I draw and how I act, and not actually getting to know me. Some have been easy to manipulate and not very good at the job they are supposed to do. All I wanted to do was talk to someone, to get them to listen to what I was going through, not to make me do IQ tests as if I was thick. I was at a girls' school, I had to be relatively bright to get in there. So why the need for IQ tests? All I wanted to be was normal. The social worker that helped me find Tanya was the only "professional" whom I'd come into contact with that was ever any good.

Meeting my birth mother

I was living on the streets of London when I was about 16–17, with a boyfriend who came and went over the next few years, and invariably got me into trouble when he was around. I felt that something was missing and as I had nothing to lose I felt that it was the right time to try and find Tanya. In many ways, if it had not been for me running away with him and ending up on the streets of London, I don't know if I would have ever had the courage to go and find Tanya. I contacted the wonderful social worker that my mother found, and with whom I am good friends now, and she helped me to find Tanya.

About a week later she got back to me to say she had found Tanya and would I like to phone her. I did and we had a very tearful conversation. A little while later she went with me to meet Tanya in the pub that she was running with her latest bloke. I stayed with her for a week or so, and all was well, until Tanya ran off with one of the punters from the pub. I followed her for a while but did not fit into her new lifestyle. I sometimes wonder if I had not turned up, whether she would have left the fellow that she was with and run off.

I got myself a grotty flat in the town where she lived and settled for a while. I saw Tanya from time to time. I heard through the grapevine that she was getting married to this new fellow of hers, and when I asked her, she said she was but that I was not invited. We had a few words and decided that we were better on our own. Well I phoned my social worker again and she mopped up the tears. She saw me through some really hard times after Tanya and I parted.

The fellow I had been with found me again, and because I was so low after what had happened I took him back. This was not such a good idea but I had had all the fight taken out of me. Well, a couple of years had gone by and I started to think that although Tanya's life had been hard she still had managed to make the best of things, so why couldn't I? So I put myself into college and although I didn't finish the course it gave me the courage to start to stand up for myself. The only problem was that the man I was with was violent and I had to take a few beatings before I learned to give one back. I know you probably think that that was not the right thing to do but it was my way of dealing with it. When I was strong enough I gave him the beating of his life and packed my bags and went and have not seen him since. The only thing that I regret is that I did not prosecute!

There is always a positive in every negative no matter how bad the outlook seems – that is the one thing that Tanya taught me, to survive. I was never shocked at what I had learnt – it all fitted into place and I never would blame Tanya, she did what she felt was best.

I know I am just rambling on but it is all so jumbled up in my mind. I have been over so many different periods of my life at different times and with different people that it is hard to separate what's what at times. I got in with a wrong crowd when I was in the last years of secondary school and after that got into everything Tanya had said she wanted me not to do, like drugs and crime. In many ways I have lived her life and have now understood why she did what she did and why she had no option. I really don't know how you can understand something like this from a textbook – there are no real symptoms, only a reason. I think that if you have grown up not quite knowing who you are, where you belong, even did you look like them, you tend to feel lost and a sense of belonging is very important to a child.

I know that I was not a nice person to be around as I was hitting puberty. It was even worse because I had a huge chip on my shoulder and thought that the world owed me something. I just felt all I needed was to belong, but as much as my parents loved me and cared for me, they could not give me the sense of belonging to a birth family. I wanted to know how it felt to have the bond between a real parent and child. So I really wanted to meet Tanya, to find out why someone could give me up, and when I couldn't find out I went on self-destruct.

I know that it probably sounds simple, but they were some really hard years. I skip over so much of what happened, because this chapter is to do with whether substance misuse in a parent rubs off onto a child. I suppose it doesn't matter whether you are adopted or not. If you are around drugs as a young child and growing up in a household where drugs are common-place, you don't see it as wrong. In spite of growing up in a well-educated environment, going to church and being respectable, and knowing that drugs were wrong, I always knew that there was a very different part of me that needed to get out.

I ended up on crack cocaine by the time I was 19, but I still don't know if it was because my birth parents were using around me as a young child that I automatically used, or whether it had had any effect on it. I think that I managed to get myself on the bloody stuff due to wanting to know too much, although it was indirectly to do with my adoption, as I ended up on drugs through meeting people in my search to get to know Tanya and what she went through. It was my quest for knowledge that led me into leading their lifestyle, and so finding what life was like. I was smoking dope when I was in care, but only moved on to the harder drugs at about 18 when I left Tanya again. I think that I needed to escape, and as alcohol held no appeal for me, I tried drugs as a way to escape from the pain that I had gone through. I ended up hooked and in many ways lived the life that Tanya had lived for many years – the rollercoaster ride of parties, highs and lows, everything being very surreal and living through it and out the other side only to find not much has changed – the grass is not always greener on the other side! I think in retrospect Tanya's life was a rollercoaster such as mine, started out good, hit a lot of rocky patches but always bounced back. It is strange now that we have quite a few of the same friends but never meet up. I expect that at some point she or I will be curious and will find each other again, probably walking round a supermarket, but we respect that we each have our own lives. Maybe a case of each meeting our "Waterloos".

My life as a young adult

The next few years were very fast. I lived with a violent alcoholic boyfriend who was absolutely no help whatsoever. I think that part of my cycle of boyfriends has to do with my having been given up for adoption, as genetics are a lot stronger than people think. Tanya had ended up in situations because she had thought so little of herself. Now I was repeating the cycle because I thought so little of myself that I could allow these things to happen, because I didn't love myself, as I thought that Tanya did not care for me or herself. All I had wanted was to feel my real mother's love, even if it was briefly.

The relationship with my boyfriend lasted for four years and I got myself into trouble with the police. I was on benefit and generally could not be bothered to work my way out of the dump I had managed to get myself into. One day I had been at a friend's house when I was supposed to have been shopping, so knew I was going to be in trouble when I got back, as I was at least two hours late. I had decided before I had got home where I lived with my boyfriend that enough was enough and I was going to get out. I didn't know where, but I had had "a gut's full"! I got home and there were two empty bottles of brandy on the back doorstep. I knew it was going to "kick off". It did kick off and I got badly hurt, the police were called and I left with my cat and a few black bags. I have never looked back since then. In many ways I needed to go through it to come out the other side. It made me realise so much about myself, and the harm I was doing to myself by being there.

I found myself a little bed-sit where I lived for six months while I was getting my head together. I was still on drugs and in many ways doing a lot more than I had been previously. I suppose my newfound freedom was to blame for that. It was like being a kid again with the nous of a young adult. I managed to get myself addicted to crack and that was not good. If it had not been for some very good friends who helped me turn my life around I might not be writing this today. But being me, and as independent as I was then, I got off it by going "cold turkey" alone in my bed-sit.

I got a flat with the help of the Council due to me being a recent care-leaver and a victim of domestic violence, and that was the turning point for me. I came off drugs as I had vowed to myself that this would be a fresh start, and it was. That was three years ago now and it has been an uphill struggle. You have to really go right back to go forwards again, and that was hard. I realised so many things, positive and negative, that taught me to love and understand myself. To start to trust people again as I never was one for trusting someone. From a very early age I used to say 'I do it 'aself' and that was before I was three.

Now I am a successful businesswoman working in a good job with a good salary. I am a confident person who can hold her head up high, and say I've made something of myself. OK, so I've been round the houses and over the fields and down in the valleys, but I'm getting there. If it were not for my adoptive parents being behind me all the way, and now a wonderful partner who I trust and who understands me, I don't know if I would have made it this far, without him being there for me and encour-aging me to fulfill my dreams. We have just moved out of my flat to a four-bedroom detached in a nice neighbourhood. It makes me giggle when I think of the days that I didn't have enough money to eat and now I am in pinstripe and pearls daily. So it can be done, but it is a hard road that you have to walk and a lot of soul-searching that has to be done to achieve what I have. It has been hard paying off debts and I am still not squeaky clean and doubt if I ever will be.

The last few years have taught me a lot and I have done a lot of growing up. If only one person reads this and only one person realises they are not alone and that one person talks to a friend and shares her pain like mine, it will have been worth it. The older I get the more I am realising that you can't do it alone and that at some point you have to ask for help and advice and actually listen to what you are being told, and only then can you really start to grow as an individual.

16 Substance misuse, attachment disorganisation and adoptive families

Caroline Archer

Introduction

Children who are fostered or adopted experience the twin traumas of separation and loss (Verrier, 1993; Archer, 1999a and b). The majority have also been exposed to disorganised parenting or maltreatment in their early years, whether or not overt abuses have been identified initially (Vaughan, 2003). Without a sophisticated assessment of their therapeutic and placement needs, it is difficult to anticipate outcomes for children in their new families. This may be particularly relevant to the discussion of the impact on children born or raised in environments where substance misuse is prevalent, where almost by definition their parent(s) will have demonstrated a disorganised lifestyle.

Although the concept of resilience, attributing sufficient inner resources to the child, seems attractive, we must recognise that 'children are not resilient, children are malleable' (Perry, 1997, p 124), as they adapt their responses to their earliest environments. It therefore seems more realistic to adopt the perspective which assumes that even minor differences at the outset can have major influences on outcomes and that each individual follows a unique, iterative path (Satinover, 2001). Youngsters' developmental pathways are complex, dynamic and self-reinforcing, as perceptions and responses based on their earliest experiences continue to be influential. Thus the self-organising properties of the developing brain are especially vulnerable to early, distressing experiences and in particular the lack of early attachment organisation.

This knowledge allows us working as practitioners, or parents of traumatised children, both to anticipate the worst yet hope for the best. Since the brain's capacity for self-organisation retains some malleability throughout life, this approach sustains hope that focused remedial inputs, within the healing attachment relationships of family and therapist, can have very positive long-term effects. Becoming more aware of patterns of parenting that best fit, and can eventually alter, the behaviour and relationship styles of traumatised children can provide the essential edge to enhance these children's chances of fulfilling their social and intellectual potential (Archer, 2003a; Burnell, 2003).

Developments in attachment theory

Attachment theory has evolved greatly over the past 60 years, having experienced periods of both popularity and challenge. Many of Bowlby's original propositions (e.g. 1969, 1973) are still invaluable today. Interestingly in the past 'decade of the brain' (Greenfield, 1999), the concept of attachment has increasingly become woven into neurodevelopmental and trauma theories to provide a more complex (and less linear) understanding of children's life-paths. Defining attachment as a two-way, interactive relationship between parent and child that continues evolving over time (often referred to as the 'dance of attunement or attachment') and taking trauma to mean a wound to body or mind that implies the need for healing (Waites, 1993), we might express the interactions of trauma, attachment and development through the diagram below:

Figure 1
The trauma triangle

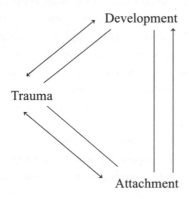

Note the fundamental, protective nature of attachment relationships. It might be possible to predict that seemingly minor distress experienced in the earliest stages of development (including gestation), when attachments are still being established, would have inordinately greater effects on the youngster's development than would later traumatic events. This is borne out by neurobiological studies of the developing brain and nervous system (e.g. Schore, 1994, 2001; Perry, 1999; Siegel, 1999). Although human infants come into the world with a full complement of brain cells (Eliot, 2000), this must be subject to uterine experiences, including the emotional, physical, nutritional and health status of the mother, since this is the organising "growth medium" of the child's developing neural systems. The mother's partner's state of mind may also impact on the unborn child, albeit more indirectly, unless there is physical aggression against the expectant mother.

Beginning at the beginning

Children who are born to parents who misuse drugs, including tobacco and alcohol, are vulnerable to a "double whammy" of adverse effects at every developmental stage. Firstly, these youngsters are likely to have been exposed to toxic substances during extremely sensitive developmental periods, when cell division and differentiation (specialisation) are greatest. Research into the long-term effects of uterine exposure to addictive substances has tended to focus on the extreme end of substance misuse. Whilst the peri-natal distress of the heroin or cocaine-affected neonate, and the identifiable syndromes associated with chronic, severe alcohol misuse are well documented, less attention has been given to the immediate traumatic impact and life-long effects of exposure to binge-drinking and occasional, or mixed, drug misuse. Eliot (2000) provides a cogent account of such influences, making the significant points that the "cocktail" effect of exposure to several risk factors can multiply risks to the unborn child, whilst lower dose effects may not be obvious for several years. Tobacco is said to increase susceptibility to other harmful factors – even "passive smoking" can adversely affect the foetus. However, direct chemical toxicity may be just the tip of the iceberg of physical and socio-emotional toxic effects, brought about by maltreatment from primary caregivers.

Since the world of the foetus, as of the emergent youngster, is experienced predominantly through physical and emotional sensations within the maternal caregiving environment (Schore, 1994), I explore these areas in some detail. I discuss some areas of development that are often not given high profile, yet may have powerfully destructive effects on children's developmental pathways. These include quite subtle sensory, motor, emotional and intellectual functions which, in neurobiological terms, are undergoing greatest growth and organisation during pregnancy and the first three years of life and are particularly sensitive to environmental challenges (Schore, 1994, 2001; van der Kolk, 1996; Siegel, 1999). It is essential that we take into account these less obvious, or less direct, factors since they may have as great an impact on the health and well-being of developing children as recognised stressors such as rubella, radiation or drug toxicity.

Individuals who demonstrate addictive behaviours are unlikely to inhabit optimal living environments (Home Office, 2003), nor are they at peace with themselves or their bodies. According to Schore (1994), an individual's vulnerability to drug misuse is strongly linked to poor early nurturing experiences – the "disorder" thus reflects an impaired capacity for self-regulation (Khantzian, 1978). This leaves the person vulnerable and ill-equipped to manage further stresses in life, of which there are likely to be many. Such individuals are often attempting to "self-medicate" deep psychological pain that has affected their lives for many years (Ruscombe-King and Hurst, 1993), as a consequence of impoverished organising and regulating interactions in their own childhoods (Schore, 1994; Archer, 1999b). Such parents are unlikely to be emotionally or physically available to their children consistently: the stage is therefore set for the cycle of disorganisation and poor self-regulation to repeat itself in subsequent generations.

Neurobiological distress

Borysenko and Borysenko (1994) describe the "foetal–maternal" dialogue that occurs throughout pregnancy, whereby the maternal neurohormone system (through which information about emotional and physiological states is transmitted and developmental sequences regulated) communicates with, and therefore directly influences, the child's developing system. Verny and Kelly (1982) explored the effects of extended periods of rejecting or ambivalent parental feelings on the child's well-being and found that these negative emotions caused lasting distress to the youngster. More recently, Eliot (2000) discussed the destructive influence of prenatal parental stress, as expressed through raised levels of specific neurohormones. We can understand these effects in terms of corresponding neurophysiological changes to the foetus, brought about by "toxic" levels of maternal stress hormones, and raised sympathetic nervous system activation, such as in the familiar adrenaline-fuelled "fight or flight" response. This would be particularly likely in mothers whose own regulation of physical and emotional states has been compromised in early childhood. It has also been suggested that some raised neurohormone levels interfere with neural development by reducing oxygen and nutritional supplies to the foetus (Eliot, 2000).

The neurobiological development of infants is "experience dependent". Their brain and nervous system organise according to environmental influences, to optimise their survival. Thus infants who are exposed to parental distress, or rapidly altering moods, will mirror these patterns in their own responses, both in the womb and after birth. Spangler and Grossman (1999) found that poor neurobiological organisation in neonates is highly correlated with attachment disorganisation by school age; attachment disorganisation is itself highly predictive of long-term social and emotional difficulties (Liotti, 1995; Fonagy, 2002), including the propensity to addictions in adulthood (Schore, 1994).

One major stress neurohormone known to have adverse effects on neurological systems is the corticosteroid cortisol. According to Begley (1997), excess cortisol secretion, as part of the "fight or flight" response, leads to neural "pruning" – the destruction of neural pathways and specific neural structures, such as the hippocampus, a structure in the brain responsible for verbal memory storage and retrieval. Thus cognition and explicit memory functions are frequently affected. Since Fisk (2000) found raised levels of cortisol in foetuses as early as 20 weeks after conception, it is clear that the foetus is not as protected from vulnerability to traumatic distress as we would like to imagine. Just as a child who has experienced trauma is adaptively primed to perceive and respond to cues of further trauma, so the foetal nervous system is set on "red alert" to react to a potentially hostile environment, both before and following birth. Such infants do not make easy babies and require particularly sensitive handling, yet are more likely to provoke rejecting or aggressive responses in drug-misusing, emotionally needy or unstable parents. This is consistent with Spangler and Grossman's findings (1999) that raised neonatal cortisol levels are associated with attachment disorganisation in infancy.

Turning to consider in more detail the effects on the growing youngster of being raised in a household with substance misuse, I explore the young child's internal and external sensory, motor and emotional experiences, since this provides insights into the potentially destructive effects of living in a sub-optimal environment. It is worth reminding ourselves that, in Oliver James's words (2003), 'early experiences set our emotional thermostat'. It is perhaps even more essential that we recognise the effects of these formative experiences on the child's developing body-based, sensory and motor systems. Brain and nervous system development is described as 'bottom up' (Porges, 1998): that is, the basic physiological functions that keep us alive mature first, in the "reptilian" brainstem. The sequence of brain maturation continues with the growth of the "mammalian" midbrain and limbic system, providing awareness of, and the capacity to, regulate sensations and emotions and offering greater individual choices over behaviour. Finally, the "human" neo-cortical areas develop so that mature individuals can use thinking, reasoning and negotiating skills in psycho-social interactions. However, under stress, these newer more mature capacities can be lost (Porges, 1998), forcing the individual to rely on the increasingly primitive response patterns of "fight or flight", or "freeze" (physical and psychological shut-down). According to Siegel (1999) and Schore (2001) the presence of a "good-enough" primary caregiver is essential for healthy maturation and organisation of neurological systems. Here, specific parts of the right side of the "human" brain, located behind the forehead and known as the orbito-prefrontal cortex, are particularly implicated in the organisation and "downloading" of essential information between parent and infant. It is through this interactive process that the youngster acquires a sense of self, including the capacity for physical and emotional self-regulation (Schore, 2001).

Meet the family

Let us consider what may happen to these developing systems in a young child raised within a substance-misusing household. In our imaginary family, mother (Sian) is 18 years old, single and a regular user of "street" drugs and tobacco. She has already had several partners, living a chaotic, transient existence in a series of bed-sits. She often leaves her baby, Karl, alone as she goes in search of drugs. At other times the room is crowded with casual acquaintances, smoking, drinking and talking loudly.

Karl, born prematurely, is five months old when we first meet him. He is lying on the floor surrounded by discarded drinks containers, decaying food, soiled nappies and cigarette ends. The threadbare carpet is stained, the room is chilly. Sian is lying on the bed listening to loud music, oblivious to Karl's whimpering. Emotionally, Sian is unable to provide Karl with the consistency of nurturing care he needs to begin to develop attachment security. Instead he frequently experiences unpredictability and powerlessness, as his attempts to connect with his mother are ignored, or responded to arbitrarily. This reinforces Karl's feelings of terror and despair. His burgeoning, internal working models (Bowlby, 1973, 1988), or inner "road maps" (Archer, 2003b), formed from real-world experiences, reinforce his perceptions that he is worthless, helpless and abandoned.

Living through the senses

Looking more closely at Karl's immediate sensory world, we can identify the levels of sensory distress to which he is regularly exposed. The floor is cold and hard under his thin clothing. He has not yet fully mastered rolling over, so he spends much of his time immobile, staring up at the uncovered light bulb, watching clouds of cigarette smoke coiling upwards, or frantically moving his own hands in front of his eyes. His bottom is very sore since Sian does not change his nappy regularly, even when it is heavily soiled. Faeces and urine burn into Karl's skin, at times the pain becomes unbearable and his sensitive tactile system becomes overloaded. He has no choice but to "switch off" (dissociate) from his discomfort in order to bear the distress and survive (Perry *et al*, 1995; Liotti, 1999; Archer, 2003b). The odour of decaying food, dirt and excrement, the constant pounding music and raised voices are also overwhelming: Karl gradually adapts by over-riding his olfactory and auditory awareness, "closing his senses" to this terrifying world.

Karl is hungry but his increasingly distressed cries elicit no yearned-for comfort, and pain gnaws in his belly. He sucks hopelessly on the cuff of his filthy, threadbare cardigan, grimacing at its harsh taste and texture. Over time he learns to ignore his body's expressions of hunger and discomfort. His back aches from remaining in one position and his movements range from frantic and unco-ordinated to impassive. Karl frequently closes his eyes to escape the harsh glare of the bare bulb. His days and nights seem endless and beyond endurance. Day by day he is becoming increasingly disconnected from his body's internal and external sensations and movements, just as he is becoming disconnected from his emotional needs, including intimate bonds. These responses are typical of disorganised attachment patterns in very young children (Archer and Burnell, 2003).

The world of the young child is essentially a body-based sensory world. Without sensitive attunement and continuous feedback from his attachment figure, he cannot make sense of these internal and external sensations, nor will he learn to understand himself or 'put himself in the shoes of others' (Siegel, 1999; Schore, 2001; Hughes, 2002). Instead, highly polarised patterns of behaviour are frequently observed that reflect differing patterns of dysfunctional caregiving. Emotional neglect provides the child with distorted "road maps" of his social world, and bimodal behaviour patterns are frequently observable by school age (Lyons-Ruth *et al*, 1999). Similarly, the assault on a young child's senses, including internal sensations, movement and body position, brought about by physical neglect leads to poor self-organisation and impaired self-awareness (Schore, 2001; Bentovim, 2002; Archer, 2003a and b). Here, too, we typically observe polarised patterns of sensory and motor response, in which the child demonstrates increased (hyper) or decreased (hypo) sensitivity and responsiveness through one or more of his senses, as a direct result of his traumatic early experiences (Archer, 1999a). Lacking a reliable source of co-regulation for his aroused physiological states, the child is unable to organise his neurobiological systems well. Poor self-regulation and neural disorganisation then render him highly susceptible to subsequent external and internal stresses (van der Kolk, 1996; Bentovim, 2002) and further interfere with his acquisition of developmentally appropriate social, emotional and intellectual skills. Traumatic sensitisation and these persisting "negative feedback loops" (van der Kolk, 1996; Balbernie, 2001) mean that change to a healthier environment, such as placement within an adoptive family, may not in itself heal the child's physiological and psychological wounds. It is therefore essential that we begin to "learn the language of trauma" if children are to be understood, and learn to understand themselves, empathically.

Three years on, Karl has a younger sister (Lara, aged nine months). Karl has learned to "take care" of himself and Lara. He frequently forages for food scraps, which he attempts to prepare and share. The children are often hungry, cold, tired and scared; their home remains squalid and chaotic. Karl knows how to "look after" Mum and is highly vigilant for cues that she is depressed or angry, relaxed or comatose. Increasingly he uses verbal or physical threats in attempts to control his unpredictable world, particularly his mother. He can be very demanding of her attention, although frequently he "doesn't listen". However, Karl has also learned to charm or cajole many of the casual visitors to his home into giving him money, sweets or attention. Sadly this has included inappropriate sexual attention. Karl is a very "busy" child who likes to play in the street, where he often gets into squabbles. Most of the children avoid Karl, complaining that he has nits, smells, is oddly dressed and can be unpredictable, aggressive and destructive. Karl moves awkwardly and seems poorly co-ordinated, tending to rush about, bumping into people and objects. At other times Karl spends long periods inside watching television, often rocking and pulling at his face as he sits in the noisy, dank, chaotic room.

In control or out of control?

Karl displays the overt organisation of behaviour in children with disorganised attachments described by Lyons-Ruth *et al* (1999) as "controlling-punitive". Such children often act in verbally or physically threatening ways when interacting with parents and others. Research (Schore, 2001) is beginning to support anecdotal evidence that boys more frequently demonstrate hostile behaviour patterns, including swearing, kicking and destroying possessions, whilst girls tend to display "controlling-caregiving" patterns, in which they attempt to meet the needs of parents and others. Lyons-Ruth *et al* (1999) also found links between types of poor maternal caregiving and dominance of one of these patterns: "absent" or "helpless" mothers tending to raise hostile offspring, providing some symmetry in this "dance of disorganised attachment". In time Lara, being female, is likely to display some controlling-caregiving behaviours. However, her experiences of maternal unavailability and helplessness and sibling position are both predictive of "controlling-punitive" patterns. It is important to remember that traumatised children can exhibit behaviours at either pole of the "helpless-hostile continuum" in differing social situations (Lyons-Ruth *et al*, 1999) and that beneath the apparent organisation of these behaviour patterns resides a deeply disorganised neurobiological system containing distorted perceptions and expectations of the self and of the world.

Disconnection, connection and reconnection

Children's mental representational systems ("road maps"), originally adaptive to their "caregiving" environment, bring with them a unique constellation of perceptions and expectations of the self and the social world that are resistant to change (Perry, 1997, 1999), since perceptions of the current world are viewed through the lens of early formative experience (Waites, 1997; Archer, 1999b; Siegel, 1999). Thus the destructive effects of an early drug-misusing environment can become inter-generational: the parent's lack of external connection, and powerful connection to her own internal needs, seriously inhibiting the development of healthy external and internal connections in the child. The youngster's "organised disorganisation" continues to distort his experience and response patterns: closeness and dependency remain terrifying concepts. Simultaneously, the child's sensory systems and capacity for self-regulation remain vulnerable to challenge. He or she continues to experience frequent, distressing "overload", perpetuating early "fight or flight" patterns (often evoking labels such as hyperactive or impulsive) or "freeze" behaviours (commonly labelled oppositional, lazy or daydreaming). Switching into aggressive "control mode", or "switching out" through dissociation (physiological and psychological "shutdown") are classic bimodal features that attempt to confer security and order in a world experienced as terrifying and chaotic (Putnam, 1997; Liotti, 1999; Archer and Burnell, 2003).

Without a great deal of specialised therapeutic input, incorporating developmentally-based attachment reparenting strategies (Archer, 1999c; 2003a; Jernberg and Booth, 2001; Hughes, 2002), a child's distorted "road maps" will continue seriously to compromise his or her capacity to recognise, or make use of, positive experiences of nurture and containment within the adoptive family (Gordon, 2003; Vaughan, 2003). The adoptive parents' role here is unique and vital. Only the current parental attachment figures can provide the ongoing healing environment within which opportunities for the re-organisation of neural pathways, perceptions, expectations and patterns of relating can occur, since it was in the original caregiving relationship that maladaptive patterns were established. Even the most experienced adopters may find this task challenging unless they are provided with the support and understanding that empowers them to translate their child's real needs from his or her language of distorted behaviours. It is through the provision of developmentally sensitive attachment interactions that newer, more positive interpersonal connections can eventually be forged, and internal connections "rewired", conferring better physical, socio-emotional and mental health (Hughes, 2002; Archer, 2003a and b; Gordon, 2003). Irrespective of chronological age, the child will need, yet may struggle desperately to avoid, repeated experiences of the closeness and dependency of babyhood and toddlerhood (Archer, 2001). Reciprocally, parents may need encouragement to feel comfortable identifying and meeting these early sensory and emotional needs appropriately in resistant or older children (Gordon, 2003). This can pose challenges for all those involved.

Clearly, the earlier these interventions begin, the better the outcomes will be (Balbernie, 2001; Archer, 2003b). It is therefore essential that thorough multi-disciplinary assessments of children's attachment patterns, and physical and mental health, are undertaken *prior* to placement and that this information, along with complete early family histories, is explored with potential adopters, alongside parents' own attachment histories (Burnell, 2003; Price, 2003). This too is no easy task. However, if we, as child care providers, can give adopters sufficient understanding and informed support they, in their turn, will be more able to provide the optimal secure, predictable, containing environment that is essential for the improved well-being of our most vulnerable children (Archer, 2003b; Briggs, 2003; Gordo, 2003).

References

Archer C (1999a) *First Steps in Parenting the Child Who Hurts: Tiddlers and toddlers*, London: Jessica Kingsley Publishers

Archer C (1999b) *Next Steps in Parenting the Child Who Hurts: Tykes and teens*, London: Jessica Kingsley Publishers

Archer C (1999c) 'Re-parenting the traumatised child: a developmental process', *Young Minds Magazine*, 42, pp 19–20

Archer C (2001) 'Thinking toddler – whatever the age of the child!' *Adoption Today*, 97, pp 14–16

Archer C (2003a) 'Weaving together the threads: families with futures', in Archer C and Burnell A (eds) *Trauma, Attachment and Family Permanence*, London: Jessica Kingsley Publishers

Archer C (2003b) 'Weft and warp: developmental impact of trauma and implications for healing', in Archer C and Burnell A (eds) *Trauma, Attachment and Family Permanence*, London: Jessica Kingsley Publishers

Archer C and Burnell A (2003) *Trauma, Attachment and Family Permanence*, London: Jessica Kingsley Publishers

Balbernie R (2001) 'Circuits and circumstance: the neurobiological consequences of early attachment experiences and how they shape later behaviour', *Journal of Child Psychotherapy*, 27:3, pp 237–55

Begley S (1997) 'How to build a baby's brain', *Newsweek* (special edition) Spring/ Summer, pp 28–32

Bentovim A (2002) 'Dissociative Identity disorder', in Sinason V (ed) *Attachment, Trauma and Multiplicity*, Hove: Brunner-Routledge

Borysenko J and Borysenko M (1994) *The Power of the Mind to Heal*, Carson, CA: Hay House Inc

Bowlby J (1969) *Attachment* (Volume I of *Attachment and Loss*), London: Hogarth Press

Bowlby J (1973) *Separation: Anxiety and Anger* (Volume II of *Attachment and Loss*), London: Hogarth Press

Bowlby J (1988) *A Secure Base*, London: Routledge

Briggs A (2003) 'Adoption and permanence today', in Archer C and Burnell A (eds) *Trauma, Attachment and Family Permanence,* London: Jessica Kingsley Publishers

Burnell A (2003) 'Assessment: a multi-disciplinary approach', in Archer C and Burnell A (eds) *Trauma, Attachment and Family Permanence*, London: Jessica Kingsley Publishers

Eliot L (2000) *What's Going on in There?* New York: Bantam Books

Fisk N (2000) 'Does a foetus feel pain?' Burns E, London: *The Times* (28 March)

Fonagy P (2002) 'Multiple voices versus meta-cognition: an attachment theory perspective', in Sinason V (ed) *Attachment, Trauma and Multiplicity*, Hove: Brunner-Routledge

Gordon C (2003) 'Hands on help', in Archer C and Burnell A (eds) *Trauma, Attachment and Family Permanence*, London: Jessica Kingsley Publishers

Greenfield S (1997) *The Human Brain*, London: Phoenix (Orion Books Ltd)

Home Office (2003) *Hidden Harm*, Hidden Harm Summary. www.homeoffice. gov.uk/docs2/hiddenharmsummary.pdf

Hughes D (2002) 'The psychological treatment of children with PTSD and attachment disorganization: Integrative dyadic psychotherapy', Submitted to *American Journal of Orthopsychiatry* (February 2000)

James O (2003) 'Children before cash', *The Guardian*, p 21, Manchester (17 May)

Jernberg A and Booth P (2001, 2nd edn) *Theraplay*, San Francisco, CA: John Wiley & Sons

Khantzian E (1978) 'The ego, the self and opiate addiction', *International Review of Psychoanalysis*, 5, pp 189–98

Liotti G (1995) 'Disorganized/disorientated attachment in the psychotherapy of dissociative disorder', in Goldberg S, Muir R and Kerr J (eds) *Attachment Theory: Social, developmental and clinical perspectives*, Hillsdale NJ: Analytic Press

Liotti G (1999) 'Disorganization of attachment as a model for understanding dissociative psychopathology', in Solomon J and George C (eds) *Attachment Disorganization*, New York/London: Bantam Books

Lyons-Ruth K, Bronfman E and Atwood G (1999) 'A relationship diathesis model of hostile-helpless states of mind: Expressions in mother–infant interaction', in Solomon J and George C (eds) *Attachment Disorganization*, New York/London: Bantam Books

Perry B, Pollard R, Blakely T, Baker W and Vigilante D (1995) 'Childhood trauma, the neurobiology of adaptation, and "use-dependent" development of the brain: How states become traits', *Journal of Infant Mental Health*, 16:4, pp 271–91

Perry B (1997) 'Incubated in terror: neurodevelopmental factors in the "cycle of violence" ', in Osofsky J (ed), *Children, Youth and Violence: The search for solutions*, New York: Guilford Press

Perry B (1999) 'The memories of states: How the brain stores and retrieves traumatic experience', in Goodwin J and Attias R (eds) *Splintered Reflections: Images of the body in trauma*, New York: Basic Books

Porges S (1998) 'Love and the evolution of the autonomic nervous system: the polyvagal theory of intimacy', *Psychoneuroendocrinology*, 23, pp 837–61

Price E (2003) 'The "coherent narrative": realism, resources and responsibility in family placement', in Archer C and Burnell A (eds) *Trauma, Attachment and Family Permanence*, London: Jessica Kingsley Publishers

Putnam F (1997) *Dissociation in Children and Adolescents: A developmental perspective*, New York: Guilford Press

Ruscombe-King G and Hurst S (1993) *Alcohol Problems*, London: Jessica Kingsley Publishers

Satinover J (2001) *The Quantum Brain*, New York: John Wiley & Sons

Schore A (1994) *Affect Regulation and the Origin of the Self*, Hillsdale NJ: Lawrence Erlbaum Associates

Schore A (2001) 'The effects of early relational trauma on right brain development, affect regulation, and infant mental health', *Infant Mental Health Journal*, 22, pp 201–69

Siegel D (1999) *The Developing Mind: Towards a neurobiology of interpersonal experience*, New York: Guilford Press

Solomon J and George C (1999) 'The place of disorganization in attachment theory: Linking classic observations with contemporary findings', in Solomon J and George C (eds) *Attachment Disorganization*, New York and London: Bantam Books

Spangler G and Grossman K (1999) 'Individual and physiological correlates of attachment disorganization in infancy', in Solomon J and George C (eds) *Attachment Disorganization*, New York and London: Bantam Books

Van der Kolk B (1996) 'The complexity of adaptation to trauma: self-regulation, stimulus discrimination and characterological development', in van der Kolk B, McFarlane A and Weisaeth L (eds), *Traumatic Stress: The effects of overwhelming experience on mind, body and society*, New York: Guilford Press

Vaughan J (2003) 'Rationale for the intensive programme', in Archer C and Burnell A (eds) *Trauma, Attachment and Family Permanence*, London: Jessica Kingsley Publishers

Verny T and Kelly J (1982) *The Secret Life of the Unborn Child*, Glasgow: Collins

Verrier N (1993) *The Primal Wound*, Baltimore: Gateway Press

Waites E (1993) *Trauma and Survival*, New York: Norton & Co

Waites E (1997) *Memory Quest*, New York: Norton & Co

Planning and supporting placements

17 Care planning for children looked after as a result of parental substance misuse

Dr Di Hart

Introduction

This chapter is concerned with the need to make effective plans for children who become looked after as a result of parental substance misuse. The emphasis within much of the literature, and the focus of practitioner attention, is rightly given to the question of assessment and family support to enable children's needs to be met by their parents (see Local Government Drugs Forum and the Standing Conference on Drug Abuse (SCODA), 1997; Harbin and Murphy, 2000). We know, however, that significant numbers of children whose parents misuse drugs or alcohol become looked after by local authorities or by friends and family. Exact numbers are impossible to obtain but the recent report by the Advisory Council on the Misuse of Drugs (2003) suggests that, of 77,928 drug-using parents where information was available, only 64.4 per cent of mothers and 37.2 per cent of fathers actually had their children living with them. An increasing number of these separated children were living "in care": 3.8 per cent of parents had children in this category in 1996; this rose to 5.6 per cent in 2000. There are no equivalent estimates relating to alcohol-using parents although Harwin and Forrester's (2002) study suggests that they also give rise to serious concerns. Children may become looked after for a variety of reasons: as part of a planned assessment, following a crisis such as a parent's arrest, or because of concerns about harm. Some return home while others are placed long term with alternative carers.

There is no specific guidance to practitioners about how they can effectively plan for such children. Of course, it could be argued that guidance is unnecessary: children's needs are universal and the care planning system should ensure that every child is looked after in a way that provides them with the best life chances possible. However, the chapter on assessment (Chapter 10) indicates that practitioners may lack confidence in working with substance-misusing parents. This chapter, therefore, attempts to explore some of the particular features of formulating plans for looked after children.

Effective care planning

The Looking after Children System (LACS) (Department of Health, 1995) requires that a clear plan should be made for every child entering the care system, to provide them with a safe, stable and caring home, either with their birth family or alternative carers, and outlining the strategy needed to achieve this goal. These plans should be written down and regularly reviewed. This system came about in response to concerns that children were drifting within the care system and that the long-term outcomes were poor (Department of Health, 1991; Parker *et al*, 1991). The extent to which these problems have been eradicated is questioned in recent studies (Department of Health, 1998; Harwin and Owen, 2000; Lowe and Murch, 2002). Care plans may be inadequate or not implemented, or may be implemented but fail to improve the outcome for the child. In awareness of this, the process of reviewing care plans has been strengthened in a recent amendment to the Adoption and Children Act 2002, and Reviewing Officers and Children's Guardians have been given new powers to challenge plans which do not meet the child's needs.

It must be acknowledged that, however robust these arrangements are, an essentially "administrative" system cannot guarantee the quality of planning in itself (Grimshaw and Sinclair, 1997). Sound professional judgement and skilled practice are also essential if children are to be well served by the planning process. A "good" care plan will be based firmly on the assessed needs of the individual child, rather than slotting the child into the cheapest or most readily available provision. The desired outcomes for the child in all areas of their development will be spelled out, with the services provided to achieve them within child-centred time-scales, and planning will be seen as a dynamic process rather than a single event. The child and their family should be involved in the formulation of the plan, receive a written version of it and actively participate in its review. This process of review should be clear to all, but flexible enough to respond to changing circumstances.

There are a number of factors arising from parental substance misuse for the practitioners concerned to take into account in order to achieve the best plan, and thus the best outcome, for the children. Some of these factors relate to the planning process itself, and others from the specific needs the children are likely to have.

Agreeing the plan

Perhaps the most crucial element of the care plan is whether a particular child can be returned to the care of parents. Thresholds for judging "good-enough" parenting when parents use drugs/alcohol are particularly problematic and Harwin and Forrester's (2002) finding that social workers respond differently to parents who misuse drugs from those who misuse alcohol suggests that differences may be partly attributable to professional attitudes and levels of awareness rather than parental capacity per se.

Keeping the focus on the child

It is important that decisions are based on each child's needs and experiences, not on stereotypical views about the characteristics of "good" parents. The complexity of work with substance-misusing families, where there may be several "clients", brings particular difficulties. Social workers may feel out of their depth if there are gaps in their knowledge or skills about drugs or alcohol and they are unable to judge their effects. A consequence may be an over-preoccupation with the substance misuse itself rather than the needs of the child. The crucial question should be: 'What is this child experiencing?' not 'How much methadone is this mother taking?' If a medical model is allowed to predominate, the focus of work becomes whether parents have stopped drinking or taking drugs rather than the quality of care they could provide for their children if they were returned home. Of course, the extent and pattern of drug use *is* relevant but will not provide all the answers. Instead, a judgement needs to be made about the likely impact of a parent's drinking or drug-taking on each child, depending on age and development. This stage in the analysis must not be overlooked amid the chaotic demands that are often a feature of the work.

Substance misusers inevitably have many problems of their own – financial, legal, physical or psychological – that demand attention. It is right that they should receive help to resolve these, but it is essential not to forget the child in the process. For example, the following notes were made by a social worker assessing whether an unborn baby could safely be discharged home to his drug-using parents:

> *Sharon missed appointments because Mike was arrested (from her home) on robbery (armed?) – flat searched – nothing found – Mike to appear in identity parade. Car was impounded by police with diary of appointments inside.* (Hart, 2002)

Such incidents inform judgements about parenting as they provide evidence about parents' availability, however well-motivated, to their children. A child living within a household where there are constant crises with parents being arrested, or drugs being sold, is unlikely to be getting the level of attention they need to thrive.

Not only is there is a danger of professionals allowing adults' crises to dominate the agenda, but the children of substance-misusing parents may be particularly "invisible". At the point of contact, they may be very young – or even unborn – and unable to speak for themselves. Alternatively, they may have taken on the role of carer and protector of their parent or may have learned to mistrust authority. Older children can be further confused, and thus silenced, by the conflicting values they are presented with in drug education sessions, or by media representations of substance misuse. Such children may cover up the difficulties they are experiencing:

> *I just couldn't tell anybody 'cause it's like . . . it's hard to tell someone and if they find out, they like phone the police and you might get took off your Mum and your Dad and the Police will get involved and that.*
> (Advisory Council on the Misuse of Drugs, 2003, p 50)

Uncertainty and prediction

The task when planning for children is not only to examine the quality of parenting *now*, but also to predict how it will develop in the future. This is a particular challenge when dealing with substance-misusing parents, who may have intrinsically good parenting skills but be unable to exercise them consistently. Behaviour may vary from hour to hour depending on the nature of the substances used: a parent can be competent and loving during the day but belligerent and negligent at night (when professionals have gone home) after using crack or alcohol. Similarly, parenting capacity may fluctuate from month to month as parents go through a cycle of escalating use, treatment and relapse. In the current climate of scarce resources, there is a real danger that professionals will withdraw when all is well and fail to see signs of deterioration. This problem of prediction is particularly important in planning for very young children, where there may be little "hard" evidence but huge concern. The birth of a new baby or the initiation of care proceedings may galvanise parents into seeking treatment and resolving some of their difficulties, but the crucial judgement is whether this is likely to be maintained. A particularly common scenario is for a substance-misusing parent to apply for a rehabilitation programme during care proceedings, but unfortunately such places are scarce and the waiting lists long. The professionals must advise the court, firstly, of the likelihood of the programme being effective and, secondly, the prognosis for long-term stability.

The same may apply to residential or other specialist assessments:

There were examples where excessive attempts to rehabilitate children home, including family assessments, appeared to contribute to case drift. (Department of Health, 1998, p 33)

In my study of pre-birth assessments (Hart, 2002), there were indications that practitioners may recommend residential assessments not because they think they will demonstrate positive parenting but to provide a safe place for parenting to fail, or additional evidence for care proceedings. This is not to say that further assessments are always pointless; they may provide information about the pattern of care over 24 hours, which is both difficult to obtain and vitally important.

A degree of uncertainty is inevitable (Parton, 1998), but practitioners must make a decision. Where parents are well intentioned, and battling with their own demons, there is a temptation to 'give them one more chance' or to 'wait and see what happens'. This may be compounded by a cautious approach to care proceedings, with practitioners deferring to legal advisers as to the meaning of "likely" harm and waiting for the major crisis which will bring clarity to the situation. Meanwhile, the child may be subjected to changes in placement and repeated assessments.

This brings us to a further consideration: whether the child can wait. Given the young age of many children in this situation, their urgent need for stability may have to take precedence, and plans be based on a timescale which reflects this. Because of this imperative to avoid unnecessary delay, there are clear benefits to twin-track planning, where alternative plans are being made alongside any attempts at rehabilitation; or concurrent planning, where children are placed with carers who are committed to working towards rehabilitation but will also provide a permanent home if this is not achieved. As a minimum, every child should have a contingency plan in case there is a need to change direction; for example, retaining the child's short-term placement if the family enters a residential unit.

Partnership and professional boundaries

There is no consensus across, or sometimes within, agencies about the threshold for good-enough parenting. The more chaotic the family, the greater the number of professionals likely to be involved. Yet deciding whether substance misuse is impeding parental capacity relies on professionals being able to work together. Staff who have expertise in the field will have knowledge of the specific effects of the substances being used, the pattern of use and the prospects of treatment being successful. Health professionals will be able to identify whether the child's health has suffered as a result of antenatal exposure to drugs or alcohol and whether they are receiving adequate physical care subsequently. Hospital staff often have valuable information about the quality of care parents have provided to babies being treated for withdrawal syndrome. Police will know whether parents' substance misuse is connected with criminal activity likely to lead to imprisonment or whether there is a pattern of violence. The probation service often has knowledge of a parent's ability to comply with plans. Finally, child care social workers or Child and Adolescent Mental Health teams will have an understanding of the child's individual needs.

All of this information should contribute to decision-making, but can this be guaranteed? Agency priorities or culture may get in the way: for example, substance misuse workers may close the case because parents have dropped out of treatment, or they may (mistakenly) insist on maintaining confidentiality with regard to the parent. Planning a child's future is a serious responsibility and professional networks may be disabled by a reluctance to participate in such a final decision, particularly if there is fear of violence or of getting it "wrong". As with all multi-agency work, communication is key and protocols for sharing information and joint working may support professionals in their task.

The need for a multi-agency approach does not stop once the decision is made. If rehabilitation is to be attempted, it is crucial that a detailed plan is agreed to address the needs of both parent and child, with roles and responsibilities defined. For example, the plan for one drug-using mother was that she should be reunited with her baby in a residential setting, but the child care social worker failed to establish that she had dropped out of treatment. The placement took months to arrange, and meanwhile the baby had several changes of short-term foster carer. On arrival at the unit, the mother left the baby alone to go out and "score" and the placement immediately broke down. Even if the plan is for the child to be placed with alternative long-term carers, there is still likely to be a need for ongoing support from a range of professionals. Parental substance misuse will continue to have an impact on the child, possibly physically and certainly emotionally, and plans need to reflect this.

The children and parents themselves should also be recognised as partners in agreeing the plan. This will need skill and perseverance to overcome the problems of stigma and mistrust.

Making the plan work

Effective care planning is inextricably linked with a thorough assessment of the needs of the child. There will be differences according to the substances used and Harwin and Forrester's (2002) study suggests that drug use is most likely to give rise to concern about neglect in babies, while alcohol use is commonly associated with concern about older children experiencing violence. The range of possible effects on children are well documented elsewhere (Cleaver *et al*, 1999; Harbin and Murphy,

2000; Tunnard, 2002a, 2002b) but some of these may have a particular impact on care planning. Of particular value are the few studies where children, and their parents, have been allowed to speak for themselves (see Hill *et al*, 1996; Advisory Council on the Misuse of Drugs, 2003) in highlighting the implications for children.

Finding the right placement

Where it is decided that parents cannot provide adequate care, the task is to consider the type of placement that will best meet the child's needs throughout childhood. Worryingly, the children of substance-misusing parents may already have experienced some drift and delay so that existing emotional, behavioural and attachment disorders may have worsened or new problems been created, making the task more difficult. Surprisingly, there is evidence that babies under the age of one year are the most likely to have had multiple placements (Ward and Skuse, 2001) and some of these babies may also have had the adverse start in life caused by neonatal withdrawal syndrome. Stability is essential so that the child can form healthy attachments as soon as possible.

The first option should always be to consider placing the child with family or friends and, if the care planning process has been effective, they should already be active players in discussions about the child's best interests. Yet there are factors in substance-misusing families that may serve to exclude them. Firstly, substance misuse is surrounded by shame, stigma and recrimination. Parents may not have disclosed the extent of their problem to family members, or may have been rejected as a result of it. They may not co-operate with attempts to make contact with extended family, or there may be professional concerns about breaching confidentiality. Practitioners may also be sceptical about the quality of care that grandparents can provide, given the problems that their children display; or a fear that they will be unable to protect the child from the ongoing impact of parents' substance misuse, allowing the child to be exposed to volatile scenes or to return home. There is an increasing body of evidence about the value of kinship placements, however (see Broad, 2001; Flynn, 2002), and many children of substance-misusing parents are successfully cared for by extended family members with little professional involvement. Where a child is placed with friends or family, there has been a tendency to leave them to get on with it, but the need for ongoing financial, practical and emotional support is being recognised and may result in more such placements.

Wherever the child is placed, carers are likely to have specific fears arising from the child's exposure to drugs or alcohol. The most obvious of these is the fear that the child will have sustained some lasting damage, particularly if the mother used alcohol or drugs during pregnancy. The research is somewhat confusing, ranging from reports of screaming "crack babies" who will grow into disordered adults to suggestions that most babies will develop perfectly normally. Carers are entitled to full and honest advice from expert paediatricians before deciding to take on a child, and agencies should be clear about their commitment to offering ongoing support. Carers may also have fears about whether the children are at increased risk of developing drink or drug problems, about HIV and hepatitis, and about how best to talk to the child about their history.

Contact

It is always difficult to judge the "right" level of contact with children placed with alternative permanent carers, but particular concerns arise if parents continue to misuse substances. They may turn up drunk or fail to turn up at all. It is particularly upsetting for a child who has taken on a caring role to see their parent deteriorating, which may well happen. Parents who were struggling to keep it together for the sake of their children may go into a downward spiral once there is no hope of the child being returned, or they may feel so guilty about their failure that they use alcohol or drugs to block out the pain.

If contact is a difficult experience, it will add to the carer's fears and they will want to protect the child (and themselves). Given these difficulties, it may be tempting to let contact lapse, often a very easy option with substance-misusing parents whose lifestyle may be highly mobile and chaotic. Yet it is likely to be in the child's interests to have some ongoing contact, whether direct or indirect, because the child will continue to wonder how their parent is faring. This may generate fears or guilt which are more damaging than exposure to a parent's erratic (but probably familiar) behaviour. Substance misuse workers may have a role here in maintaining contact or providing updates.

Meeting children's needs

This brings us back to the implications for children's developmental needs of having a parent who misuses drugs or alcohol. Each child's experiences will be unique: some may have entered the care system as babies and have had little direct exposure, others will have witnessed disturbing scenes, or been neglected. The Report of the Advisory Council on the Misuse of Drugs (2003) describes the theme of parents "not being there" for their children, either physically or emotionally, because of the demands of the drug. The implications of these varied experiences need to be recognised within care plans and the child may need support with the following tasks.

Relinquishing responsibility

Many children will have been burdened by feelings of responsibility for their parents, and this will not disappear because they are removed. In fact, the child may feel guilty and anxious because they have left the parent to fend for themselves. Apart from the need to provide reassurance through some form of contact, the child may need help to relinquish this caring role and learn other ways of being. Often they have been overly involved with the care of siblings, and again will need support to allow others to take over this role. Accompanying this responsibility, they may also have experienced a great deal of autonomy, and may struggle with the constraints of a more structured household:

> *Children's anecdotes and even interaction witnessed during interviews revealed that some completely disregarded parental requests and attempts to guide or discipline them. It appeared that when parents had done "stupid things" or broken up furniture, their authority was undermined.* (Hill *et al*, 1996)

The fact that children cannot be responsible for the behaviour of adults can also be an important lesson, with many children reporting that they thought parents were drinking or using drugs because of them.

Making sense of the story

All children in the care system are likely to experience conflicting emotions about their parents but substance misuse brings an extra dimension. Being the child of socially excluded parents may provoke questions for the child about their own identity, and they can veer between fierce loyalty and protectiveness to shame and disgust (Hill *et al*, 1996). Sensitivity will be needed, not just from carers but teachers and other professionals, when talking to the child about their parents' behaviour. It is tempting to fall back again on a medical model, suggesting that 'mummy was ill and couldn't help it', but this may be at odds with other messages to the child, particularly if parents' behaviour has been defined as criminal or a child receives fiercely anti-drug messages at school which are clearly based on the notion of free choice. A child may also have unspoken fears about whether their carers will follow in the parents' footsteps, and one foster mother reported giving up alcohol altogether because of the distress it caused the child. Some children may even have fears about their own future use of substances, and may need specific help to explore this.

This process of reconciling conflicting emotions can be hindered by a pattern of secrecy and mistrust and considerable support may be needed before the child can talk about and hence make sense of their story.

Forming new attachments

These are daunting issues to face, but are essential if the child is to form new attachments. The pattern of frequent moves, inconsistent care, separations and chaos are likely to have had an impact on the child's ability to rely on the adults in their life to respond to their needs. There may, however, also be grounds for optimism. The studies described earlier indicate that substance-misusing parents want the best for their children, and will have given them a legacy of positive as well as negative experiences on which to build. It must also be recognised that children will rarely have responded by being passive victims within the family. In their conversations with children affected by parental drinking, Hill *et al* (1996) found that children had adopted a number of strategies to manage their situation. These ranged from pouring drink down the sink, to avoidance, to channelling energies into activities outside the home. Some of these coping strategies may have contributed to resilience while others could be problematic, but they will need to be recognised and worked with in order to help the child develop.

Conclusion

The impact of parental drug or alcohol misuse on children makes planning for those who enter the care system a complex task. Although the plan should be determined by the individual and holistic needs of each child, parents and carers are also entitled to support so that they can, in turn, help the child make sense of what has happened. The level of chaos, secrecy and fear which surrounds substance misuse needs to be tackled head on to make sure that plans are effective in genuinely improving the long-term outcomes for this increasing number of very vulnerable children.

References

Advisory Council on the Misuse of Drugs (2003) *Hidden Harm: Responding to the needs of children of problem drug users*, London: Home Office

Broad, B (ed) (2001) *Kinship Care: The placement choice for children and young people*, Lyme Regis: Russell House Publishing

Cleaver H, Unell I and Aldgate J (1999) *Children's Needs – Parenting Capacity: The impact of parental mental illness, problem alcohol and drug use and domestic violence on children's development*, London: The Stationery Office

Department of Health (1991) *Patterns and Outcomes in Child Placement: Messages from current research and their implications*, London: The Stationery Office

Department of Health (1995) *Looking after Children: Assessing outcomes in child care*, London: The Stationery Office

Department of Health (1998) *Someone Else's Children: Inspections of planning and decision-making for children looked after and the safety of children looked after*, London: The Stationery Office

Flynn R (2002) 'Kinship foster care', *Child & Family Social Work*, 7:4, pp 311–21

Grimshaw R and Sinclair R (1997) *Planning to Care: Regulation, procedure and practice under the Children Act 1989*, London: National Children's Bureau

Harbin F and Murphy M (2000) *Substance Misuse and Child Care: How to understand, assist and intervene when drugs affect parenting*, Lyme Regis: Russell House Publishing

Hart D (2002) *The Contested Subject: Child protection assessment before birth*, Unpublished PhD thesis, University of Southampton

Harwin J and Forrester D (2002) *Parental Substance Misuse and Child Welfare: A study of social work with families in which parents misuse drugs or alcohol*, Interim Report for Nuffield Foundation

Harwin J and Owen M (2000) 'A study of care plans and their implementation and relevance for *Re W and B and Re W (Care Plan)*', in Thorpe J and Cowton C (eds) *Delight and Dole – The Children Act 10 years on*, Bristol: Jordan Publishing Limited

Hill M, Leybourn A and Brown J (1996) 'Children whose parents misuse alcohol', *Child & Family Social Work*, 1, pp 159–67

Local Government Drugs Forum and the Standing Conference on Drug Abuse (1997) *Drug Using Parents: Policy guidelines for inter-agency working*, London: Local Government Association

Lowe N and Murch M (2002) *The Plan for the Child: Adoption or long-term fostering*, London: BAAF

Parker R, Ward H, Jackson S, Aldgate J and Wedge P (eds) (1991) *Looking after Children: Assessing outcomes in child care*, London: The Stationery Office

Parton N (1998) 'Risk, advanced liberalism and child welfare: the need to rediscover uncertainty and ambiguity', *British Journal of Social Work*, 28:1, pp 5–27

Tunnard J (2002a) *Parental Problem Drinking and its Impact on Children*, Research in practice

Tunnard J (2002b) *Parental Drug Misuse – A review of impact and intervention studies*, Research in practice

Ward H and Skuse T (2001) 'Performance targets and stability of placements for children long looked after away from home', *Children & Society*, 15, pp 333–46

18 **Meeting placement challenges**
One local authority's response

Jennifer Bell and Margaret Sim

Introduction

This chapter covers a range of issues relevant to substitute family placements of children whose birth families are affected by substance misuse.
This will be done from a practice base, informed by our experience as
Senior Officers in the 'Families for Children' Team – the fostering and
adoption section of Glasgow City Council's Social Work Services.

We shall be highlighting issues relating to sibling groups, sexual abuse
and education which arose out of a survey undertaken recently by the
team. We also examine other areas including: caring for children from
substance misuse backgrounds, care planning and contact with birth
parents, and recruitment and retention of carers.

The Glasgow context

Glasgow City Council has, at any one time, an accommodated population
of around 1,100 children and young people. In July 2003, 807 of these
children and young people were in 380 foster care households. The numbers
of children and young people accommodated in foster care has grown year
on year (by 150 since April 2000). This seems to be a trend experienced by
many local authorities and, while some of this increase may be attributed to
the shift from residential care to family placement, there is also a recognition
that the accommodated population per se is increasing.

In her excellent paper, Marina Barnard (2001) quotes the Greater
Glasgow Drug Action Team estimate that there may be as many as 10,000
children living with a drug-dependent parent in Glasgow alone, which
has four times the average registration of known drug users. If this is
correct, we are dealing with only a very small tip of a very large iceberg.
It would be fair to assume that the children in our foster care service
come from families where chronic substance misuse is only one factor,

albeit perhaps the deciding factor, in their inability to care for their children.

The Families for Children team, divided into specialist sub-teams, provides placements for all accommodated children requiring family-based care across the spectrum from emergency placements through to adoption. One of the sub-teams operates the Glasgow and West of Scotland Adoption Service (GWSAS) which provides placements for all children aged up to the age of two years who are referred from Glasgow and other members of a local consortium. At any one time up to 30 children are waiting for GWSAS placements. The total number of children currently on referral for adoptive placements is 50. Almost all of these are under five years old reflecting, as highlighted in a previous chapter, the young age of the children needing adoptive placements.

In this chapter our focus is on the provision of foster placements, both temporary and permanent. Approximately two-thirds of our 400 carers provide exclusively either short-term or permanent placements. The remaining third, mainly our experienced fee-paid carers, provide long-term placements for more challenging children, especially those whose needs appear to be complex at the point of accommodation. Sometimes, due to shortage of resources, these carers are used for temporary placements. We acknowledge and promote the long-term benefits of successful adoptive placements. However, there is no doubt that permanency planning for children over five years is influenced by our long experience of the range of supports that the complex children described in this chapter need in order to sustain family placements. These supports, in our experience, are more readily available in long-term foster care where carers are able to share the responsibility of the challenges the child presents. While not all the children who might potentially be placed for adoption could be described as complex, the high number of pre-school children "use up" a lot of available adopters, who favour them over older children.

During the period which saw the increase of children in foster care, our family placement team climbed a steep learning curve. Without another comparable authority in Scotland, and with only limited research available on the impact of parental drug misuse, our knowledge base has developed as a result of experience over time. The first few children under the age of five, who proved too challenging in two or three consecutive placements with experienced carers, were the subject of much debate. We are now more able to identify the young children who are so affected by early neglect and trauma in their birth family that they remain in a high state of anxiety and arousal for a prolonged period after being accommodated and placed in foster care. For example:

Claire, aged 4, placed with experienced carers after an adoption disruption lived with chronically drug-misusing parents prior to accommodation. Getting her dressed is a daily power battle. Despite negotiation and distraction by her carer she regularly urinates on her clothing if her demands to wear certain items are not acceded to.

John, aged 9, when placed (from a residential unit) with very experienced carers initially settled well. After a year in placement John began to react very badly to quite trivial requests from his carers. This escalated quickly till he was regularly out of control. He would run out of the house and disappear for hours at a time. If "grounded" he would climb out of windows to escape from the house. He needed physical restraint on several occasions and was clearly happier roaming the streets. John spent his earliest years as a "street child" cared for by his mother who had a severe drug problem.

Caring for children from substance misuse backgrounds

Our working knowledge of the psychosocial effects of early life trauma, disrupted attachments and separations is very recently acquired. Only in the last ten years has it become part of some social workers' repertoire, in trying to assess risk in relation to removing or returning children. Likewise, our working knowledge of recent research into brain development is very limited indeed, so pronouncements about the long-term effects of drug exposure *in utero* need to be made with great care. Whatever the interplay of organic, environmental or genetic factors may be, the reality is that many of our carers are looking after children whose behaviour is very complex, hard to understand and hard to manage. There is a need to ensure that the developing knowledge about trauma, attachment and brain development is made relevant and available to carers, family placement workers, field workers, drugs workers and professionals in education and health.

It is important to clarify the kind of neglect we term "chronic". There are many parents who attempt to manage their drug use in a way that ensures one adult remains capable of caring for their children's needs. Many of these parents are helped and supported through their involvement in Glasgow's Methadone Programme. The parents of the children we accommodate either use drugs chaotically, or also have other problems such as a "dual diagnosis" of substance misuse and mental illness (Scottish Executive, 2003) and chronic poverty. Their lifestyles combine to create circumstances which are as toxic to a young child's physical and emotional development as any that can be imagined in our society. Some of the behaviours of the young children that give us most cause for concern are reminiscent of the first distressing footage of children placed in Romanian and Chinese orphanages.

The link between early trauma, chronic neglect and behaviours associated with lack of attachment is now well documented (Keck and Kupecky, 1995; Hughes, 1997). The most common behaviours reported as problematic by our carers are related to control and anxiety. This can lead to the "distorted perception" with which children from chronically neglected backgrounds view substitute carers' attempts at nurturing as a threat to their ability to be in control or a precursor to further abuse. This is fully illustrated in *Healing the Child who Hurts* (Adoption UK, 2000). We have found that this distortion is at the root of many of the complaints and allegations against carers which are, after investigation, considered unfounded. The desire that pre-school children can express for control of their environment can be astounding at times. Children who use hyper-vigilance as a coping mechanism in an unpredictable and dangerous adult world perceive physical and emotional closeness as a threat. As children become less fearful of their carers in placement, their need to control increases, as they believe this is their only means of protecting themselves from possible further rejection or abuse.

Many of the children whose behaviour is most challenging in family placements do not show this behaviour in respite care and relate well to departmental staff. Their fears and defences are rooted in their birth families, and it is substitute *family care* that continues to trigger these fears. We have struggled with decision-making for young children who have had to leave two or more placements, even when these placements are with carers experienced in managing challenging behaviour. The underlying causes of serial placement breakdowns, such as both attachment disorder and post-traumatic stress disorder, often come to light when children are finally accommodated in residential care (Giller, 2000).

The survey

The number of children

In order to quantify the problem of drug misuse, we surveyed all the social workers in the team to identify the numbers of children currently in placement with foster carers, where drug misuse was one of the reasons for accommodation, or was preventing rehabilitation. The results of this survey will inform much of the discussion in this chapter.

At the time of the survey, as highlighted above, 807 children were being supported in family placement by Families for Children staff. This constitutes 73 per cent of Glasgow City Council's accommodated child population. The survey covered children in both pre-adoptive and foster placements. The latter were by far the greater in terms of numbers, but young children in pre-adoptive placements were just as likely to come from drug-misusing families. The survey did not look at parental alcohol misuse as a reason for accommodation. The experience of our team, carers and area team colleagues was that alcohol misuse was still a significant factor but no more so than it had been traditionally. We have worked longer with alcohol misuse and are more familiar with its effects such as Foetal Alcohol Syndrome. However, we were clear that we were not seeing any significant proportionate increase in alcohol misuse as a causal factor in the increase in numbers of children being accommodated. On the other hand, there has been a substantial increase in accommodated children whose parents misuse drugs. Experienced workers and carers were commenting widely on the severe nature of their neglect. Given our limited knowledge and understanding at present of the adverse long-term effects of drug misuse, we did not want to dilute the data by including alcohol misuse in our survey.

Of the total 807 children, 395 were identified where parental drug misuse was either a reason for accommodation or a factor preventing rehabilitation. This constitutes 48 per cent of all the children in family placements. This figure has not previously been readily available in relation to drug misuse alone, as the Council's information system does not currently contain a category for recording "drug misuse" as a reason for accommodation. The category most often used is that of "neglect". This will be relevant to drug-misusing families but also includes those with a range of other problems, such as parents with learning disabilities who are unable to adequately parent their children. The survey included children in our many long-term foster placements, which were made several years ago, before parental drug misuse had such a significant impact. It is our belief therefore, that within the population of children currently being accommodated, the proportion of those who are directly affected by parental drug misuse is much higher than the quoted figure of 48 per cent. To test this a detailed analysis of one area team's accommodated children was carried out over a six-month period.

Glasgow City Council is served by nine area social work teams. The East Area Team (covering a large part of Glasgow's east end) accommodated 32 children between April and September 2003. Of these 32 children, 82 per cent or 26 children, were under 11 years old.The reason for accommodation was directly related to drug misuse for 19 of the 32 children, or 60 per cent of accommodations. This team's figures, albeit on a small scale, but in all probability replicated in the other eight Glasgow teams, seem to give some objective evidence that our accommodated population is getting younger and this is related to drug misuse amongst parents. Thirteen of the 32 children were in the age-range 0–4, and 11 of these were accommodated because of drug-related problems.

Sibling groups

One of the questions in the survey focused on children who were part of a sibling group of three or more. Of the 395 identified as having drug-misusing parents a total of 179 (45 per cent) came into this category. This is a much higher percentage than sibling groups in the accommodated population as a whole. The team has often struggled with the placement issues presented by such groups. We have placed several groups of four, and two groups of five together. We have been involved in the separate placements of four other sets of five siblings, and two groups of six. Clearly parental drug misuse was a more common factor in these children's lives than we were able to identify amid the dilemmas and debates their situations generated. It is unlikely that any of these children's parents planned to have such large families. Few had any real extended family supports and many of the mothers were the victims of domestic violence. One can only assume that the chaotic nature of the parents' lives, as well as their struggles with parental responsibilities, have contributed to their inability to avoid further pregnancies. In most instances the large sibling groups we have placed in foster care have been accommodated together after a crisis. Others have come into care at different periods, creating the dilemma of whether to remove children from existing placements, to be reunited with siblings.

Some of the placement needs of individual children within large sibling groups have often of necessity been compromised, in order to plan for the whole family. Even if an exceptional family can be found, who can parent siblings permanently, the flexibility and levels of contact appropriate for a 13-year-old intent on eventually returning to her mother's care, is unlikely to be as positive for her three-year-old brother. Separate adoptive placements for younger siblings in many instances lead to the severance of contact with older siblings who may feel intensely the loss of brothers or sisters for whom they have been the primary carer. Many adoptive parents are committed to maintaining the relationships between their adopted child and older siblings in foster or residential care, but it can be difficult to manage the siblings' desire to share information about the birth family with whom they may have regular contact.

Sibling relationships in families where children have experienced chronic neglect can be complex. Aggression between siblings close in age has presented particular challenges. Descriptions from social workers who knew the children at home with their birth parents suggest competition, from an early age, for the little available attention and nurturing. Parents, struggling with their physical addiction, are often unable to contain the escalating aggression between their children. Normal sibling rivalry is then compounded by the children's individual unmet emotional needs and they come to believe, often accurately, that whatever their parents are able to give to their brothers and sisters diminishes what they receive. Siblings, whose foster placements together have disrupted, often end up with experienced carers who look after several non-related children. Interestingly, they seldom show the same level of competition or physical abuse towards these other foster children as they did towards their brothers and sisters.

The problem of sexualised behaviour is discussed below, but it is worth noting that this behaviour between siblings seems all too common where there is a history of chronic neglect and parental drug misuse. The Halt Project in Glasgow, which works with children who have been the victims of sexual abuse, has identified mutual sexual behaviours between siblings as the most difficult to treat. Lack of adequate parental comfort and exposure to strangers may combine to give children a level of emotional need and inappropriate knowledge, which is expressed within the sibling group.

It is often hoped that younger children in an accommodated sibling group will have the benefits of being "rescued" earlier. While security hopefully can be provided sooner in their development, the youngest have inevitably been the most vulnerable, as their parents' drug misuse increased to the stage that care and protection measures were required. Older siblings may have more positive memories and a stronger attachment, resulting from parenting which was less dominated by drug misuse.

Sexual abuse

The number of children reporting sexual abuse and the level of problematic sexualised behaviour children present in placements has, in the team's experience, increased considerably during the last few years. Eighty-seven children out of the 395 identified as having drug misuse fell into either or both of these categories. At 22 per cent, this is probably a conservative estimate, as 60 of the children were under the age of four and less able to verbalise their experiences. There are studies which link substance misuse with sexual as well as physical and emotional abuse (Hampton *et al*, 1998; Hawley *et al*, 1995, quoted in Barnard, 2001). The levels indicated in our survey are high in comparison to the accommodated population as a whole, and probably reflect the nature of the drug misuse and other issues which contributed to the children's accommodation.

It is generally accepted that, unlike physical abuse, sexual abuse within the family setting is not more prevalent in any one socio-economic group, but the lack of protection in drug-misusing households is evident in many of the accounts children give to their carers. The eldest two children in an accommodated family of six recall the constant stream of unknown adults who would arrive at their door at night threatening them and their mother, presumably demanding payment. In some cases, in their desperation to fund their habit, parents have accepted payment for allowing sexual abuse to be perpetrated on their children. In addition, when heroin was almost twice as expensive as it is to purchase now, many mothers turned to prostitution to finance their habit, further exposing their children to risk of abuse by unknown males.

Children often manage to avoid adult discovery of their sexualised behaviour well into their first and often into their permanent, placements. This behaviour may pose a risk to other younger children in the household, the extended family or the community. Few behaviours children present in placements generate such difficult emotions for carers as sexualised behaviour, particularly if the child attempts to engage other younger children. Foster carers often feel very ambivalent: on the one hand, there is empathy for the child as victim; on the other, they may, as people who are motivated to protect children, feel rejecting towards the child and fearful of the future. We have only been able to manage the overall increase in the numbers of children we have placed by asking our most experienced carers (who traditionally took older, more challenging children) to take on multiple placements of non-related children, including younger ones who may have already experienced a disruption. This has been alongside ongoing advertising and recruitment to attract new carers. The operation of multiple placement foster homes poses the constant need to attempt an assessment of risk with each new placement. This can be very difficult when permanent carers, or those we have tried to use for specific task-centred placements, have to be used for emergency admissions, and there is limited knowledge about the child who is joining the family.

Education

Of the 395 children affected by parental drug misuse, 60 were too young to receive nursery education or attend school. Supervising social workers were asked to identify how many of the remaining 335 children were presenting either behavioural or learning difficulties in their educational setting: 199 were recorded as experiencing difficulties, representing 68 per cent of the school-age children in the survey.

There is certainly a feeling amongst our workers that this group of children, who make particular demands on the education system, is growing. Most classroom teachers in Glasgow would recognise the description of the children we are placing. The prevalence of short attention span and lack of concentration amongst this group of children from chaotic drug-misusing families has obvious implications for any teacher in a classroom with 25 children, if one of them shows these symptoms of chronic neglect.

Many of the children in the study had erratic school attendance prior to accommodation. But equally, for many of these children, school may have proved to be the one stable, calm and safe area of their life. Because we place children across a wide geographical area, moves of school are almost inevitable at the point of accommodation. When this happens, children will sometimes lose the connection with a school environment which has been nurturing, and particular teachers who have been very committed and supportive. When we are negotiating "out of authority" placements, there is a recognition that additional education supports may be necessary. This is often done through the provision of finance to provide a classroom assistant to support particular children.

With the emphasis currently on "social inclusion" there is a real need to quantify the demands on the education system that are being made and which will, we suggest, increase. Along with the usual, often forlorn, plea for more money and more resources to be targeted at this particularly vulnerable group of children, it is vitally important to incorporate the growing body of knowledge about trauma, attachment and the impact of drugs on brain development (see Cairns and Stanway, forthcoming, 2004) into teacher training. More opportunities for joint teacher/social worker training are also much needed.

Contact and care planning

Contact with birth parents and extended family members is crucial for most of the children and young people in foster care. It is necessary to help social workers assess the likelihood of a return home and, where not possible, it is vital to help children and young people work out who they are and where they came from. Contact with parents who are chronic substance misusers brings its own set of complex dilemmas, which have to be assessed and worked with by social workers, and lived with by children and their carers.

Heroin, the most widely used class A drug in Glasgow, does not in itself induce aggression, but will, like most similar substances, exaggerate the user's existing moods and coping mechanisms. Children are quick to determine whether a parent is under the influence when contact takes place – all the anxieties present at the time of the child's removal from the parent's care can be triggered. Many very young children have an almost adult knowledge of the mechanics of drug misuse, having seen and been involved with their parents' and other people's drug habits. Older children may be aware of the expectation that their parent will address their drug misuse before rehabilitation can be considered, and are then faced with possible disappointment.

There is widespread knowledge now, within schools and within the media at large, about the implications of drug misuse. This knowledge is perhaps of necessity crude and simplistic, and often equates drug misuse with death. Children in foster care, who know their parents are drug misusers, often feel chronic anxiety about their well-being. This makes contact essential to ensure that their parents are still alive, but given the chaotic lifestyle of many of them, consistent contact patterns are rare, and the implications of several missed contact visits can be devastating for some children.

The use of a combination of different drugs, or methadone with other substances, can make it difficult to determine a parent's ability to take part in contact. This is often managed by an agreement that the parent appears for their condition to be assessed, prior to the child being collected for the meeting. Communication between the child's workers, addiction workers and the health professionals who prescribe substitutes such as methadone is clearly essential to the care plan for any child whose parents misuse drugs. The single shared assessment, outlined in *Getting our Priorities Right* (Scottish Executive, 2003), is a useful tool in ensuring that the advocacy role of addiction workers with parents does not come into conflict with the need to protect and plan for children. We would argue that family placement workers need to be familiar with the treatment programmes available for drug users and also involved in any multi-disciplinary case conferences.

Arguably the most difficult aspect of parental drug misuse is the "two clocks" analogy referred to by the National Centre on Addiction and Substance Abuse, USA (1999), one showing the child's need for security and permanent care and the other the slow, relapsing nature of recovery from drug dependency. Successful recovery often involves two or three periods of detoxification treatment. How long should young children remain in short-term foster care while their parents undertake a second attempt? Should existing permanency plans be abandoned if a parent continues to remain drug free and shows other signs of stability? How do we help children to accept that they cannot return to a parent, who may have finally recovered from their addiction, if permanency has been legally secured? We work within the Children's Hearing system which struggles with the concept of permanency. Often the Panel system seems to focus primarily on the current wishes and needs of parents and children at any given point in time, rather than taking a considered, long-term view.

The disappearance of parents after their children are accommodated is a major cause for concern to our area team colleagues and carers. This produces almost intolerable anxiety for many children, who as they get older are given more education about drug misuse and fear for their parents' lives. This fear is not unjustified – we identified 11 children who have lost a parent through drugs-related death. Helping a child grieve for a parent from whom they have been separated, and towards whom they may have all kinds of ambivalent feelings, is an onerous task. Most of the children who have suffered such bereavements have shown behaviours such as self-harming that have led to referrals to child and adolescent mental health services. The sometimes devastating impact of missed contacts must surely evoke very angry and ambivalent feelings in the carers who have to watch, apparently helpless, while the child struggles with the misery of not knowing whether a parent is dead or alive.

Recruitment and retention

Our practice in all areas of this work, including baby adoption, is to discourage any potential applicants unable to consider a background of parental drug misuse. All the case material sent out to initial enquirers includes case histories of drug-misusing parents and explanations of the likely implications of this kind of background. Whether applicants are interested in temporary care or adoption, we stress that our population of children, whatever their age and where they might be in their "care career", have very similar early life experiences and many have a range of behaviours which reflect this. This message is particularly important for prospective adoptive parents to hear as they, as well as some social workers, retain a belief that the younger children will have escaped the worst damage which might result from living with drug-misusing parents. The truth is that, given our current state of knowledge, we cannot identify with any degree of accuracy the young children who will indeed triumph over an early damaging start in life, and those who will carry the scars for the rest of their lives.

Case material in preparatory groups is based on actual children who lived with drug-misusing parents during their first months or years. Our agency medical adviser does a specific presentation at all baby adopters' preparatory groups, giving detailed information about possible implications for a young child's future development of intra-uterine exposure to drugs and alcohol, and of spending their first few months in a family where such misuse has occurred. At the stage of a possible link to a child with this kind of profile, potential adopters can be offered an individual consultation with the medical adviser. Payment of adoption allowances may be considered if there is a significant developmental delay as a result of substance misuse.

There is a growing belief amongst our team members that those chaotic and very challenging young children, who seem to be becoming a common feature of our accommodated population, need a period of "professional" family placement before any thought is given to permanent family placement. Providing the numbers of such placements which we will need in the future – and assuming that, for many of these children, what is needed is a "singleton" placement so that competing demands from other damaged and needy children are not part of the equation – is one of the greatest challenges facing Families for Children. While voluntary and private agencies many find it easier to provide these placements, this comes of necessity at a very high cost , which has huge implications for our already over-stretched fostering budget.

We are currently trying to develop a "high tariff" foster care scheme, in an attempt to place young children who have had multiple fostering disruptions and are currently living in residential units or schools. This small group of full-time and part-time carers was recruited specifically to work with some of the children we are discussing. This scheme hopes to pay carers enough, in fees and allowances, to ensure that there is one full-time carer at home and that each family is asked to care for only one child over a time-limited period. The other possible solution could be the development of well-staffed and supported small children's units whose remit would be to contain them, and begin to move them towards family placement, working in conjunction with family placement teams.

Supporting those much-needed carers, who seem able to manage the most challenging children from chaotic drug-using families, is a time and skill consuming business. Given Glasgow's current shortfall in area team child care social workers, we are often the only ones in regular contact with the carers and the child, with caseloads of 18–20 families each across the spectrum of family placements, as well as carrying out assessments. Because of the numbers of multiple placements our carers manage, each family placement worker will have contact with and knowledge of 40–50 children. This creates a working environment where crisis is a daily occurrence and planned work becomes harder and harder to manage.

Our duty system, which attempts to place children being accommodated from the city, usually due to child protection issues, routinely accommodates 20–30 children per month. The demands of this system resonate across the whole team. Nevertheless, one of the benefits of this situation is that our workers have become knowledgeable and skilled in identifying the complex placement needs of the children in our accommodated population, and in providing the support carers need to maintain placements. Families who care for the children we have been discussing need to be paid appropriately, trained well, and supported in a way that is recognised as helpful by them. That support needs to continue beyond 5 pm and be available over weekends and holidays. We are currently looking at having dedicated family placement staff who will be able to offer "out of hours" support to all our carers.

Conclusion

The underpinning basis of the work with drug-misusing parents, across all the "helping" agencies, is one of encouraging openness and partnership and discouraging stigma and exclusion. For the benefit of the estimated 10,000 children in Glasgow who live in families where there is a drug-misusing parent, this is without doubt the only way to approach the provision of services.

For the 395 children accommodated because of their parent's drug misuse, a more targeted and explicit approach is necessary. We need to be very clear about the kinds of damage we are seeing amongst this group of children, in order to highlight the specific services they and their carers need. Until we have the knowledge to identify at an early stage the children most vulnerable to the longer-term effect of their parents' substance misuse, and all the indications are that this is a growing population, then we cannot argue for the resources, therapeutic, educational and health, which will be needed.

Identifying this group of children, and making the very hard decision that is sometimes necessary, to separate them from their parents, demands co-operation between social workers, drug workers, teachers, doctors, carers and family placement workers. It has been our experience that practice is developing towards this co-operative model, but carers and their workers have been on the periphery of these developments. There is an inevitable tension between those who care for the children and, for instance, drug workers, whose focus is the parents. It is also inevitable that a number of children in our care will not return to their parents because of the latter's continuing drug use. In order to make the best decisions for these very vulnerable children, it is essential there is an exchange of information between family placement workers, carers and the drug workers who are often the only people who have any relationship with parents. Both family placement workers and drug workers have a great deal to learn from each other – in this Council we need to address the issue of joint training, as a matter of urgency.

The children we have identified make immense demands on our foster care service and on a daily basis we struggle to recruit and retain carers skilled enough to care for them. The number and the complexity of the children in foster care, particularly those from chaotic drug-misusing families, need to be highlighted if we wish to continue to offer a family placement service to all those children who require it, no matter how challenging their needs may be. There must be a general recognition at all levels of our service, including the political one, that foster care can no longer be provided "on the cheap". It is not unreasonable to suggest that some of the monies currently available to fund various drug projects across the country might be targeted specifically to a service which provides family-based care for those children most severely affected by their parents' drug misuse.

References

Adoption UK (2000) *Healing the Child who Hurts*, Adoption UK

Barnard M (2001) *Intervening with Drug Dependent Parents and their Children: What is the problem and what is being done to help?*, Centre for Drug Misuse Research, University of Glasgow

Cains K and Stanway C (2004, forthcoming) *Learn the Child* (working title), London: BAAF

Giller E (2000) *What is Psychological Trauma?*, SIRDAR Foundation

Hampton *et al* (1998) 'Substance abuse, family violence and child welfare', *Issues in Children's & Families' Lives*, 10, Thousand Oaks, CA: Sage

Hawley *et al* (1995) 'Children of addicted mothers: effects of the "crack epidemic" on the caregiving environment and the development of preschoolers', *American Journal of Orthopsychiatry*, 65

Hughes D (1997) *Facilitating Developmental Attachment*, Northvale NJ: Jason Aronson

Keck G and Kupecky R M (1995) *Adopting the Hurt Child*, Colorado Springs, CO: Pinon Press

National Center on Addiction and Substance Abuse, USA (1999) *No Safe Haven: Children of substance abusing parents*, New York: C.A.S.A, Columbia University

Scottish Executive (2003) *Getting Our Priorities Right: Good practice guidance for working with children and families affected by substance misuse*, Edinburgh: The Stationery Office

19 **Therapeutic interventions**

Alan Burnell and Jay Vaughan

Family Futures was set up in 1998 to specialise in working with children who had been traumatised in their birth families and, as a result of which, were placed in adoptive or foster families. Family Futures offers a multidisciplinary service providing assessment, therapeutic programmes of parent mentor support and parenting strategies as well as training. The work of Family Futures is described in its first book, *Trauma, Attachment and Family Permanence* (Archer and Burnell, 2003).

Results of an evaluation

In August 2003 an independent evaluation was carried out on families who have received therapeutic help from Family Futures over the past five years. Sixty-nine families took part, involving 100 children who were living in foster care or adoptive families. The average age of the children seen by Family Futures was nine years.

- 48 per cent were seen post adoption;
- 34 per cent pre adoption;
- 11per cent were long-term fostered;
- 50 per cent of the children had more than five previous placements;
- Of the children in the survey, 41 per cent had a disorganised attachment style and 26 per cent an ambivalent attachment style. (These two styles of attachment are classified as being insecure rather than secure attachment styles – they represent the two most disturbed forms of insecure attachment);
- 37 per cent had parental alcohol misuse in their background;
- 36 per cent had drug misuse by their birth parents in their background.

It was not possible to do a cross-variant analysis, which would have isolated a range of variables and correlated their relationship to one another. However, the therapists who had worked with the children with a parental alcohol and substance misuse background have derived from their clinical work, a belief that there is a significant difference between

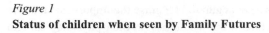

Figure 1

Status of children when seen by Family Futures

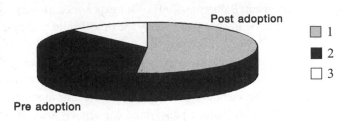

Post adoption

☐ 1
■ 2
☐ 3

Pre adoption

Figure 2

Drug and alcohol abuse in birth mothers of children in Family Future's survey

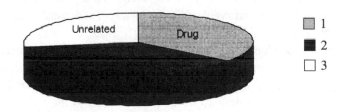

Unrelated   Drug

☐ 1
■ 2
☐ 3

children whose parents misused alcohol, children whose parents used Class A drugs (opiates, cocaine and cocaine derivatives) regularly and children where there is no history of drug or alcohol misuse. Our experience concurs with that of other contributors to this book, that although it is common to find that drug misusers also misuse alcohol, there are many alcohol misusers who do not also misuse Class A drugs. The importance of this will be explored later in the chapter.

The significance of thorough multidisciplinary assessments of children prior to placement

As is now realised, many of the symptoms in the child born to substance misuse are not visible and take the form of neurological damage, which is often difficult to detect in young children. It is only in recent years, since Tom Verny's ground-breaking book, *The Secret Life of the Unborn Child*

287

(1982), that professionals have begun to recognise the importance that the experience of the child while in the womb has on their physiological and psychological development (Balbernie, 2001). Our experience of working with adoptive and foster families is that only by the time a child is eight or nine years old and has been in placement for two or three years, do the symptoms of parental substance misuse begin to present themselves. The early symptoms of withdrawal are picked up by doctors. However, once withdrawal programmes are completed, there appears to be little monitoring of the long-term effects. Adoption panel medical reports may make reference to maternal substance misuse and panel medical advisers may draw attention to this, but they usually talk in terms of probabilities and percentages when it comes to the possibility of long-term damage. Parents find it hard to relate this information to the reality of their child and it is often, in our experience, only later on in childhood that they truly recognise the manifestations of the maternal substance misuse. These usually take the form of behavioural problems and learning difficulties.

Up until three or four years ago, Family Futures would have perceived most children who came from backgrounds involving abuse and neglect as having attachment difficulties as a consequence of this early trauma. However, we are increasingly aware that, in addition to the attachment difficulties that may result from early trauma, where there is a parental history of alcohol or drug misuse the child may be suffering from neurological and physiological damage. This impacts on the child's behaviour, their cognitive development and their attachment patterns over and above the effects of post-traumatic stress disorder (PTSD), which are rooted in the child's psychology.

It is well documented that Foetal Alcohol Syndrome has long been associated with behavioural and learning difficulties (Cundall, 2003). Recent studies on babies born to Class A drug-using mothers have shown a different range of physiological and neurological outcomes for the children. This literature suggests that opiates, cocaine and cocaine derivatives have different effects on the development of neonates. What is interesting to look at here is not only the neurological and physiological impact of being born addicted, but the consequences of the post-birth nursing care and withdrawal programme for the child or baby's ability to make attachments.

In general terms, opiate-addicted babies are now withdrawn gradually with the use of methadone over a six- to eight-week period. The literature also suggests that sub-acute withdrawal symptoms are now recognised which may only occur after a baby is returned home and manifest themselves through a failure to sleep, excessive demands for milk, severe colic and vomiting. The point of significance here is not the detail of the medical implications of opiate withdrawal, but the impact that it has on the baby and its developing relationship with its mother. Such babies are hard to care for and have parents who are struggling. It is likely that opiate-addicted babies will remain in hospital longer, experience multiple care-taking and be in a soporific state when medicated and an agitated, distressed state when experiencing withdrawal. This immediate post-partum experience is different from that experienced by babies of alcohol-dependent mothers and also different again from cocaine or crack-using mothers. In the latter case there is an association between cocaine addiction and sleep disturbance in a baby, and in the longer term, the possible development of ADHD. The neurological damage which may be caused by alcohol misuse during pregnancy is well documented and described in the medical literature as Foetal Alcohol Syndrome or Effects (FAS/FAE) (Rennie and Roberton, 1999).

The quality of the birth mother's attention, attunement, affect, and state of arousal will also be affected by the type and degree of drug or alcohol consumption or addiction. The picture that begins to emerge, therefore, is of a highly complex and differential pattern of effects of parental drug and alcohol misuse. These in turn, we believe, will impact on the child's very earliest experience of attachment formation. Such differing patterns have consequences for the subsequent re-parenting of this group of children and upon the psychotherapy that they will require. Our thinking on this is in its early stages; however, we are able to suggest certain hypotheses based on the framework outlined below.

Our hypotheses regarding children of alcohol-misusing birth mothers are as follows:

- Children whose birth mothers misused alcohol during pregnancy are more likely than not to experience some form of FAS/FAE. As these syndromes are not easy to detect at birth and manifest themselves as the child develops, it may be that they are not diagnosed or diagnosable until the child is already placed in a permanent home. The consequence of this is that an assessment for foetal alcohol-related disorders needs to be carried out as part of a pre-therapy assessment as children suffering from alcohol effects may require a more behaviourally orientated therapeutic programme due to learning difficulties and slow development. As FAS is associated with severe learning difficulties, intervention programmes need to be more concrete, structured and focused on the child's behaviour. Such programmes need to be organised so that there is a close integration between home and school environments.

- Children born to birth mothers who misuse alcohol are more likely to have an ambivalent attachment style as there is a potential for positive affect and attachments being formed despite the alcohol dependency of the birth mother. Furthermore, it is likely for the baby to have remained in the care of the birth mother for longer than with a drug-misusing parent because of the greater cultural acceptance of alcohol misuse. As a hypothetical generalisation, the birth and post-birth period, though not conducive to secure and positive attachments, may not always be an environment in which extreme neglect and abandonment may occur.

Our hypotheses regarding children of drug-addicted birth mothers are as follows:
- This group of babies, in general, will have more traumatic births and post-birth experiences of hospitalisation and multiple care-taking.
- There is a higher likelihood of parental abandonment.
- Drug withdrawal will induce in the baby a post-birth experience of extreme discomfort and agitation, which cannot be ameliorated by maternal comfort.
- Babies and children brought up by drug-misusing parents are more likely to be raised in conditions of extreme material deprivation due to the high financial cost of drug dependency. This will result in the baby being reared in a physically impoverished environment, with inadequate quantities of food.
- Class A drug use incapacitates the birth mother for longer and more frequent periods, thus further reducing the potential for secure attachment formation.
- In addition to incapacitation of the parent, "mad and crazy" delusional

thinking is often associated with drug-induced states. These are, therefore, potentially "downloaded" into the baby and become part of the
child's developing thinking.

- The high financial cost of drug use means that drug dependency is
associated with a criminal sub-culture.
- A further consequence of the high financial cost of drugs is for birth
mothers to resort to prostitution. This has a consequence for them and
their lifestyle, but also, in our experience, makes children highly vulnerable to sexual abuse by clients or acquaintances at a very young age.

To summarise, we believe that hypothetically, children born to alcohol-
misusing mothers will have a propensity towards an ambivalent attachment style, compounded by behavioural problems and learning disability
resulting from neurological and physiological damage caused by alcohol
in utero. Children born to drug-misusing mothers, because of the *in utero*
effects of Class A drugs, post-birth hospitalisation, difficulties with
nursing and the more chaotic and "crazy" sub-culture, are more likely to
have disorganised attachment styles with possible ADHD-type cognitive
and behavioural difficulties. Using the following framework of substance
misuse and impact, the different experiences of babies and young children
can begin to be compared.

Table 1 is a crude and simplistic attempt to illustrate the different
factors that may impact upon a growing baby and child and how they may
differ depending on the form of substance misuse. When looked at in this
way, the need for a detailed paediatric and social history of the pregnancy
and the immediate post-birth period becomes crucial in order for appropriate psychological and medical care and therapy to be offered to the
baby and child as they grow up. This understanding of their background
should not just be held within the medical domain, but must also be part
of the awareness of the social worker, foster carers and prospective
adopters of any child where substance misuse has been a feature of their
past. Adoptive parents are often perplexed as children from substance-
misusing backgrounds can have a confusing array of difficulties and
disabilities. Many adoptive parents had not realised at the time of
placement that they were adopting a child who, because of the parental
history of substance misuse, had potentially dormant (and therefore

Table 1

The impact on the child of parental substance misuse

	Substance misuse	
Impact on baby and child	*Alcohol-misusing birth mothers*	*Cocaine-misusing birth mothers*
Pre-birth *in utero* impact	Foetal Alcohol Effect	Suffers high levels of adrenalin *in utero* and other chemical consequences of cocaine abuse.
Post-birth medical care	Discharged after 3 days to care of mother who returns home.	Is born cocaine addicted. Birth mother discharges herself from hospital leaving baby in care of medical staff who provide institutional care and drug withdrawal routine.
Quality of mother–baby interaction	Baby receives variable but just about good enough care for the first few months of life. Baby is hard to care for.	Hospitalisation and drug withdrawal. Little or no mother–baby contact.
Sub-cultural lifestyle	Erratic behaviour due to intoxication, deprived conditions, crime.	Crime – theft, prostitution. Erratic behaviour, deprived conditions, food shortages, sexual abuse.
Quality of foster parenting	Baby is fostered short term after a violent drunken argument between the birth mother and partner. In foster care, baby continues to be undemanding, withdrawn and under-stimulated.	After three weeks, baby discharged to foster care. Baby is agitated, has poor sleep patterns, is hard to regulate, showing all the signs of cocaine withdrawal. Due to demanding nature of baby's behaviour, may be resentfully and roughly handled by an unsympathetic carer.

"invisible") special needs which would only manifest themselves fully as the child grew older. For this reason Family Futures operates a model of an integrated multidisciplinary team where a consultation with a paediatrician has become routine, either at the point of initial assessment or during the treatment process. We have become very reliant upon our paediatric consultants' help to advise professional staff and parents as to the possibility of a child suffering some consequence of birth parental substance misuse. Often parents need reassurance and factual information regarding the genetic transmission of alcoholism and drug misuse.

Implications for therapeutic interventions with children and their new families

There is a period of mourning for parents as they come to terms with the unseen damage their child has suffered and may not be able to ever completely recover from, despite the best efforts of the parents.

The three case examples in this section are real cases, but names and some details have been changed to protect confidentiality.

Case study

Mr and Mrs P were in a state of shock. They knew that they could not continue as they were with Jessie (aged 8), but hoped that she would get easier to manage as she got older. She had appeared to be a perfectly healthy baby. Maybe she cried quite a bit, but don't all babies do that? She had always seemed a very particular sort of child; could not bear rough materials on her skin, hated bright lights and struggled to remember basic instructions. It was just the way Jessie was, something she would grow out of, wasn't it? They had her life story book, they had the original form. It seemed so straightforward: domestic violence, parents could not cope, so Jessie was removed. They had felt the time was right to find out just a few more details to help Jessie understand.

But this? Nothing had prepared them for this. Mrs P's sister had always had the odd sherry during pregnancy, but that amount of wine? They knew that mattered. Why had no one thought to mention this? Maybe they should have asked. She seemed . . . well . . . Jessie-like. They had accepted it as a stage, something she would grow out of. But now they had to rethink. The social worker did not seem to know that much about Foetal Alcohol Syndrome but they had researched on the Internet. And then wished they hadn't. That was it, full stop. They moved between blaming social services and blaming themselves. Sometimes they felt angry with Jessie's birth mother. Didn't she realise what she was doing to the Jessie growing in her tummy? Didn't everyone know that so much alcohol during pregnancy damaged the growing baby? Mrs P cried and cried. She cried for Jessie, her perfect beautiful daughter who was hurt but looked fine. She cried for the baby she would have liked to have had. She held on to the knot in her stomach that told her over and over how carefully she would have cared for Jessie. She cried about how she would explain this to Jessie. What would it mean? Would it ever feel better? She was scared by the immensity of all the questions she had. Mr P withdrew into days of silence and longer hours at work. They began to feel their lives failing apart while Jessie continued Jessie-like as if nothing had happened.

The therapy team needs to be acutely aware of the implications for the child of any cognitive and neurological damage so that the therapy can be finely tuned to the child's understanding and abilities.

There is a need for long-term interventions for children and their families. The child's difficulties and their understanding of their past changes at every stage of their development and they will need help at each stage. There is also a period of mourning as they become aware of the number of difficulties they have at home, at school, and in their ability to make sense of the world. This is particularly marked in middle childhood.

Case study

Jim (12 years old) had been studying human development at school, carefully making mental notes of the effects of drugs on unborn babies. Yes, that was him. Damaged before he could even cry out *'NO!'* He closed his eyes and tried to imagine what it would be like to be a baby in an incubator on methadone. He could only think of the very bad flu he had had the previous winter when he felt as if he was dying and he could never imagine feeling better. Maybe it felt like that. Sometimes when he was feeling particularly bored with a lesson he would drift off and try to imagine the "drugs" in his body still working through his system. He even thought about what it would be like to try some drugs. For some strange reason the teachers concerned usually got very angry with him for not concentrating. How could he concentrate when he had these things to think about? How could he concentrate with his "dyslexia"? No one had said, but he blamed that on his birth mother. If she had not had drugs then maybe he wouldn't find school so difficult. It felt sometimes as if he was wading through treacle to try and understand what he was meant to do. Sometimes, even worse, it was hard to understand other things, things he did with his friends. It seemed so unfair. Everyone said that he was fine. But he didn't feel fine.

One English lesson he made up a story about his life (he didn't say it was about his life, but it was). He called it "Bruise". It was about a boy aged 11 years old who had the nickname Bruise. This was because of a mark on the side of his face that looked like a bruise. Bruise was not happy and lived alone just outside of town. No one knew much about Bruise and that was the way he liked it. People avoided Bruise because he looked so strange with his purple scarred face. Everyone understood that the bruise was a bad sign and it meant bad things had happened. Bruise knew that he could keep all his worries to himself because nobody dared ask about the bruise and how he came by it.

That evening Jim showed his adoptive father the story of Bruise. He read it and smiled at Jim: *'It would be easier, wouldn't it, if your bruises showed. Do you think everyone would understand then how hard it is for you?'* Jim nodded. *'It is so hard for you to have all your bruises hidden inside.'* Jim replied, *'I don't feel normal like everyone else. All this stuff happened to me that affects me. Not just that she didn't look after me and was scary but she messed up my head. I don't know how I can ever forgive her for that.'*

During the years that followed Jim kept the story of Bruise in his desk at home and created more and more adventures for him. Bruise could do all sorts of things Jim didn't dare do. And from time to time Jim still wished that he, like Bruise, wore his damage on the outside for the entire world to see.

A significant difference in this group of children, who may also have experienced other forms of abuse and neglect, from children who do not suffer the long-term neurological and physiological effects of substance misuse, is the sense of anger, outrage and powerlessness. Many children who have experienced early abuse and neglect feel empowered, during the course of therapy and with the help of their new parents, to overcome the traumas and deficits of their early experiences. Though they may have experienced these as primal wounds, they are enabled to see that they can be healed (Verrier, 1993). They have a sense that they can overcome their past and make different choices from their birth parents. Birth parents who have handed their children a physiological and neurological legacy (through substance misuse), which will not heal in the same way, leave this group of children with the greatest challenge.

Case study

There had always been the three of them. They had stuck together: Gemma, Lee and Angie (13, 11 and 8 years). They talked in therapy about their experiences and their different memories of what had happened in their birth family. They tried to piece together a shared understanding of how it was. Angie struggled most with this because she did not remember. At home, at school and in the therapy sessions they easily reverted to their roles in the birth family: Gemma as mum, Lee as Dad and Angie as the baby. Gemma and Lee both remembered very clearly changing Angie's nappy and trying to make sure she got fed. Angie hated that bit of the discussion as she found the whole idea of nappies so embarrassing. They all remembered the fear. It still startled them to think about it. Curled up together on the old mattress in the bedroom. Comforting each other, hoping it would all go away. Hearing the grown-ups next door and fearing what may happen. Gemma and Lee could not really see why it was so scary but they knew it felt scary. Something about the way the grown-ups started behaving strangely. It wasn't just the Halloween masks, it was the horror film feel it all had. They hated horror films now. It was so terrifying – even now all these years later. Angie could not remember in the same way but she somehow knew something about what her sister and brother described. They still felt sad that their birth mother had died of a drugs overdose. When they had visited her from their foster carers she had seemed rather sad and pathetic and then she had died.

Trying to put together all the mixed feelings of love and anger and fear they had about this mother was the hardest thing of all. They fell out about it between themselves again and again. She was so many different people. They used the therapy to piece together the fragments they all held of their shared history. They mourned the mother they had lost to drugs and finally to death. They shouted at her for lack of care and love of them. They cried and clung to the memory of what might have been. Gemma and Lee knew that they would never be able to completely forget what had happened to them. Especially because when they looked at little Angie's face she did not look quite right and they were old enough and wise enough to know that, in her strange little pixie face, their sister would carry their history forever.

In addition to this, these children often struggle, because of the cognitive impairment and the degree of disorganisation, to make sense of and integrate their beliefs and the emotions that derive from their earliest experiences. For these reasons, therapists need to modify their approach and their interventions for this group of children. There is a huge need for parent mentoring – peer support from other more experienced adoptive parents and foster carers who have undergone a parent mentor training. This would be as part of the support for foster and adoptive families, to run in parallel with the therapy, because of the high incidence of behavioural problems that goes with the damage.

A recent and hopeful development in our service at Family Futures to children who have, for whatever reason, some degree of cognitive and neurological malfunction, has been the inclusion in the therapy team of a neuro-developmental therapist. There has been a growing awareness that abuse, neglect and neurological damage in the early years causes immaturity in the neurological pathways. Neuro-developmental and sensory-integration therapies have been developed to re-stimulate and help recreate early patterns of neurological development that have been damaged. These body-based, parent–child exercise regimes appear to go a long way towards helping children overcome early neurological damage. It is now increasingly recognised by different specialists that the plasticity of the brain means that there is the potential for rewiring (Schore, 1994, 1998, 2001a, 2001b, 2002; Glaser 2000; Glaser and Balbernie, 2001).

Children also particularly need educational testing as part of the therapeutic package because, inevitably, they will have some form of specific learning difficulty. Educational testing can also throw light not just on levels of IQ, but on the form of cognitive organisation. Many of the children tested at Family Futures show high degrees of disorganisation on the Executive Functioning Test, irrespective of their IQ. The Executive Functioning Test measures the children's ability to integrate the different areas of cognitive functioning, which is essential for the completion of many complex tasks. The implications of this for parents, teachers and therapy teams is profound as it highlights the need for a very structured, concrete approach to helping children organise their lives at a very practical level. For example, remembering the order in which one gets dressed in the morning to go to school can be problematic. The child's ability to orientate themselves around their school and to remember the sequence of a timetable can also be problematic. The strategies required to address this may be lists in the child's bedroom of the order in which to put on their clothes and a diary for the day. In school, colour coding rooms and providing maps would also help. This way of thinking and the development of strategies for coping will be crucial in the future as the children mature into adulthood and need support around independent living and career choices. Much of the acting out and behavioural difficulties, both at home and at school, can be seen to emanate from the basic frustration that these children experience in organising themselves and understanding how school and family organise themselves.

Conclusions

Without a sensitive approach from therapists and support for parents, this group of children is more vulnerable to repeating patterns from their birth families. Over and above these neurological and physiological issues, we have become aware that the nature and pattern of attachment that children have towards their alcohol- and drug-misusing parents is different. The psychological issues arising from these attachments need also to be addressed in therapy. Generalising, we would now see children who have had purely alcohol-misusing parents and children who have had drug-misusing parents as having had quite different experiences, from different subcultures, which lead to variations in the nature of their attachment difficulties. This needs further research.

We would say that children whose parents misuse alcohol tend to show the following features.

- More ambivalent attachments to parents who were at times warm and affectionate.
- A tendency to be "parentified children". The oldest child in particular will often have assumed responsibility for both the parents at times and for younger siblings. This has implications for placing children together or apart and for the way that contact plans are made with birth parents. Such children tend to be wanting or "needing" to have contact in order to maintain their role as a caretaker.
- A tendency to come into care later due to the ability of many alcoholic parents to maintain a just about acceptable level of child care and because of society's acceptance of alcohol as a drug of choice. The consequences of this are that children have experienced longer periods of deprivation and have more entrenched patterns of attachment and stronger loyalty to the birth family.

We would say that children whose parents are Class A drug misusers tend to show the following features.

- Their attachment patterns tend to be more disorganised as their experience of their birth parent has been unpredictable, moving wildly between scared and scary.
- There is a nightmarish quality that they bring to their new families and interactions with people.
- The disinhibiting nature of drug misuse is that the child often ends up experiencing a much more "mad-making" family life in which anything, at any time, can happen. Drug misuse is often associated with criminality, police raids and paedophile rings.

- They tend to show higher levels of self-reliance, disassociation and a desperate need for psychic survival. There is a more instinctive, feral child quality to their interactions.

This is very tentative generalisation but at the anecdotal level there does appear to be a qualitative difference in the experience of these two groups of children, who often require different forms of remedial parenting and different forms of therapeutic intervention.

References

Archer C and Burnell A (2003) *Trauma, Attachment and Family Permanence: Fear can stop you loving*, London: Jessica Kingsley Publishers

Balbernie R (2001) 'Circuits and circumstance: the neurobiological consequences of early relationship experiences and how they shape later behaviour', *Journal of Child Psychotherapy*, 27:3

Cundall D (2003) Contact a family: for families with disabled children, www.ca-family.org.uk

Glaser D (2000) 'Child abuse and neglect and the brain – a review', *Journal of Child Psychology and Psychiatry*, 41:1, pp 97–116

Glaser D and Balbernie R (2001) 'Early experience, attachment and the brain', in Gordon R and Harran E, *'Fragile Handle with Care'*, Leicester: NSPCC

Rennie J and Roberton N (eds) (1999, 3rd edn) *Textbook of Neonatology*, New York: Churchil Livingstons

Schore A (1994) *Affect Regulation and the Origin of the Self*, New Jersey: Laurence Erlbaum Associates

Schore A (1998) 'Affect regulation: A fundamental process of psychobiological development, brain organisation and psychotherapy', London: Tavistock 'Baby Brains' Conference

Schore A (2001a) 'Effects of secure attachment on right brain development, affect regulation and infant mental health', *Infant Mental Health Journal*, 22

Schore A (2001b) 'The effect of early relational trauma on right brain development, affect regulation, and infant mental health', *Infant Mental Health Journal*, 22

Schore A (2002) 'Dysregulation of the right brain: a fundamental mechanism of traumatic attachment and the psychopathogenesis of Post-traumatic Stress Disorder', *Australian and New Zealand Journal of Psychiatry*

Verny T (1982) *The Secret Life of the Unborn Child*, London: Sphere

Verrier N (1993) *The Primal Wound*, Baltimore: Gateway Press

20 The vulnerable child in school

Patricia Daley and Sandra Johnson

Introduction

Over the last four to five years, education departments and schools throughout the country have reviewed their remit in relation to looked after children, in order to work more effectively in a corporate parenting role with social services departments. In Sheffield where we live and work, educational psychologists have been allocated an increase in time with this vulnerable group of children, and specialist teachers and school support assistants are included in the education department's generic support team. As part of this team, educational psychologists have worked with all schools in the city in the training of teachers and support assistants, focusing on the educational and emotional needs of looked after children. Educational psychologists also contribute their knowledge and experience of child development and applied psychology to the adoption and fostering panels, and work alongside mental health professionals in providing a service for the city's residential units. We have a specialist project in our city, "The Support Service For Looked After Children", which is managed by the National Society for Prevention of Cruelty to Children (NSPCC) (2002). It consists of a range of professionals, including one of us on a part-time basis, engaging directly with young people, teachers, social workers and carers. Based on experience, this chapter offers information and observations about looked after and adopted children in schools, including those who are, or have been, subject to parental substance misuse.

What the child brings to the situation

Children growing up in favourable circumstances have opportunities not only to form good attachments, but also to receive a wide range of appropriate stimulation, particularly of language and play experiences that form the basis for future development. They attain their developmental milestones and develop their ability to understand, to reason and to learn as a result of these experiences. The combined environmental influences of parenting, home and community are of crucial importance.

For children who have been affected by parental substance misuse, it is likely that their developmental progress and learning ability will have been compromised by a combination of prenatal and postnatal factors. Every child is individual, bringing to the school situation a unique combination of inherited characteristics and environmental experiences, which have begun to shape the person they will become. Their experiences in school will, in turn, form part of these influences. Research findings show that children who have been exposed prenatally to various substances – nicotine, alcohol, marijuana, cocaine, heroin, amongst others – are likely to be vulnerable to difficulties which will affect their developmental progress, their learning abilities and their behaviour, which will impact on their progress in school. The difficulties described in the literature (McNamara *et al*, 1995; Alison, 2000), include the following:

- **Attention and memory deficits**
  Children are likely to find it hard to be physically well settled and to focus their attention, especially in large groups or when needing to listen. They are likely to be easily distracted by the actions of other children. This can be a particular problem as children move up in school and there is greater expectation that they will be able to sit still, attend and listen to the teacher for longer periods, and to absorb larger amounts of spoken information at one time. They may easily forget instructions or information, as they have not actually been able to "take in" and process the information. It may be that children will seem to have a good memory for some things and not for others, and this is likely to be related to the degree of attention they have given to the information. Similarly some will have good attention levels when playing on the computer, but cannot concentrate for more than a few seconds when in a lesson. This is likely to be because the visual medium, individual nature, rapid action and immediate feedback provided by computer games are able to engage attention, whereas the teacher standing

talking to a roomful of children is much less effective as an attention-getter. This may be true for all children, but those who have attention difficulties are much less able to screen out the "distracters", unless the subject matter and the way it are presented is very compelling.

- **Poor co-ordination**
  Difficulties in this area may affect children's gross motor skills, for example, their ability to walk down a corridor without banging into others, to sit on a chair without sprawling, to learn ball skills, or to ride a bike. It may also affect their fine motor skills, such as handling a knife and fork, getting dressed, or learning to draw and write. In addition to appearing "clumsy" the children may be disorganised in their motor skills, and this will show in difficulties with, for example, organising their belongings and their work. They need help with getting their things ready for school, getting ready for work in class, setting out their work.

- **Visual or hearing problems**
  These difficulties may be relatively mild and managed by the prescription of spectacles or hearing aids. However, in cases of brain damage as a result of the effects of substance misuse, the difficulty may lie with the ability of the brain to process and interpret the information being received from the eyes or ears. These difficulties are usually termed "sensori-neural" deficits, and are not likely to be remedied by glasses or hearing aids alone. In these cases more specialist support and advice from the Local Education Authority (LEA) advisory teachers (in Scotland – "specialist" teachers) is likely to be needed. Most LEAs employ such teachers for children with sensory (visual or hearing) impairments. They provide assessments, advice and training to schools and parents, regarding the teaching strategies and aids which will help the child's development and promote inclusion of the child in local mainstream education.

- **Difficulties with cause and effect and abstract thinking**
  As they develop, children learn to make connections between things and between actions (their own and those of others), and the

consequences of those. As an illustration, at a very early age, young children begin to find out that shaking a rattle will produce a noise, and if they do it again it will happen again. Children in nursery will learn that, if they pour water on the wheel in the water tray, it will go round. So what begins as a random action or "play" becomes a deliberate one in order to make something happen. From these early beginnings children continue to learn about how things relate and how one thing leads to another – first with real objects and later by using the knowledge they have gained to think things through. When children have difficulties with these aspects of learning, they are not able to think things through to a logical conclusion. They will need to be shown in practical ways much more than might be expected, and will require opportunities to try things out and to be "talked through" what is happening.

- **Communication and social difficulties**
  These may take the form of a speech problem, for example, in the articulation of sounds and words. There may be a delay in the development of speech and language so that children begin to talk at a later age than is normally expected. They may have a particular problem with language, struggling to express themselves, to explain what they mean and to describe events or answer questions. In relation to understanding language, requests, instructions or explanations need to be simplified and repeated. If children have a problem with the broader aspects of communication, this can affect the way they interact with other children. It can be difficult for them to understand the non-verbal aspects of communication, such as facial expressions, tone of voice and body language, thus misunderstanding the intentions of others. They may find it hard to communicate and interact in a group, so sharing and taking turns could be a problem.

- **Emotional and behavioural difficulties**
  These difficulties are seen when children have problems regulating their emotional state and adjusting behaviours appropriate to a situation. They may show excitable behaviours, be over-demanding of attention, become easily frustrated and be unable to deal with failure and criticism. They may repeat unwanted behaviours, be unsociable,

steal and lie and be aggressive towards other children. They may also be withdrawn, passive and too eager to please. There is a range of strategies and approaches that schools employ when promoting positive social, emotional and behavioural development in all children and when tackling particular difficulties shown by some children. The most successful schools in this respect are those which have a clear and comprehensive behaviour policy and parents should be involved and fully informed about this. Educational psychologists and, in some LEAs, specialist advisory behaviour support teachers will be involved in advising and supporting schools in this area.

The above descriptions of difficulties indicate that children affected by parental substance misuse may show any of a wide range of problems, for a multiplicity of reasons. The most clearly documented findings are in relation to the effects of alcohol, where a clear link is found with cognitive deficits (that is, thinking and reasoning skills) and learning difficulties. So it is possible that children with Foetal Alcohol Syndrome or Spectrum Disorder (FAS/FASD) will have difficulty with understanding, with remembering and with working things out. In this case they would be likely to score at a lower than average level on tests of cognitive functioning or intelligence. Because of this they may have difficulties in learning, especially of the more complex kind, for example, to read and understand such material. Difficulties in literacy, and in numeracy, will have a fundamental effect on the child's ability to learn and progress in many school subjects. Not all children of substance-misusing parents demonstrate symptoms at birth – some become manifest in later childhood, and some children never develop symptoms at all.

Supporting the child

Hayley

Hayley is three years old, currently in local authority care in England. She was born with FAS, and in the first few months of life experienced a chaotic pattern of care and neglect. This combination of factors means that Hayley's development is significantly below the average range for her age. She has already been identified by the LEA as a child with special educational needs who will require some form of special provision. Currently this is provided by a Portage Home Visitor, who works with the foster carer on structured play activities to stimulate and support Hayley's learning and development. Portage (www. portage.org.uk) is available in many LEAs in the UK. It is a home visiting service which works in partnership with parents, providing carefully structured play activities to encourage pre-school children who are experiencing developmental difficulties or delays.

It is likely that Hayley will move on to a local nursery and school, where she will continue to receive some individualised support, through the provision of a Statement of Special Educational Needs (in Scotland – a Record of Special Educational Needs). Such a Statement is provided by LEAs for children whose needs cannot be met from the resources and provision normally available within mainstream schooling. A multi-professional assessment is carried out and the resulting statement specifies the nature of the child's needs and the provision which is required to address them. The law and code of practice governing this statutory process requires that parents are fully informed and involved, and there is an appeal process for parents if disagreements arise. Most LEAs have criteria for which children need a multi-professional assessment and a statement, and these may vary between authorities. All LEAs must provide for a Parental Partnership Service to assist parents whose children are undergoing a multi- professional assessment. A statement may result in the child's existing school receiving additional funding or resources, or it may result in alternative provision being recommended, for example a move to a more specialised unit or school.

Hayley will continue to have long-term learning difficulties associated with FAS, but the provision of a stimulating environment and an appropriately differentiated curriculum will ensure that her learning progresses and that her educational needs are met. The provision of a differentiated curriculum will mean that while Hayley will work on the same broad aspects of the National Curriculum as others in her year group, the learning targets which teachers will be working towards with her will be adjusted so that they are within her capabilities. For example, if all the children are working on a topic in numeracy to do with shapes, Hayley may be sorting squares and circles into the right piles, while other children are drawing round the shapes or copying them. Teachers will also differentiate the way in which they present tasks. Hayley will need to be given more individual attention and to be shown and guided through tasks more carefully. It will be important that her teachers know about both the education of children with learning difficulties and also the nature of FAS.

In school, it may become very obvious from a child's progress or behaviour that he or she has been affected by their experiences, or, as in the case of Hayley, the knowledge may already be clear and available. However, it may also be that signs of damage are subtle or that they occur at particular times or stages of the child's development. The way that difficulties present will be different at different ages, as with Kyle's case described below.

Kyle

An adopted six-year-old, Kyle had a trouble-free time in the pre-school setting, where he was described as a 'lively and adventurous' child. When he moved into the reception class, it became apparent that he was less able to settle and sustain concentration than other children of his age, and this began to be viewed as a barrier to his learning and progress. Discussion with his parents led to the teachers receiving the information that Kyle's birth mother had been an intravenous drug user during her pregnancy. Kyle had shown withdrawal symptoms for a few weeks after birth, and had needed medication for this. While this knowledge did not, of itself, make a difference to the approaches and strategies that the teachers used to support Kyle, it did help them to gain a greater understanding of the underlying causes of his difficulties. Their increased awareness of the possible effects of parental substance misuse on a child's development, meant that they were able to view Kyle's difficulties more objectively, and were less likely to attribute his behaviour to "disobedience" or "naughtiness". In particular, they had a better understanding of some of Kyle's difficulties such as sitting still during "carpet time" and listening to a story, carrying out simple requests ('put your book away and get your milk'), sitting in a group and completing a piece of work (drawing a picture and writing or copying the words) without interfering with other children's work. They were able to appreciate that Kyle's difficulties in focusing his attention and ignoring or "screening out" distractions going on around him were likely to be because of an underlying difficulty caused by the parental substance misuse during pregnancy.

Children have difficulties in school for many and varied reasons and there can be numerous different explanations for similar presenting difficulties. For instance, a child may not be experiencing success in learning to read because of absence from school due to illness, because of emotional distress impeding the learning process, or because of brain damage causing lowered cognitive ability. Any of these factors may apply to a child from a background of parental substance misuse, but may also be factors for children from quite different backgrounds. In this sense the child from a parental substance misuse background may not have unique problems affecting their educational and social development, but will have their own profile of strengths and difficulties.

A good and caring school will seek to gain insight into the causes for the difficulties and this may facilitate decisions about the best actions to take. However, this is not to imply that the school should always think that what is necessarily required is specialised "therapy", or provisions they are not qualified or experienced to make. They should not fail to appreciate the great deal they can do, and that provisions made as part of the children's local mainstream school are often the most effective in helping them to progress and to feel part of the wider community. By offering routine, structure and consistency, the school can help to mitigate against disruption or disharmony in other aspects of the child's life.

So schools should seek to directly address problems. In the example given above, this would be by providing more support for the teaching of reading. In some cases the very act of addressing the presenting problem may help to ameliorate the underlying factors. The child whose emotional difficulties are affecting learning may be helped by receiving extra attention and teaching – the success generated will also have the positive psychological effect of increasing motivation and raising self-esteem.

Sometimes the school can have the most therapeutic effect by doing what they do best, raising attainment and promoting achievement, as in David's situation.

David

David who is 12, lived for eight years with parents who were inter-mittent drug users. He experienced many disruptions in his care and some periods of acute neglect. His attendance at school had been very poor and he moved school three times. He had considerable behav-ioural difficulties and had been excluded from one school. He was taken into local authority care, and after two short-term foster place-ments, found permanence in a long-term foster home where he has been since he was ten years old.

David's primary school had focused their intervention and support around his behavioural difficulties, providing in-class support and an Individual Education Plan (IEP) with behavioural targets. An IEP sets out some individual targets for the staff to work on with the child over a period of half a term or a term. These targets will be focused around one or two particular difficulties, in addition to the other class or group targets, which all children will be working on as part of the National Curriculum. In David's case the targets for his final term in primary school were: to stay in his seat and put his hand up instead of standing up and calling out; to work in his group for 15 minutes without disrupting the work of the others; to seek help from a lunch time supervisor instead of fighting. The teacher, classroom assistant and lunch time supervisor were all involved in helping David work towards these targets, but they saw only a small amount of progress. They remained very concerned about David's low level of self-esteem and confidence.

When David moved to secondary school (Y7), the focus of his support was switched to learning, in particular to the development of literacy skills. At 11, David had a reading age of about seven. The school's Special Needs Co-ordinator (in Scotland – Learning Support Manager) and the Learning Mentor (in Scotland – Classroom Assistant or Special Needs Auxilliary) became involved. (The Special Needs Co-ordinator is a teacher who has responsibility for co-ordinating the provision in school for children or young people who have special educational needs or are experiencing particular difficulty in learning or behaviour; the Learning Mentor is a member of school staff, not a teacher, who works with children who are showing low motivation, are under-achieving or at risk of exclusion.) Together they planned a programme of support involving daily periods of reading tuition, with either a special needs teacher or a support assistant. In addition, the Learning Mentor saw David very regularly to give feedback and encourage motivation. David's foster carers were included in the programme and were taught how to use a paired reading approach. This involves the adult and child reading aloud together, with the adult providing the correct model for the reading and giving support and building confidence through frequent praise. This is in contrast to the often-used approach where the adult listens, waits, and corrects the child's mistakes. The paired reading approach is well researched (Topping and Lindsay, 1992) and is a proven method of boosting children's reading skills. David's reading age improved by 12 months over a six-month period – by the time he entered Y8 he was reading at almost a nine-year level, and still improving. There was a very positive effect on David's confidence and self-esteem; his behavioural difficulties decreased considerably and there was also an improvement in his attainment levels in other areas of the curriculum.

This example shows how vital it is that schools understand the implications that the lack of appropriate experiences have for a child's learning and development, and that they seek to compensate for missed opportunities and to enrich the child's environment. An understanding of the particular difficulties associated with the effects of parental substance misuse will also contribute to the detailed planning of the kinds of approaches and strategies that are needed. For example, a child with FASD is likely to have difficulties with attention and listening skills. Thus they will find it hard to sit still, focus their attention on the adult speaker, ignore any distractions (for example, noises outside the classroom, someone else moving around) and take in and "process" what the adult is saying. Teaching staff will therefore need to make use of visual cues and

supports for any auditory input. At primary level this could mean providing a child with a picture version of the day's timetable and activities, to
supplement the spoken instructions and explanations. At secondary level
it may mean using a multi-media approach to the teaching of, for example,
history. This could be done through the use of relevant video or computer
programmes and providing students with illustrated worksheets in addition
to written information. Similarly the students could be asked to record
their responses on tapes, to use cameras or video, such as recording a
discussion about the aspect of history being taught. All these are ways in
which the student's attention may be more readily engaged and held, more
use is made of the visual medium, learning is more active and there is less
reliance on the "sitting and listening" and "sitting and writing" method of
teaching and learning.

Including parents and carers

The behaviour of children who have lived through adverse early life
experiences can appear incomprehensible to teachers, carers and parents.
When a child seems unresponsive to the tried and tested approaches in
developing learning, emotional stability and social skills, negative or
despairing feelings for both adults and the child inevitably develop. A
vital psychological need for every person is to be understood, but for the
parents and carers of these children there is often only limited access to
information about the early stages of their development. They need to
have as much knowledge as possible about the child's personal history,
together with an awareness of children's development and the impact of
adverse circumstances, including parental use of drugs and alcohol on
normal child development. When parents, carers and social workers share
their knowledge of the child with receptive and sympathetic education
staff, then the child's behaviour can become more comprehensible. From
this basis, previous negative energies and emotions can be re-directed to
addressing children's difficulties and removing barriers to their learning.
Similarly, schools need to reassure parents and carers that they are aware
of the child's needs, and that they acknowledge their responsibility and
commitment to being flexible in their use of strategies to support the
child.

Parents and carers of vulnerable children need opportunities for frequent and lengthy contact to talk with their child's teacher in relation to curriculum, homework, learning programmes, behaviour management strategies, etc. Teachers need to be aware of significant life events, anniversaries, and contact with siblings or birth parents. The process of sharing information needs to be carried out sensitively and regular meetings of the child's professional network, including educational psychologists and LEA support services, can ensure that a range of perspectives about the child's needs are considered and consistent approaches of support and management are facilitated.

The inclusive school

In providing for children in the care system, schools are required to implement good practice as recommended by government reports (Department of Health/Department for Education and Employment, 2000; Her Majesty's Chief Inspector of Schools, 2001). The Social Exclusion Unit report (2003), *A Better Education for Children in Care*, which accompanies The Children's Green Paper *Every Child Matters* (Department for Education and Skills, 2003), further emphasises the vital role that schools have in improving vulnerable children's life chances. There is also practical advice and guidance available on "including" children at risk of social exclusion (Centre for Studies on Inclusive Education, 2000). In Scotland a report arising from joint inspection services in social work and education highlighted the lack of training for teachers, social workers, residential workers and foster carers on the education of looked after children (HM Inspectors of Schools/Social Work Services Inspectorate, 2001). The Scottish Executive subsequently commissioned a number of agencies (including BAAF) to produce appropriate training materials (Hudson *et al*, 2003).

All the above reports emphasise the requirements of a high level of commitment to raising achievements, the allocation of resources to needs and regular monitoring of progress, so that effective additional support for vulnerable children is put in place. The descriptions of inclusive school practices in this section of the chapter may give foster carers and adoptive parents useful guidelines regarding what to look for in their child's school.

Inclusive schools ensure raised awareness and sensitivities towards vulnerable children by all the adults. They place a strong emphasis on building secure and high-quality relationships between the children and their teachers. Each school has a trained designated teacher (to support and monitor the welfare and progress of looked after children) and there is allocated time for increased opportunities for planned and regular contacts with carers and social workers. The school makes good use of education support services and other adults to support class times, lunchtimes and after school periods. Most schools will be able to provide support arrangements such as withdrawing a child to a smaller group for some periods in the week. In secondary schools, alternative arrangements for GCSEs can be made, and tailor-made learning packages included for individual children. Post-16 planning with Connexions Services (a careers mentoring and advisory service) will also be available.

For children with special educational needs, as discussed above, an Individual Education Plan (IEP) is put together, which details the child's needs, learning targets, specific teaching methods and materials and ways of checking on progress. For children who present behavioural difficulties and who may be at risk of exclusion, a Pastoral Support Plan (PSP) (in Scotland – Individual Behaviour Plan [IBP]) is put into operation. A PSP defines problem areas, sets targets and assigns responsibilities for action, including a designated key worker. The programme is tightly set within timescales and reviewed regularly with external support from the education support services. The school will involve parents and carers when devising and monitoring the IEP and PSP. For children who have been assessed as having exceptional special educational needs, the LEA will usually make a Statement of Special Educational Needs (discussed above), if they decide that all the special help the child requires cannot be provided from within the school's resources. Additional resources could then include funding for staff time and/or special equipment. In a very small number of cases a child may be provided with a place in a special school.

Active attention to emotional and personal development

Providing a safe and predictable context for learning is important for all children and is vital for vulnerable children. Effective teaching and learning take place when teachers are acutely aware of the significant impact of a range of factors within the teaching and learning arena. Including vulnerable children in the classroom requires that the teacher "actively attends" to the management, organisation, style and pace of teaching and makes use of a range of strategies to maintain engagement and a sense of belonging.

Active attention to emotional and personal development is essential when including emotionally fragile children in the classroom. Teachers need to be informed about the children's history and how their behaviours can be an understandable response to adverse circumstances and as a means of coping with distress. The adults working with children need to have knowledge and understanding of the psychological impact of parental substance misuse, attachment difficulties, trauma and movements in the care system. An assessment of children's behaviours in the school context may provide information about environmental triggers that maintain both positive and troubled behaviours.

- In providing a secure base and encouraging healthy emotional development, adults will need to model and teach tolerance and acceptance of individual differences.
- It is important to make sure that the curriculum content is not uncomfortable for children, for example, that it is sensitive around "family" topics and sex education.
- Adults need to make sure that implicit and explicit expectations and routines are understood, and give clear prompts and reminders before actions or transitions. Children's understanding of the rules, rewards and sanctions requires regular checking.
- Adults need to use a genuine, warm, assertive, "holding" style in relating to the children, demonstrating their personal appreciation of the child's words and actions and to be acutely aware of the impact of body language and voice tone and of the power of deflection and humour to defuse difficult situations. Confidence in the child can be demonstra-

ted by acknowledging the child's efforts in developing new adaptive behaviours and social skills.

- It is important that there is a validation of the child's feelings and the recognition of "triggers" of frustration. Children can be taught to develop an awareness of tense physiological states and safe ways to express feelings. It is helpful when the modelling and practice of relaxation and calming strategies take place during non-crisis times. The child can then be prompted to use these strategies during times of distress. If practically possible there needs to be a quiet, private, secure space in or close to the classroom.

Emotionally vulnerable children need active adult attention to make and maintain relationships with others. Inclusive schools encourage the development of relationships by sensitive engineering of social groups – pairing and grouping more vulnerable children with socially skilled children. Adults can actively teach negotiation skills and introduce creative social activities that encourage win/win outcomes. Schools that make regular use of "Circle Time" activities nurture peer relationships and give opportunities to foster self-esteem, co-operation, listening and speaking skills (Mosley and Tew, 1999). Educational psychologists and support services can aid schools in the development of these initiatives. Timetabled Circle Time meetings have received excellent OFSTED reports in the area of personal, social, cultural, spiritual and moral education. Circle Time sessions always involve a group or a class of children seated in a circle and usually last forty minutes to an hour. Sessions are structured to include a fun warm-up or guided imagery phase, then a round of the circle when each child has a turn to speak. The next phase of the session will usually focus on issues of concern (curriculum, behaviour, social interaction), and then a closing phase of co-operative activities to ensure a positive closure. "Circles of Friends" is an intervention which recognises the importance of relationships for psychological well-being and resilience, and is underpinned by the recognition that student culture is a powerful influence on behaviour and the development of belief systems. It is essentially the engineering of a meaningful contact group promoting understanding and empathy, building friendships and support networks for children at risk of peer rejection or exclusion (Newton and Wilson, 1999).

The nurturing school

The same experiences which foster developmental progress and achieve-ment can also help to develop children's trust in others and enable them to become more emotionally resilient. Children who have lived through difficult and damaging circumstances may have less resilience, or more brittle resilience, than others. This means that they are likely to be more vulnerable to further stress when faced with demands, challenges or difficulties. Their responses may be highly defensive and hostile with behaviour that in turn creates further difficulties. Children can then become caught in a downward spiral of their own negative behaviour and the school system's negative responses. For these children, therefore, school can be a less than happy place, and even a place which further impedes social and emotional development and learning.

However, this does not have to be so, as school can be a place which contributes to a building of resilience and repairing damage. A school which recognises this capacity and which takes positive steps to provide the right environment and experiences can perform a very valuable function in the child's social and emotional development. It is important to note that such a school – a nurturing school – will be committed to doing this for *all* the children and adults who cross its threshold.

A nurturing school is one that places as much importance and emphasis on the social and emotional development of children as on their academic achievement. The ethos and values are about the nurturing of the whole child, and the primacy of the mental well-being of all. The two strands of raising attainment and the promotion of social, emotional and behavioural skills are seen as interdependent, each depending on the other if real progress is to be made. The curriculum for the development of social, emotional and behavioural skills will be as carefully planned and thor-oughly taught as the curriculum for literacy, numeracy, science, IT and so on. All the adults in the school setting will have worked to develop shared understandings and approaches to the social and personal development of all children. There will be an acceptance that the establishment of positive relationships with children is crucial. Staff will have training opportunities to further their understanding and skills in the promotion of children's social, emotional and behavioural development. There will have been careful consideration of the way resources are allocated and provision made for children who have particular needs in this area of development.

An increasing number of schools are taking steps, for example, by setting up nurture classes or groups, to make particular and special provision for children who have had damaging and difficult experiences and who enter school with little trust in adults, without a secure sense of self-worth, and whose emotional development is impeded by unmet needs during their infancy. Children from a background of parental substance misuse often fall into this category because of the chaos, inconsistency, neglect or abuse they have experienced.

The usual model for a nurture class is a group of ten to 12 children in a mainstream primary school (i.e. not a special school). They register each day with their age group class but then spend up to four-and-a-half days each week in the small group. The nurture group is staffed by a teacher and a teaching assistant who have usually been specially trained. In addition to providing many of the normal early years educational experiences the nurture group incorporates some "home and family" type situations, for example, the room or rooms will be furnished and decorated with curtains, easy chairs, etc., there will be a dining and kitchen area where breakfast and other meals are eaten daily. In this setting it is more possible for the adults to be flexible in their interactions with and expectations of the children in ways which meet the children's emotional and developmental needs. The aim is to help children to experience care in a predictable, positive and loving environment, by forming trusting relationships with warm, caring adults. In this way it is hoped that they will be able to relearn their knowledge of adults and of themselves.

It is not expected that nurture groups will provide a complete substitute for the unsatisfactory experiences within the child's life, and neither should a dramatic change in the child's demeanour, behaviour and progress necessarily be anticipated. However, there is an accumulating body of action research findings pointing to the positive effects of nurture groups on children's behaviour and social adjustment in primary and secondary schools (Bennathan and Boxall, 1996; Cooper et al, 2001; Boxall, 2002; O'Connor and Colwell, 2002). These studies indicate that nurture groups can be instrumental in ensuring the continued inclusion of troubled and distressed children in mainstream schools, and that schools develop a greater capacity to cater for the needs of children with social, emotional, behavioural and learning difficulties. Schools which do not have a specific nurture class or group can still incorporate nurture group principles and values into their approaches. For children who are fostered or adopted the approaches of the nurturing school can support the healing processes that foster carers and adopters are providing for the child in the family.

For children from a background of substance misuse the importance of a school that is nurturing and inclusive is paramount. In such an environment it is possible for children to have experiences and relationships which will foster positive self-esteem, the growth of trust in others, the development of resilience and the achievement of potential.

In conclusion teachers and staff in schools need to be knowledgeable about the underlying causes and difficulties of vulnerable children, including those with a background of substance misuse. However, it is also important that children's difficulties are not over pathologised or seen as fixed and unchangeable. Teachers, parents and carers need to be realistic *and* optimistic that a practical and positive joint commitment can make a very real difference to children's lives.

References

Alison L (2000) 'What are the risks to children of parental substance misuse', in Harbin F and Murphy M (eds) *Substance Misuse and Child Care*, Lyme Regis: Russell House Publishing

Bennathan M and Boxall M (1996) *Effective Intervention in Primary Schools: Nurture groups*, London: David Fulton Publishers

Boxall M (2002) *Nurture Groups in School*, London: Paul Chapman Publishing

Cooper P, Arnold R and Boyd E (2001) 'The effectiveness of nurture groups: preliminary research findings', *British Journal of Special Education*, 28:4, pp 160–66

Centre for Studies on Inclusive Education (2000) *The Index for Inclusion – Developing Learning and Participation in Schools*, Bristol: CSIE

Department for Education and Skills (2003) *Every Child Matters*, London: DfES

Department of Health/Department for Education and Employment (2000) *Guidance on the Education of Young People in Public Care*, London: DH/DfEE

HM Inspectors of Schools/Social Work Services Inspectorate (2001) *Learning with Care: The education of children looked after away from home by local authorities*, Edinburgh: Scottish Executive

Hudson B, Furnivall J, Paterson S, Livingston K and Maclean K (2003) *Learning with Care: Training materials for carers, social workers and teachers concerning the education of looked after children and young people*, Her Majesty's Inspectorate of Education and Social Work Services Inspectorate, Glasgow: University of Strathclyde

McNamara J, Bullock A and Grimes E (1995) *Bruised before Birth*, London: BAAF

Mosley J and Tew M (1999) *Quality Circle Time in the Secondary School*, London: David Fulton Publishers

NSPCC/Sheffield Social Services (2002) *Support Services for Looked After Children: Third annual report,* Sheffield: National Society for the Prevention of Cruelty to Children

Her Majesty's Chief Inspector of Schools (2001) *Raising Achievment of Children in Public Care*, London: Office for Standards in Education

Newton C and Wilson D (1999) *Circles of Friends*, Dunstable: Folens Publishers

O'Connor T and Colwell J (2002) 'The effectiveness and rationale of the nurture group approach to helping children with emotional and behavioural difficulties remain within mainstream education', *British Journal of Special Education*, 29:2, pp 96–100

Social Exclusion Unit (2003) *A Better Education for Children in Care*, London: SEU

Topping K J and Lindsay G A (1992) 'Paired reading: a review of the literature', *Research Papers in Education*, 7, pp 3199–246

Further reading

Bliss T (1994) *Managing Children Managing Themselves*, Bristol: Lucky Duck Publishing

Brandes D and Ginnis P (1990) *The Student Centred School*, Oxford: Blackwell Education

Department of Health (1998) *Fostering Good Mental Health in Young People*, London: DoH

Department for Education and Science (2001) *Promoting Children's Mental Health within Early Years and School Settings*, London: DfES

Department for Education and Science (2001) *Special Educational Needs, Code of Practice*, London: DfES

Gross J (2002) *Special Educational Needs in the Primary School*, Buckinghamshire: Open University Press

Jackson S (ed) (2001) *Nobody Ever Told Us School Mattered: Raising the educational attainment of children in care*, London: BAAF

Morgan R (1986) *Helping Children Read: The paired reading handbook*, London: Methuen

Topping K J (1987) *The Peer Tutoring Handbook: Promoting co-operative learning*, London: Croom Helm

Wolfendale S (ed) (2002) *Parent Partnership Services for Special Educational Need*, London: David Fulton Publishers

National Portage Association

www.portage.org.uk, or National Portage Association PO BOX 3075, Yeovil, Somerset BA213FB, Tel. 01935 471641

Notes on the contributors

Caroline Archer, as a long-standing member of Adoption UK, was responsible for writing much of their literature relating to adoption and attachment. More recently she has been developing the concept of parent mentoring in collaboration with Family Futures Consortium. Caroline also carries out independent parent mentoring work in South Wales.

Joy Barlow is the Head of STRADA (Scottish Training–Drugs and Alcohol) in Scotland, a partnership between the University of Glasgow and DrugScope, providing regional training, academic programmes and leadership development for professionals working with drug and alcohol misusers.

Joy has a background in the design, development and management of services for children and families affected by substance misuse. She has contributed to research in this area – *Children Growing Up in Drug Dependent Households*, with Dr Marina Barnard at the Centre for Drug Misuse Research, University of Glasgow. As a long-serving member of the Advisory Council on the Misuse of Drugs, she contributed to the *Hidden Harm* Inquiry, and was a member of the advisory group for *Getting Our Priorities Right*, the Scottish Executive guidance for working with children and families affected by drug and alcohol misuse. She is currently involved in assisting with the implementation of these guidelines. Joy was awarded an MBE in 1998 for services to drug prevention and treatment.

Jennifer Bell qualified as a social worker in 1981. She worked in an area team in Glasgow for four years doing generic social work, followed by two years in a child guidance clinic. She has worked in family placement for the last 15 years.

Alan Burnell is a qualified social worker who began his career in a local authority social services child care team. He was a counsellor at the Post Adoption Centre in London for 13 years and helped pioneer the development of post-adoption services to all parties in adoption. For the past four years he has been a Co-Director of Family Futures Consortium, an innovative service dedicated to developing therapeutic support to families who have adopted or are fostering traumatised children. The project offers a collaborative, family-based approach using a variety of techniques.

Kate Cairns is a social worker and teacher. For 25 years, with her partner Brian and their three birth children, she provided permanence for 12 other children who had all experienced significant adversity in their earlier lives. All 15 are now adult, and the family continues to grow as partners and children are added to the numbers. She is the author of *Surviving Paedophilia* (Treatham Books, 1999) and *Attachment, Trauma and Resilience* (BAAF, 2001), as well as several articles.

Dr Tagore Charles, MBBS, MRCPCH, was born in Salford. He grew up and went to school in Westminster, living in the Cloisters of the Abbey. Tagore studied medicine in King's College London. He has worked in England, Australia, Wales, Mozambique and Jamaica. In Wessex he worked under the supervision of Dr Cathy Hill where he developed his interest in looked after children. He is presently a Specialist Registrar in Paediatrics in London, with an interest in respiratory medicine.

Valerie Corbett qualified as a probation officer in 1988, working in Liverpool and then Sunderland. During her time in the probation service, she gained experience as a practitioner and manager working with substance use and child protection. She moved to work in the voluntary sector with Aberlour in 2001, focusing on the impact of parental substance misuse on children and young people. This has been an enriching period during which she has begun to actively listen and understand what family life does feel like for such children and how best to work effectively alongside both parent and child.

Dr Catherine Cosgrove, MBBS, MRCP, was born in Bedford and grew up and went to school in the West Country. She studied Medicine at King's College London, and has practised medicine in Oxford, London, Wales and Australia. She has a specialist interest in respiratory medicine and infectious diseases, and is currently a Clinical Research Fellow at St George's Hospital Medical School, London.

Patricia Daley, B.A. Honours Psychology, Post Graduate Certificate in Education, MSc Educational Psychology, has worked as an Educational Psychologist in Sheffield for nine years and in Wakefield for five years. She has seven years of teaching experience.

Alongside her generic educational psychologist role, she is seconded to work on a Department of Health project "The Support Service for Looked After Children", a multi-professional therapeutic team managed by the NSPCC. She provides professional advice on Sheffield's fostering panel and works with residential unit social workers, foster carers and teachers relating to the care and education of looked after children. She is a trainer for Sheffield's multi-professional Child Protection Committee. She specialises in working with deaf children and their families in Sheffield and has developed the Educational Psychology Service's Critical Incident Response Team.

Donald Forrester is a lecturer in social work at Goldsmiths College. After a number of years in practice he moved into research and lecturing from 1998. Since then he has been involved in studies of social work and parental substance misuse, care plan outcomes and re-referrals of closed initial assessments. He has published a number of articles and was co-author of a recent study of care plans, *Making Care Orders Work*. He is writing up (with Judith Harwin) the findings of their study of social work and parental substance misuse for publication by John Wiley in 2005.

Dr Di Hart worked for many years as a social worker and manager before taking up a post at the National Children's Bureau, developing practice with children in public care. She has a particular interest in children in secure settings. Di has recently been awarded a PhD following research into pre-birth assessments.

Judith Harwin is Professor of Social Work in the Department of Health and Social Care at Brunel University and Director of the Brunel Inter-disciplinary Child Focused Research Centre.

Her research interests focus particularly on public policy, law and practice for children in need and looked after. She led a study for the Department of Health published by The Stationery Office – *Making Care Orders Work: A study of care plans and their implementation*. She is currently directing a research project funded by the Nuffield Foundation on the nature, extent and impact of parental substance misuse on child welfare in social services. She and Donald Forrester are writing a final report of the study for the Nuffield Foundation as well as working on the book to be published by John Wiley (2005).

She has published widely on child care policy in Central and Eastern Europe and was an associate fellow of UNICEF's International Child Development Centre in 1997–1999. She recently completed a programme for the World Bank and UNICEF on de-institutionalisation in Central and Eastern Europe.

Dr Catherine Hill is Senior Lecturer, Child Health, University of Southampton. She has an interest in researching health needs of looked after children, with publications and authorship in the field. She is Vice Chair of BAAF's Health Advisory Group. She chaired the BAAF committee which produced practice notes for health screening of children adopted from abroad. She has edited medical notes in BAAF's journal, *Adoption & Fostering*, for two years.

Sandra Johnson BA, Postgraduate Certificate in Education, BSc, MA, is a trained and experienced teacher and has more than 20 years of experience as an educational psychologist. Her present post in Sheffield includes working with schools, and with pre-school children and their families as Portage Supervisor. She is an adoption panel member and currently doing research into the difficulties which adopted children and parents have experienced with schools and education.

Dr Mary Mather FRCP, FRCPCH, has been a Consultant Community Paediatrician since 1993. She is the Chair of BAAF's Health Advisory Group, the Medical Adviser to the Bexley Adoption and Fostering Panel and medical consultant for Parents for Children. She was a member of the Department of Health Reference Group overseeing the implementation of "Quality Protects". She is a member of the Editorial Board of *Archives of Disease in Childhood* and the peer review panel for the journal, *Adoption & Fostering*.

She is the author of *Doctors for Children in Public Care*, a textbook for medical advisers working in adoption and fostering. She has published work on the health of children being presented to adoption panels and the need to reduce delay in order to protect their physical and mental health. She has also published work on the statutory medical examination and the need to replace this formal system with a more flexible and holistic approach, which recognises the stigma attached to growing up in care and the consequences for health outcomes. She has been extensively involved in both local and national training of medical advisers.

Sara Mayer is the Project Leader for The Children's Society STARS Project, Nottingham. Having qualified as a children and families social worker in 1997, she has worked with families in the area of parental substance misuse in various settings, including Phoenix House Family Centre, Sheffield, and Nottingham City Social Services Department both as a worker and team manager.

Dr Patricia McElhatton has been a reproductive toxicologist for 30 years, a founder member of the UK National Teratology Information Service (NTIS) and the European Network of Teratology Information Services (ENTIS). She is an Honorary Lecturer in Reproductive Toxicology, Newcastle University Medical School. She lectures nationally and internationally and has over 100 publications. She was appointed to the Government's Advisory Committee on Pesticides and the Medical Toxicology Panel as the reproductive toxicity expert (2003–2005).

Jacqueline Mok is consultant paediatrician at the Royal Hospital for Sick Children in Edinburgh and part-time Senior Lecturer in the Section of Child Life and Health, University of Edinburgh. She is the lead clinician for Child Protection as well as Paediatric HIV services in the University Hospitals Division of NHS Lothian. Both remits require close working with colleagues in social work, education, law enforcement and the voluntary sector.

Moira Plant is Professor of Alcohol Studies at the University of the West of England in Bristol and Director of the Alcohol & Health Research Trust. She has a particular interest in women and alcohol and drinking in pregnancy and heads the UK section for a number of international collaborative projects in these areas.

Dr W. A. Phillips is Professor of Neuropsychology at Stirling University, where he was a founder and the first Director of the Centre for Cognitive and Computational Neuroscience. He has published extensively on vision, visual memory, perceptual learning, children's drawing, the effects of brain damage on reading and writing and the theory of neuronal computation. Recent work includes a major new theory of the neurochemical bases of cognitive disorganisation in psychosis. He teaches an advanced undergraduate course on "Drugs and the Mind".

Rena Phillips is an independent practitioner and researcher. She is currently employed by adoptive families as part-time co-ordinator of a post-adoption support service and is an adoption panel member.

Rena worked in a social work department as an adoption and foster care specialist, and was a teacher and researcher in the Social Work Unit and Social Work Research Centre, Stirling University. Her publications cover adoption, disability, children with complex support needs and social work education. She co-edited *After Adoption: Working with adoptive families* (BAAF, 1996). She was previously chair of BAAF's Research Group Advisory Committee. She is on the peer review panels of the journals *Adoption & Fostering* and *Adoption Quarterly*.

Margaret Sim has worked as a family placement worker for 26 years. She was employed for seven years as a social worker with Barnardo's New Families Project, set up to place older children for adoption. When the Project was taken over by the then Strathclyde Regional Council in 1984, she became a senior practitioner in the team recruiting carers for teenagers. She has continued to work in Glasgow since that time developing various forms of family placement, most recently a "high tariff" scheme to find families for children currently in residential schools.

Jay Vaughan is a Co-Director of Family Futures and has been working with traumatised children for over ten years. She has worked as a drama therapist with children who were terminally ill at St Bartholomew's Hospital, with children in a children's home who had been abused and neglected and with young people in psychiatric hospitals. For seven years she has specialised in working solely with fostered and adopted children. Jay says:'I was inspired by the courage these children and their foster or adoptive families had, to try to overcome early profound damage and abuse'.